STUDIES IN T

General Editor

The East Mid

The East Midlands
in the Early Middle Ages

Pauline Stafford

Leicester University Press   1985

First published in 1985 by Leicester University Press
First published in 1985 in the United States of America by
Humanities Press Inc., Atlantic Highlands, NJ 07716,
and also distributed by them in North America

Designed by Douglas Martin
Set in Linotron 202 Trump Medieval
by Wyvern Typesetting Limited, Bristol
Printed and bound in Great Britain by The Bath Press, Avon

British Library Cataloguing in Publication Data

Stafford, Pauline
The East Midlands in the early Middle Ages. –
(Studies in the early history of Britain)
1. Midlands (England) – History   2. Great
Britain – History – Anglo-Saxon period, 449–1066
I. Title   II. Series
942.5'01   DA670.M64

ISBN 0–7185–1198–0
ISBN 0–7185–1257–X Pbk

Contents

In memory of Frances Rose Greenfield and Sarah Johnson

Foreword

The aim of the *Studies in the Early History of Britain* is to promote works of the highest scholarship which open up virgin fields of study or which surmount the barriers of traditional academic disciplines. As interest in the origins of our society and culture grows whilst scholarship yet becomes ever more specialized inter-disciplinary studies are needed more urgently, not only by scholars but also by students and by laymen. The series will therefore include research monographs, works of synthesis and also collaborative studies of important themes by several scholars whose training and expertise has lain in different fields. Our knowledge of the early Middle Ages will always be limited and fragmentary, and progress will only be made if the work of the historian embraces that of the philologist, the archaeologist, the geographer, the numismatist, the art historian and the liturgist – to name only the most obvious. The need to cross and to remove academic frontiers also explains the extension of the geographical range from that of the previous *Studies in Early English History* to include the whole island of Britain. The change would have been welcomed by the editor of the earlier series, the late Professor H.P.R. Finberg, whose pioneering work helped to inspire, or to provoke, the interest of a new generation of early medievalists in the relations of Britons and Saxons. The approach of the new series is therefore deliberately wide-ranging and will seek to avoid being unduly insular. Early medieval Britain can only be understood in the context of contemporary developments in Ireland and on the Continent.

This volume is the second regional study to be published. It is intended that the series will cover all the main regions of early medieval Britain and will provide brief, well-illustrated and up-to-date syntheses of their settlement and history. The East Midlands did not form a single political unit at any time during the early Middle Ages. The fluctuating fortunes of the kingdoms of Mercia, Lindsey and East Anglia and of their Viking and English successors mean that any region defined by geography cuts across historical frontiers. Nonetheless Dr Stafford shows that there are distinct advantages in examining not only the Anglo-Saxon and Viking settlements but also other major historical developments from an East Midland perspective. Indeed her work suggests that it may be at this local but regional level that the most exciting advances in our understanding will emerge.

University of St Andrews, November 1984   N.P. Brooks

List of illustrations

Acknowledgments

This book is not simply the product of my last few years' work on the East Midlands, but of many previous years' study, especially of late Anglo-Saxon England. The debts I have incurred over those years are too numerous to acknowledge, but three in particular must be mentioned. The first is that to my students, in my Special Subject in particular, who have constantly forced me to think and rethink my view of ninth-, tenth- and eleventh-century England. The second is to the late Michael Dolley who gave so much help and advice over the years and inspired my enthusiasm for the Anglo-Saxon coinage in his role as a scholar and as a friend. The third is to Pierre Chaplais, my former supervisor, who set me exacting standards I may not always have met and to whose training and encouragement I owe much more than simply a doctorate.

I owe specific debts for help with illustrations and discussion of individual points to Marion Archibald, Maggi Solly, Christina Mahany, Rosemary Cramp, Kenneth Cameron, Peter Sawyer and Katherine East, and to all those who have allowed me to use their work for illustrative material. Sandra Lewis typed and retyped the MS with all her customary efficiency.

My especial thanks are due to Mick Jones and his colleagues at the Trust for Lincolnshire Archaeology who generously discussed the Lincoln excavations with me and provided illustrations; to Professor Martin Biddle who made available the results of his Repton excavations, much of them prior to publication; and above all to Michael Metcalf, who read an earlier draft of the chapter on towns, has patiently answered a stream of specific questions and bears no responsibility for any remaining mistakes on the subject of the coinage.

Nicholas Brooks has been far more than a general editor: he has offered essential help and criticism throughout the project and painstakingly read the entire MS twice. My thanks are due to him and to all the staff at Leicester University Press, especially to Susan Martin, without whose hard work on the illustrations this book might never have appeared at all.

My children have patiently borne constant inroads into their weekends and numerous visits to East Midlands churches. My husband has given me more practical support and encouragement than I could possibly measure, and he has taken many of the photographs. This book is dedicated to those women to whom I owe the most fundamental debts of all.

Introduction

The East Midlands is the region which stretches from the Humber estuary in the north to the Chilterns in the south, from the sea and the Fens in the east to the Pennines in the west. It comprises the shires of Bedfordshire, Huntingdonshire, Northamptonshire, Rutland, Leicestershire, Nottinghamshire, Derbyshire and Lincolnshire, and for the purposes of this book the boundaries of those shires are those before the Local Government Act of 1974. These older boundaries are much closer to those which existed and were created in the Anglo-Saxon period (below, pp. 139–42).

For much of the period between A.D.400 and 1066 the East Midlands were part of the kingdom of Mercia, incorporated in the tenth century into the kingdom of England. But the Viking invasions and settlement of the late ninth and tenth centuries drew an important new boundary through Mercia, that of the Danelaw. It is this boundary which has largely determined why Leicestershire, Derbyshire, Northamptonshire and Bedfordshire are included here in the East Midlands, whilst the neighbouring shires like Warwickshire, Staffordshire and so on are not.

Apart from the Pennines, so important a feature of Derbyshire and Nottinghamshire, the region might be considered predominantly lowland. However, within this eastern plain are significant areas of upland or hills which have played an important part in shaping local settlement and history. The river systems of the Trent and Fens both posed barriers and created lines of communication in the Anglo-Saxon period, whilst the marshes and waste around the Wash, the Witham and the Trent mouth were then more extensive landscape features than now.

The history of the region in the Anglo-Saxon period is rooted in its geography and landscape, in the exploitation of these and their potential. But it is not a simple question of economic and geographical determinism. New settlers, political control, religious history, the growth of new estates affected the most fundamental economic development. They have a broader relevance if we are to understand the shape of the region in this period, its internal and external divisions, the significance of the institutions, social structure, artefacts and buildings which survived from it. No history worthy of the name can leave the landscape unpeopled, without consideration of the ways in which local society worked, of the lives and conditions of its inhabitants, of the questions and beliefs which shaped those lives. It is these concerns which have given shape to this book.

Part One

LAND, ECONOMY AND EXPLOITATION

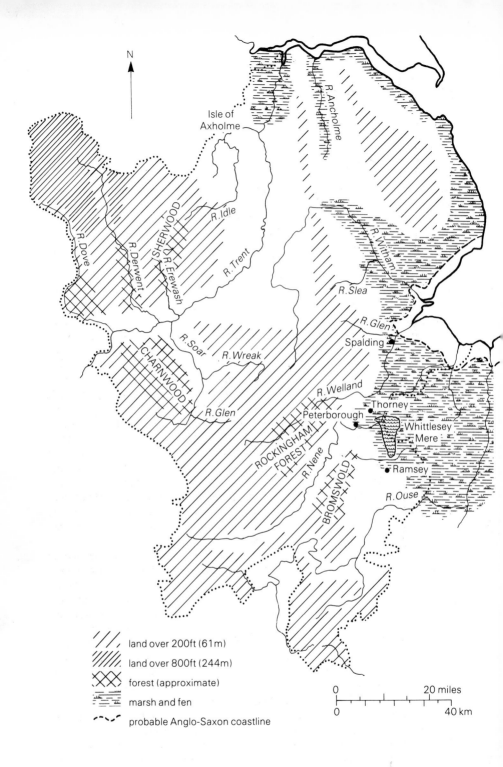

Figure 1. The topography of the East Midlands.

1 The Land

Physical Features

The landscape and its settlement was the creation of its inhabitants on the basis of its physical characteristics. Apart from Derbyshire, the East Midlands is part of the lowland zone of England, but the detailed variations of uplands of chalk, limestone, grits and sandstones with the alluvial soils and gravels of river valleys, the lowland clays and extensive tracts of fen and marsh were important determinants of its settlement and history.

To the south the poor chalklands of the Chilterns were generally inhospitable to agriculture; part of this same eastern chalk belt surfaces in the Lincolnshire Wolds. Although the chalk provided poor arable soils, the edges of such uplands were often desirable sites with access to pasture, especially for sheep; local variation like the good loam soils of the Bedfordshire escarpment warn against a too simple picture. More forbidding were the gritstone plateau and limestone uplands of the Derbyshire Peak and west Nottinghamshire, where settlement was always sparse except in the river valleys. The sandstones of upland Northamptonshire and Leicestershire proved nothing like the same formidable barrier to settlement, though here too the river valleys were favoured sites. Down the centre of the region the oolitic limestone ridge begins in Lincolnshire and runs south into Northamptonshire. It was a source of excellent building stone quarried at Ancaster and Barnack, and ironstone outcrops on its western edge at places like Scunthorpe. The limestone soils themselves might be poor, but the spring line along, for example, the western edge of the Lincolnshire ridge supported much settlement. These upland areas do not present the same impassable barriers which exist in other areas of the British Isles, but their impact on local settlement and its density is still apparent in Domesday Book (see fig. 8).

Marshes and fens did present such a barrier and were far more extensive in eastern England in the Anglo-Saxon period than now. The Fens surrounding the Wash are a flooded alluvial plain. To the seaward side sedimentation produced a silt fen bordering the Wash, whilst behind it stretched the peat fen dotted with islands capped with boulder clay. The peat fen was unstable and liable to flood, and no Domesday villages are recorded on it. Settlement here was confined to the islands like Thorney and Ramsey; Ramsey could still be approached by boat in the tenth century and Thorney was accessible only by water. Large inland lakes existed, the most extensive of them Whittlesey Mere in Huntingdonshire. The silt fen of the seaward edge was settled and a line of Domesday villages here seems to mark the original coastline, further inland than the modern one. The post-Roman flooding which produced the extended fenlands around the Wash rivers affected the courses of those rivers and altered the coastline. In Anglo-Saxon times villages such as Wisbech, Boston and Spalding were coastal settlements, South Kyme stood on an estuary formed where the Witham, Bain and Slea flowed to the sea, and marsh and fen stretched up a river like the Witham almost as far as Lincoln. The Wash rivers were an area of important settlement and Lincolnshire place-names on the high silts like Quadring, Stenning and Spalding are amongst the oldest strata of English names. But their siting demonstrates the limitations imposed by the original extent of marsh and fen.

Fen and marsh are still associated with the Wash, but during the Anglo-Saxon period they were also a feature of the lower reaches of the Humber rivers, extending the barrier to communication posed by the Humber deep inland. Small stretches of preserved reed bed are all that now remain of the fen-wastes which once stretched around the mouth of the Trent. Before the seventeenth-century drainage schemes the valleys of Ancholme and Axholme were marshy and water-logged. Heathland and blown sand joined marsh to inhibit settlement, agriculture and movement in North Lindsey.

During and after the Roman period the dangers of flooding along the Lincolnshire coasts grew as protective off-shore shoals were eroded. Before the end of the Anglo-Saxon period the Lindsey coast was protected by a sea bank, the *Hafdic* (Old Danish *haf* = sea).[1] This bank is referred to after the eleventh century at Skegness, Mablethorpe, Friskney and elsewhere, but it was in existence by 1066 since Domesday records settlements on it at such places as North Coates, Marsh Chapel and Grainthorpe. In south Lincolnshire a similar bank closed the estuary between Holbeach and Fleet; Domesday records saltpans existing at Fleet outside the sea bank.[2] Nothing is known of the construction of these banks, but they join other impressive earthworks of the Dark Ages as testimony not only to the engineering but also to the organizational skills of our ancestors.

Forest is always assumed to have been a major feature of the early landscape, but estimates of its extent by the eleventh century and earlier are fraught with problems. Domesday is the only positive source, but its statistics on woodland are patchy and difficult to interpret. Wood is recorded in the survey in rough measurements or often in terms of the number of pigs it would support. Outlying stretches of woodland are ill-recorded in a survey whose primary concern was with the central estates at which dues and renders were paid. More fundamental than the limitations of Domesday are assumptions about the history of settlement itself, which have affected ideas on early forests. A view of settlement as a story of a steady battle against waste and forest in which the Anglo-Saxons played a large part produces a tacit assumption that forest cover in the early Saxon period was extensive, being gradually reduced by clearance up to and beyond the eleventh century. Such a view of settlement history has been challenged (see below, pp. 78–9), and a theory developed that clearance and settlement had already progressed far by A.D.400. Peat pollen analysis in Derbyshire backs such a theory, suggesting that in this area at least agricultural activity relative to forest cover was actually in decline by c.A.D.400 – a decline not much reversed before the tenth century.[3] Thus assumptions that, for example, Sherwood forest in the Anglo-Saxon period covered the whole area of Bunter Sandstone in west Nottinghamshire may be gross overestimates; that sandstone may once have supported dense forest cover but how much of it remained by the eleventh century and earlier is open to doubt.

Sherwood and Charnwood forests were certainly still extensive in the eleventh century. Sherwood appears in a mid-tenth century charter granting

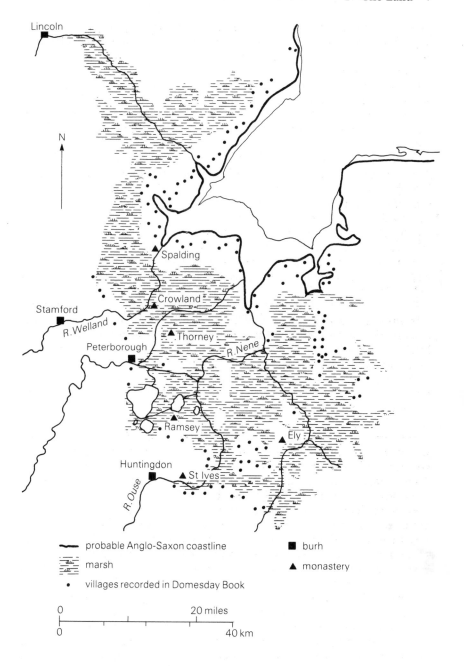

Figure 2. Marshland and settlement around the Wash (after D. Hill, *An Atlas of Anglo-Saxon England*, 1981).

land at Sutton, and its name *scirwuda* (wood belonging to the shire) suggests it may already have been royal forest.[4] In Domesday Book Leicester forest is called 'the woodland of the shire [*vicecomitatus*]', but its name is *Heres wode* (wood of the army).[5] Since the army in question was probably the Danish conquerors settled on Leicester this too may represent the preserved hunting ground of a ruling group now controlled by royal officials. Forest was once an important feature of the Derwent valley, south of Ashbourne and east of Dove; here names ending in *leah* (clearing) suggest clearance during the Anglo-Saxon period.[6] The forest of Bromswold in Northamptonshire is lacking in early place-names, and Hereward the Wake is alleged to have taken refuge there after his last stand against the Normans in the late eleventh century.[7] Records of twelfth- and thirteenth-century clearance show that the woods of the Soke of Peterborough, Yardley Chase, Salcey, Whittlewood, and the forest of Rockingham were still extensive in 1066.[8] Similar evidence shows the Chilterns well-wooded in the eleventh century, adding point to the Domesday record of a large wood at Luton sufficient to pasture 2,000 swine.[9] But this later clearance was mostly piecemeal and Hallam is probably correct in his suggestion that the East Midlands was already a well-exploited agricultural landscape by 1066.[10]

Few features have played a larger role in determining the history of the East Midlands and its settlement than rivers and their valleys. To the north the area is bounded by the Humber and its marshes, a wide estuary with difficult currents. The Trent with its broad flow cuts the region in half to the north, though like the navigable rivers of the Wash it provided a line of communication deep into its heart; at times when seaborne invasion was as important as trade such lines of penetration proved a mixed blessing. Communication along these rivers might be important but they posed formidable barriers between neighbouring communities. It is no surprise that the Trent divides Lincolnshire from Nottinghamshire for part of its course, or that the Welland is the northern boundary of Northamptonshire; the Welland already fulfilled such a role in 917 when the Viking army settled on Northampton saw it as a boundary.[11]

The Great Ouse, Nene and part of the Welland once flowed out to the sea through Wisbech at Cross Keys Wash, along the line of the boundary between Lincolnshire and Norfolk.[12] As these Wash rivers indicate, many watercourses have changed since Anglo-Saxon times, though as here their original line may be marked by old boundaries. At Newark the Trent has shifted westwards; in late Saxon times when the parish boundaries were laid out, what is now the eastern branch of the Trent at Newark was the main course of the river.[13] Other rivers differed significantly in general appearance: the Nene for example was wider and shallower before the eighteenth-century embankments.[14]

Rivers provided not only routes of communication but important settlement sites. The valleys of rivers like the Trent, Welland and Nene had fertile soils and well-drained, easily worked gravel terraces much favoured for settlement from well before Saxon times; the Nene valley's settlement history begins long before the coming of the Anglo-Saxons, in Neolithic times. Typically its gravel terraces are dry but easily tilled and have ready access to good water supply especially at spring line sites such as Irthlingborough, Twywell, Rothwell and Kettering. It was along the valleys of Dove, Derwent and Erewash that settlement penetrated the Southern Peak, and the southern tributaries of the Trent, the Soar and the Wreake offered many attractions. Indeed the eminent suitability of the Wreake valley for settlement has forced rethinking on the significance of the Viking place-names which abound here (see below, pp. 117–19).

For the agricultural communities of the East Midlands climate was of the first importance, but here our knowledge is scantiest of all. The East Midlands lacks even an annalistic chronicler for the Anglo-Saxon period who might record at least the incidence of hard winters or wet autumns – the type of annals which lay behind Simeon of Durham's remarks on the hard northern winter of 764, when snow fell early, hardened into ice and lasted until the middle of spring, withering trees and plants and killing marine animals.[15] In general the early medieval period in Europe up to the eleventh century was part of a 'Little Climatic Optimum' when the weather was on average 1°–2°F warmer than now, and drier. This should have been good for food output and allowed the growing of vines at Eaton Socon, Bedfordshire, in the late eleventh century.[16] It is at present impossible to go beyond such general statements.

Communications

Around the year 1100 two Anglo-Norman legal compilations singled out the four great roads on which travellers were to enjoy the king's special peace; they were the Watling Street, the Ermine Street, the Foss Way and the Icknield Way.[17] The *Leges Edwardi* also refer to those other important local roads 'from cities to cities, from boroughs to boroughs by which men go to markets or about their other affairs'.[18] The authors of the *Leis Willelme* and the *Leges Edwardi Confessoris* were certainly not attempting to make a definitive statement on the road system of England. The old Roman routes which these authors singled out reveal their antiquarian interests as much as the realities of the late eleventh-century communications. But in spite of their partiality these authors highlight the fact that in Anglo-Saxon times, as now, the great thoroughfares of England mostly ran through the East Midlands, a fact which has never ceased to affect the history of the area.

The East Midlands had been well served by prehistoric routes like the Jurassic Way, the Portway running through Ashford and Wirksworth in the Peak, the ancient Wolds trackway in Lincolnshire, Sewstern Lane running from East Anglia to the Midland Plain and so on. The Romans re-used and added to these to form a network of major through routes and minor roads: the Watling Street itself; the Ermine Street linking York to Lincoln and the South, crossing the Welland about half a mile upstream from Stamford; the road from Buxton to Little Chester near Derby. The roads singled out for mention by name in the Anglo-Norman sources were such major Roman routes. But the reality which these authors record is that of the tenth and eleventh centuries, periods as we shall see of rapid economic expansion. The importance of through routes by that date, and their existence in Roman times, need not argue for their continuing use and significance throughout the Anglo-Saxon period.

The Roman road connecting York and Doncaster to Lincoln was in use in the

Figure 3. Roman roads (after I. Margary, *Roman Roads in Britain*, 1967 edn).

seventh century, but it is as a military route for the movement of armies in the warfare between Mercia and Northumbria that we hear of it (see Chapter 6 below). During the sixth century burials were cut into the surface of the Ermine Street at Hackthorn,[19] and others have been found in the Watling Street at Kilsby and Aldwincle,[20] in neither case suggesting that these roads were still busy thoroughfares. The Anglo-Saxons often buried their dead, as had their predecessors, on boundaries where their spirits arguably protected the vulnerable margins and thresholds of the community. Burials associated with Roman roads underline the use of these roads as boundaries; their construction, often on a massive earthwork, made them obvious boundary marks and indeed they may already have functioned as property bounds in the

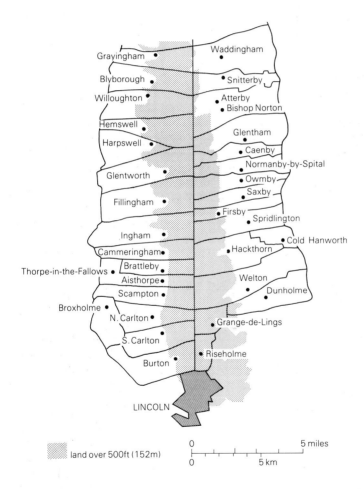

Figure 4. Ermine Street as a boundary of parishes to the north of Lincoln (after D. Owen, 'Chapelries and rural settlement: an examination of some of the Kesteven evidence', in *Medieval Settlement, Continuity and Change*, ed. P.H. Sawyer, 1976; and K. Cameron, unpublished).

pre-Saxon period. The Ermine Street is the boundary of a line of parishes in north Lincolnshire (see fig. 4) and was already a boundary of the estate of Haddon in Huntingdonshire in 951[21] and of Alwalton in 955;[22] parish bounds follow the Foss Way near Claybrooke and between Lincoln and Burgh-le-Marsh,[23] whilst the Jurassic Way is the boundary of 17 parishes in Northamptonshire, including Broughton, Walgrave and Pytchley.[24] Such boundaries may underline the continuity of property bounds and thus perhaps of social and administrative structures which are associated with property and its ownership from Roman or even pre-Roman Britain to Anglo-Saxon England, but they provide little argument for the survival of these same roads as long-distance routes in early Anglo-Saxon England.

Important tenth-century towns were often close to but not on the old Roman roads: Derby replaced the Roman site of Little Chester, to the north of the city; the Watling Street changed its course to take into account the growing importance of Northampton; Stamford is downstream of the Ermine Street's crossing of the Welland, situated at a point where the river could be forded, presumably because the Roman bridge had fallen. Important new routes had grown up by the eleventh century to serve these new sites, like the Northampton to Warwick road mentioned in a charter of 1020/2.[25] Routes serve needs as well as helping to channel them. Continued local use of Roman roads between the sixth and ninth centuries need not indicate their significance as long-distance thoroughfares; such routes may have had little relevance to contemporary economic needs. They were important for the movement of armies in seventh-century border warfare, and in the eighth and ninth centuries when Mercian kings required the owners of land to construct bridges, implying a concern for routes and communications, it was still military concerns which motivated them.[26] Source material emanating from the king and his court might be expected to stress military rather than economic use, but there are other reasons for thinking that long-distance routes were relatively unimportant at this date. Trade was apparently concentrated at coastal sites in the seventh and eighth centuries, and dealt largely in scarce, imported goods, as much a political as a mercantile activity. Through trade routes were less important, and the movements of peasants to pay dues, of wandering monks or peripatetic kings, may not have sufficed to maintain them. The elaborate method of construction of Roman roads meant that they survived and many were used again in the economic revival which marked the tenth and eleventh centuries. The important road system of the East Midlands by the eleventh century is largely a fruit of that revival. The existing routes of eastern England may have facilitated that upswing, as did undoubtedly the excellence of local river communications.

Many of the East Midland rivers were navigable to the shallow-draught boats of the early Middle Ages. The Trent was navigable as far as Nottingham and probably beyond; in the eleventh century anyone who impeded the passage of boats on the Nottinghamshire Trent was subject to a fine of eight pounds.[27] The Welland was navigable as far as Stamford, the Ouse probably as far as Bedford, the Nene well into Northamptonshire. Later in the Middle Ages Lincoln could still be reached by boat along the Witham, and the canal linking Lincoln to Torksey and the Trent was almost certainly in use before 1066, judging from the close links between Lincoln and Torksey in Domesday.[28]

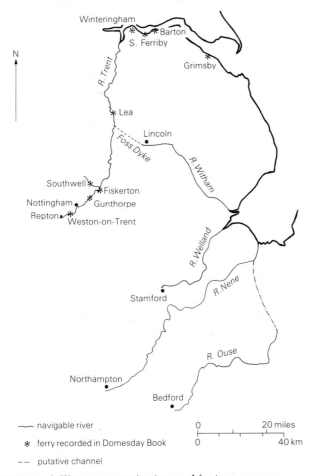

Winteringham
Barton
S. Ferriby
Grimsby
R. Trent
N
Lea
Lincoln
Foss Dyke
R. Witham
Southwell
Fiskerton
Nottingham
Gunthorpe
Repton
Weston-on-Trent
R. Welland
R. Nene
Stamford
R. Ouse
Northampton
Bedford

—— navigable river

* ferry recorded in Domesday Book

–·– putative channel

0   20 miles

0   40 km

Figure 5. Water communications and ferries.

These rivers opened the East Midlands not only to trade but to invasion. It was along the rivers of the Wash and Humber that many of the earliest Anglo-Saxon invaders came. In the ninth, tenth and eleventh centuries they facilitated Viking penetration. The Viking armies could travel along the Trent from York to winter at Torksey or to Ingleby near Repton in Derbyshire,[29] and need never be far from their boats. In 1013, during his last great campaign to conquer England, the Danish king Swegn established a base at Gainsborough on the Trent.[30] The Vikings could use Northampton as a centre because they could reach it by boat along the Nene. In their defence against the Vikings and their campaigns of conquest in eastern England the West Saxon kings of the early tenth century sought to block the passage of these rivers; Edward the Elder constructed fortified sites at Bedford, Stamford and Nottingham.[31] A remarkable concentration of earthworks in the Ouse and Ivel valleys may be associated with Viking activity, but whether constructed against Vikings or earlier invaders they underline the dangers in eastern England of river-borne invasion from the sea.[32]

Figure 6. The Trent/Humber confluence (Cambridge University Collection: copyright reserved).

By the time of Domesday the Trent/Humber route was so well established that the burgesses of Torksey were required to provide a boat to carry the sheriff to York when necessary,[33] but not all Anglo-Saxons could or did travel by boat. Useful as they were as routeways, rivers also channelled and deflected the other communications of the East Midlands. Their bridges and crossing points were the nodes of routes and urban development. Stamford was the 'stoney ford' where the Roman road now crossed the Welland. Nottingham stood where the London to York road crossed the Trent, a road so important in the eleventh century that it was accorded, along with the Trent and the Foss Way, the king's special protection in Nottinghamshire.[34] Where bridges were lacking or rivers too wide, ferries were used. Littleborough, probably the site of Bishop Paulinus' seventh-century baptisms in the Trent, was the ferrying point where the Roman road linking the Ermine Street at Lincoln to York and Doncaster crossed the river. Other ferries on the Trent by the late eleventh century existed at Gunthorpe, Fiskerton, Southwell, Lea and Weston-upon-Trent.[35] The wide estuary of the Humber was crossed by two ferries from Grimsby and two from South Ferriby, as well as from Barton and Winteringham.[36] The South Ferriby ferries were much used and yielded £3 each in tolls. The local Lincolnshire jurors complained to the Domesday surveyors in

1086 that the new Norman lords were taking new tolls on bread, fish and hides; by this date the ferries carried trade across the Humber.

As late as the eleventh century the military importance of key routes was never ignored. The routes forced through the narrow gap between the Pennines and the marshes of Axholme were always crucial to kings who aspired to control northern England. When the Norman overlord recolonized this area after its devastation by William's armies in the harrying of the North it was for strategic as much as economic reasons.[37] But by now the special royal protections accorded to the major routes of eastern England applied to the multitude of other officials and traders who regularly plied them.

Perception of the Landscape

Eastern England in the Anglo-Saxon period was an agrarian land; agriculture dominated the lives of most of its inhabitants, helped shape its landscape and provided the basis of its society and economy. The importance of the land and its agricultural exploitation recurs throughout the documents of the period, sometimes explicitly described, more often an unconscious element in the ideas, assumptions and concerns of the writers.

In 1086 Domesday Book was compiled at the order of William the Conqueror. It provides an astonishingly complete survey of England at the end of the Anglo-Saxon period, a record of the wealth and estates of the king and his great nobility. Towns are there, and already more important in eastern England than in much of the country, but in page after page of the Domesday survey the wealth of its great men and the lives of their poorer tenants appear solidly founded on the land.

> In Barnby in the Willows [Nottinghamshire] Wulfric had [in 1066] seven bovates of land subject to tax, land for three ploughs. Losoard, the Bishop of Bayeux's man has [in 1086] one plough and four freemen with two bovates of this land and nine villeins and six bordars have four and a half ploughs. There is a priest and a church to which belong half a bovate of land. One mill worth 5s 4d; meadow, thirty acres; underwood. The value in the time of king Edward and now, 40s.[38]

Even in the terseness of the Domesday entry it is clear that Barnby, like hundreds of other settlements, was an agricultural community, consisting of tenant farmers, freemen, occasionally of slaves. Its assets were its mill, its meadow, its woodland pasture, its arable land, and the rents and labour of its tenants. Many other things are important about such a community and its life; its social structure, its relationship with its landlord, its church and its beliefs, all questions to which we shall return. But the agricultural basis of life is paramount.

The land and its cultivation helped shape the thought and culture of the Anglo-Saxons. In the early eighth century Tatwine, a monk of the Leicestershire monastery of Breedon-on-the-Hill, became Archbishop of Canterbury. Tatwine was a scholar, the author of a treatise on grammar and the parts of speech. He also wrote 40 riddles, a form of literature to which the Anglo-Saxons were particularly addicted. These reflect not only the cultural interests of an eighth-century educated man but the rural roots and presuppositions of his culture. Tatwine wrote riddles on such obviously agrarian themes as 'The Sower' and 'The Winnowing Fork', but far more revealing of the influences which formed his mental picture are the images which sprang to his mind when he described the implements of a monk's literary endeavours. 'Parchment' is presented as an arable field, 'an artisan shaped me into a level field, whose fertile furrows the cultivator irrigates. My meadows yield a varied crop of balsam, a food for the healthy and a remedy for the sick.'[39] The pen which writes on the parchment is a plough 'compelled to plough wide level fields' and there the scribe forces from it ink as 'floods of tears to fill the arid furrows'.[40] Tatwine, a monk and a scholar, came from a culture steeped in agrarian imagery.

In spite of its obvious importance, straightforward descriptions of the landscape of eastern England in the Anglo-Saxon period are rare; it often appears, if at all, as a mere incidental backdrop to miraculous occurrences or to the more prosaic activities of saints. Thus the earliest description of the Fens, which stretched around the Wash and cut off eastern England from East Anglia, is from the pen of an eighth-century East Anglian monk in his life of the hero-hermit Guthlac: 'The great fen begins on the banks of the river Granta [i.e. for a man describing it from the East Anglian side] . . . swamps and bogs, an occasional black pool, exuding dark mists, sprinkled with islands of marshy heaths and crisscrossed by winding waterways.'[41] The thick fenland fogs were recorded only when, in the eleventh century, they hid from each other the rival monks of Ramsey and Ely when both were in quest of the relics of St Felix.[42] Guthlac sought out the island of Crowland for its inaccessibility, and Abbo of Fleury wrote of the Fens in the tenth century that they were 'Desirable havens of lonely life where solitude could not fail the hermits'.[43] Place-names and other sources underscore these occasional descriptions in painting the Fens of the Witham, Welland, Ouse and Nene as desolate and inhospitable.

Guthlac's island in the marshes was a place of terror, an abode of monsters and demons; his fens are those of the poem Beowulf, strongholds to which the monster Grendel tried to escape from the grips of the hero, a landscape inhabited by evil against which saints and heroes might battle. It is a picture informed by a magical view of the world, but not a solely ecclesiastical one. The wilds of fen and marsh were marginal places where enemies lurked, places shunned by all but saintly or political exiles. They held little charm for the agricultural communities of eastern England. It is their voice too which speaks through the pen of Guthlac's biographer or the *Beowulf* poet in descriptions of 'the paths of exile . . . the unknown land . . . the dangerous fen path'.[44]

The attractions of the Fens to the ascetic heroes of early Christianity has ensured that some picture of them has been recorded. In a society where churchmen had a virtual monopoly on the written word the existence of religious centres determines much of the geography of our knowledge. It is the great monastic houses, especially of the tenth century, like Ramsey, Peterborough or Thorney grouped around the Fens, which are responsible for the production or survival of such accounts. Most of eastern England is less fortunate; even stylized description is lacking. Much of our reconstruction of the landscape relies on Domesday Book, which must serve not only as a description of settled areas and forest, here to be used with caution, but also as the earliest record of most place-names, themselves a source for landscape history. But Domesday is an administrator's view of the landscape, interested in meadows, forest, even settlements only as sources of income and renders. Like the estate documents of the fenland abbeys from the tenth and eleventh centuries, it presents the land as lists of assets, so many tenants, pasturable woodland and so on. Such a view is not without its own interest, revealing as it does that for many of those who lived in it the landscape represented primarily a means of livelihood and was recorded as such.

Yet in Domesday and estate documents the viewpoint is still that of the lord, estate manager, royal official. Only in the bounds of charters do we come closer to the land as perceived by those who lived and worked in it. Anglo-Saxon charters are the records of lands granted or confirmed by the king; by the late Anglo-Saxon period most of them contain detailed boundary sections describing the property. If it is still the landlord's interest and desire to delineate his

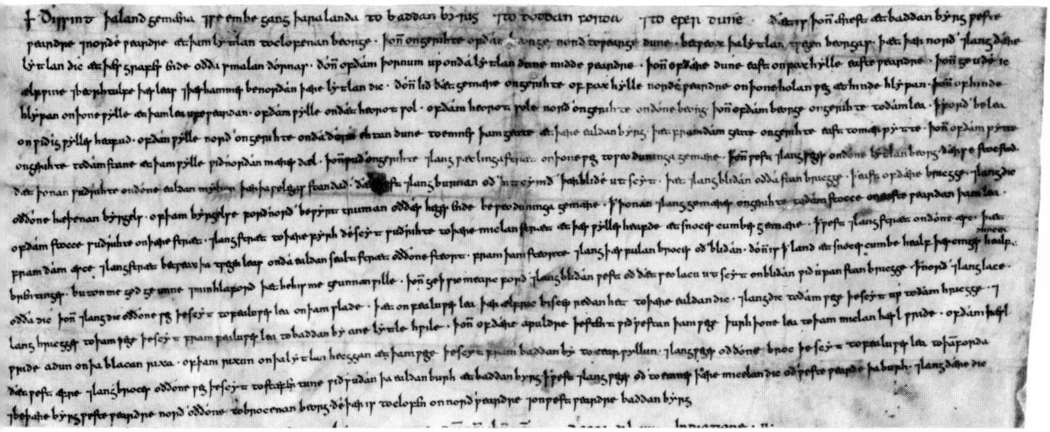

Figure 7. Boundary clause from the charter granting Badby to bishop Ælfric, A.D. 944 (BL Cotton Augustus ii.63, reproduced by permission of the British Library).

property which lies behind the production of a document, it is local knowledge which is drawn on for the detail. By the tenth and eleventh centuries the landscape they describe is one intimately known. The bounds of Badby, Northamptonshire (see fig. 7), for example, drawn up in 944, trace the estate from the hill at Studborough, via the hind's leap to the harts' wallowing place, by the mill pool where willows stand, to the heathen burial, the salt street, the hazel thicket and the apple tree.[45] The administrator's generalities of Domesday here give way to the local knowledge of the men who beat these bounds. At Ayston in Rutland in 1046 such men knew and recorded them not only by streams and trees, but by the location of badgers' setts and the lane called the Redway, coloured by the underlying ironstone.[46] But they saw it also as a peopled landscape, known in terms of its use and ownership. The boundaries of Weston-on-Trent, Nottinghamshire, included the ford on the edge of Sithrith's land and the thorn tree which marked the bound of Wulfheard's property;[47] those of Stanton in the Peak (Derbyshire) ran into dales and along spurs like Æthered's spur, on Æthered's land.[48] The ownership of adjacent property as much as geography interested those who described these boundaries. They show a landscape already well exploited in many areas; in the eleventh century the bounds of Badby and Newnham follow the headlands and furrows of the cultivated fields, the land had been cleared and ploughed up to the very bounds of the parish.[49] The boundaries of charters are unfortunately a relatively rare source for eastern England. Where they exist they take us close to a land described and known in terms of hills, streams and thorn trees, of the habits of badgers and deer, of agricultural use and ownership.

All written sources are at this date the products of specialists and of particular needs, written by ecclesiastics to celebrate saints, to record land ownership and its income, rarely concerned with landscape as such. The place-names are different. The majority of the names now in use for settlements and features of the landscape date back to the Anglo-Saxon period. These names are now fixed and often appear meaningless, but when first given they accurately described the places to which they were applied. Some give graphic pictures of the locality: Cranford, Northamptonshire, the crane's ford; Warkworth, the spider's clearing; Hartwell, the harts' spring. But if Derby is the village (*by*) of the deer, Nottingham is the village or settlement (*ham*) of the followers or family of a man called Snot. Place-names as often record ownership as physical appearance. In the names they gave to their settlements as in the descriptions of their boundaries the Anglo-Saxons seem as much aware of ownership and use as of appearance.

2 The Agrarian Economy

Population

At the end of the eleventh century the total population of England lay in the region of 1.75 to 2.25 million.[1] The source for these figures is Domesday Book, a survey which was in no sense a population census. Domesday lists primarily

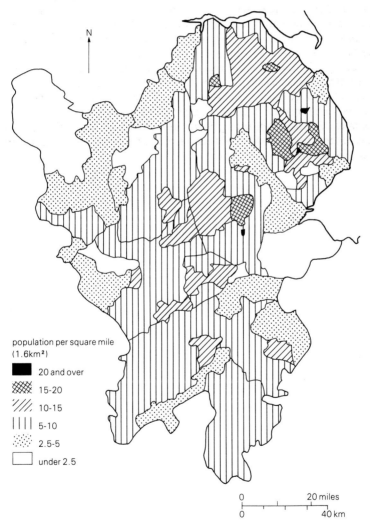

Figure 8. Population in 1086 (after H.C. Darby, *Domesday England*, 1977).

those responsible for the payment of dues, especially royal dues; as a result it omits many groups, including slaves, who did not have such responsibility and includes only the tenants or heads of households who made such payments. To convert numbers of people in Domesday into population totals thus requires a series of adjustments; estimates must be made of those omitted, a 'typical household size' (household multiplier) decided on so that lists of tenants can be expanded to a full figure of men, women and children.

Neither task is easy. There is general agreement that Domesday under-estimates the numbers of slaves, and a figure of 5 per cent is added to its rural population to allow for them. Five per cent is a proportion based on totals of slaves in counties where they *are* recorded. It is more difficult to decide how many under-tenants or rent-paying tenants have been omitted, though the question may be crucial, especially for the Derbyshire populations. Rent-payers who did not contribute to royal dues directly may often have appeared irrelevant to Domesday compilers. In Staffordshire, for example, local surveys made only 40 years or so after Domesday contain large numbers of rent-payers. Are we to argue for a spate of rapid land clearance and population change here in the late eleventh century?[2] Or simply to conclude that Domesday is an inaccurate guide to such groups in 1086?

The calculation of a 'household multiplier', or number of men, women and children who stand behind each tenant, is even more difficult since eleventh century sources give little guidance. Figures must be derived from later records and are variously estimated between three and five people to a family.[3] It is assumed that the tenants mentioned in Domesday are heads of nuclear families (father, mother and children, plus perhaps an elderly parent) and these multipliers are often based on that assumption. But if we are dealing with a wider extended family (parents, children, grandparents, aunts and uncles) these calculations are wide of the mark. The figures given here must thus be used largely for comparative purposes; they are at their weakest as *totals* of population.

The rural population of the East Midlands in 1086 was as follows:[4]

Shire	1. Total rural population in Domesday	2. × 4	3. × 5	4. + 5% for slaves
Bedfordshire	3,591	14,364	17,955	179
Derbyshire	2,836	11,344	14,180	141
Huntingdonshire	2,500	10,000	12,500	125
Leicestershire	6,423	25,728	32,115	321
Lincolnshire	21,462	85,848	107,310	1,073
Northamptonshire	7,663	30,652	38,315	383
Nottinghamshire	5,608	22,432	28,040	280
Rutland	859	3,436	4,295	43

The 'total rural population' here includes unfree tenants, prosperous peasants and small-holders, plus freemen, the so-called sokemen, and also priests, dairymaids and so on. In columns 2 and 3 these figures have been multiplied by two widely accepted family sizes (4 and 5) to produce two estimates of total population. They are all figures for rural population; town sizes will be discussed later (see below, pp. 51–3). With all their limitations they allow us, especially in conjunction with the map of population distributions (see fig. 8), to make broad comparisons of the late eleventh-century population.

The high population of Lincolnshire stands out. This is obviously a function of the sheer size of this shire, but a glance at the map shows that Lincolnshire also contains considerable concentrations of population. The shire also has a large number of tenth- and eleventh-century place-names easily identifiable by their Scandinavian forms (see fig. 47). These new place-names are not all new settlements, though some of them may be; they are certainly a sign of a vigorous land market and of economic growth in this area in the late Saxon period. The high population figures are linked in some way to this. But the large relative total for Lincolnshire population may also be one of those quirks of the Domesday figures. In this shire a large class of rent-paying tenants, the sokemen, have been included; over 50 per cent of the recorded rural population are sokemen, 10,882 all told. Leicestershire, Nottinghamshire and to a lesser extent Northamptonshire all list sokemen: 1,903 in Leicestershire, 1,704 in Nottinghamshire, 971 in Northamptonshire. We shall be returning to sokemen later, but here it should be noticed that they are a type of rent-payer, but free enough to pay their own royal dues, and that their appearance in these shires is related to that same vigorous land market and the consequent break-up of older estates. They deserve stress in these overall population figures because they are precisely that group which often slipped through the Domesday net. Economic changes had altered their position in areas like Lincolnshire, and brought them to the fore. Their inclusion in Domesday here and elsewhere may distort the population picture in these shires. In Derbyshire, by contrast, the low population figure may be partly a result of the omission of the sokemen's close cousins, the rent-payers.

The global figures by shire are less telling than the distribution of population and village sizes. In Lincolnshire, for example, population was concentrated, especially at the southern end of the Wolds and in central Kesteven around Grantham and Sleaford. This is also an area of small, irregular-shaped parishes in the Middle Ages, suggesting pressure on the land and its resources during the tenth and eleventh centuries when parish boundaries were fixed.[5] In Nottinghamshire it was the valleys of Trent and Soar which supported the largest numbers, the sandstone forest areas of Sherwood the least.[6] The Leicestershire valleys of Belvoir, Soar and Wreake were similarly well settled and by 1086 only parts of west Leicestershire and Charnwood forest remained thinly populated.[7] Charnwood forest is virtually a population blank (though a scattered population may have been included in the totals for villages on its edges), whereas the clearance of forest in the Wreake valley was well progressed; there is little or no woodland recorded here.[8] The Huntingdonshire pattern shows that the blacklands and peatlands of the Huntingdonshire fens supported little settlement;[9] by contrast the clay vale of the Ouse in Bedfordshire was well settled.

Both the global figures and the pattern of population show a well-settled landscape, the fertile river valleys already densely populated, the resources of the land often approaching full utilization by clearance. Individual village sizes, although they vary enormously, give a similar warning against under-estimating the size of eleventh-century communities. Castor by Peter-borough in Northamptonshire had 29 tenants and 4 slaves in 1086, a com-munity of between 120 and 149 souls; Brixworth with 40 tenants had between 160 and 200. Orton-on-the-Hill in Leicestershire had 28 tenants and 1 slave, a total of 113–42, neighbouring Twycross numbered between 69 and 86, Sheepy Magna between 56 and 70. A large, thriving market village like St Ives in Huntingdonshire had a population between 248 and 310. These are lowland, mixed farming communities typical of much of the region. Derbyshire, with stretches of pastoral upland, shows not only a thinner population but one scattered through small settlements and hamlets. Bakewell, for example, had an apparently large population of 216 to 268, but this figure included not only Bakewell itself but the eight hamlets of Nether and Over Haddon, Holme, Rowsley, Burton, Conkesbury, One Ash and Monyash which were attached to it; Eyam to the north had only 76–95 souls. Where Derbyshire settlements are individually described their small size is clear: Gratton with 6 tenants numbered between 24 and 30 people, Ash with 7 had little more at 28–35.

Domesday with all its limitations provides material for comparisons. To try to delve behind it into population history before the late eleventh century is to move into almost total darkness, an obscurity which makes crucial questions of population growth or decline during the Anglo-Saxon period almost unanswerable. Archaeological excavation, like that at Raunds in North-amptonshire,[10] is beginning to provide a little evidence. Here a succession of two churches and a cemetery serving a tenth- and eleventh-century com-munity have been excavated. A very small tenth-century church was destroyed and rebuilt during the eleventh century, replaced by a larger structure which housed 30 to 40 people. Church rebuilding, of course, reflects many things other than simple population growth, but the size of the new church gives some indication of that of the community. A population estimate based on the number of burials and length of use of the cemetery again gives a community of 36 ± 10.[11]

The building and rebuilding of the church at Raunds raises and fails to answer the question of population growth during the Anglo-Saxon period. Does the need for a new and larger church within a century of the construction of the old one argue an expansion of population, or simply greater wealth and rising aspirations? Does Domesday merely freeze a moment during a period of rapid population change? Recent research is suggesting that the pattern of English settlement is old, going back to Romano-British times at least,[12] and the related assumption is that the rate of population growth between the fifth and eleventh centuries was low. But to argue that a settlement pattern is old is not necessarily to prove that population within that pattern was static. The new view of settlement history certainly requires a rethink of glib assump-tions on population growth, but we are thrown back on mere shreds of evidence for its likely pattern.

The causes of population growth or decline come down to questions of birth and death rates and what causes changes within them. Some argue that population fluctuates largely in relation to resources, expanding as long as food resources do and reaching critical levels and the onset of decline when such resources are outstripped. But this crude statement has to be modified by consideration of social habits such as age at marriage, restrictions on marriage and so on which play a crucial part in determining fertility levels. For the later Middle Ages, when population statistics are fuller, a view of population change based less on resources and more on disease has been advanced,[13] and some shift of emphasis in this direction is necessary since throughout the Middle Ages the death rates of rich and poor are more similar than they ought to be if food supply and malnutrition were the sole or even major determinants. Dirt, fleas, lice, rats, impure drinking water and disease may have played a large part in determining Anglo-Saxon population levels.[14]

Translating such considerations into the reality of eastern England is difficult. Western Europe as a whole was swept by a visitation of the bubonic plague between the sixth and eighth centuries. Its local impact is unchronicled, but some protracted population decline as a result of this endemic disease occurred widely. The cemetery evidence suggests that throughout the Anglo-Saxon period the age structure of the population and its mortality rates would have discouraged any spectacular growth. Of the 368 burials in the Raunds cemetery, 304 have been subjected to detailed analysis.[15] The village community had a very high infant mortality rate. One-sixth of all children died before the age of two, most in the first 12 months of life, whilst one-third were dead by the age of six. This high infant death rate was not apparently due to still-birth or premature delivery (though the evidence here may be distorted by different burial rites for such babies) but to the problems of birth itself and the months after, arguing for poor hygiene and nutrition as significant factors. The female mortality rate was high during the crucial years of child-bearing. Of the 70 women who survived to the age of 17, 30 were dead by the age of 25 and another 20 before they reached 35. Men showed a more gradual rise in mortality rates: a half of those who reached 17 survived into the age range 35–45. At Raunds the average life expectancy at birth was 21, a figure brought down by high levels of infant mortality; for those who reached the age of 12 the expected life span was 33, though some individuals reached 60 or more. The age structure and mortality rates of the Raunds population are similar to those found in much of the Third World today. If this picture of a late Anglo-Saxon community in Northamptonshire is at all typical its high mortality of infants and women of child-bearing age must have acted as a natural brake on population rise.

Premature ageing and heavy over-work was a factor in this picture. Osteo-arthritis was the rule rather than the exception in the bones of adults examined, present throughout the limbs but especially in the vertebrae of the spinal column, where two or three vertebrae were often fused, restricting movement and leading eventually to immobility. Such features argue a life of constant, heavy manual labour for men and women. What little work has been done on the early cemeteries of the settlement period points in the same direction. A far from complete analysis of the cremated and crushed bones from Loveden Hill[16] again shows a sixth-century population of people who died young after a life of heavy labour. From Raunds at the end of the period and Loveden Hill at the beginning the same results of inadequate medical knowledge emerge: fractured bones often not set but allowed to heal in a broken position, long-standing bone infection. Such research is still far too fragmentary to base a theory of population change on it. Unknown changes in marriage patterns and other social change could still have had their effect. But infant and adult mortality rates on this scale are unlikely to have encouraged anything but a gradual population upswing. The broad pattern of the Domesday map at the end of the eleventh century may be much older than is often allowed.

Agriculture

This population of the East Midlands lived chiefly on and by the land. Agriculture was the single most important activity. We have already seen how in Domesday when the wealth of the area was recorded in the late eleventh century, that wealth was overwhelmingly agrarian, set down in lists of villages and agricultural tenants, of ploughteams, pastureland and grain mills. Agricultural life was the basis of the imagery of much Anglo-Saxon literature, of the wealth of religious houses and lay families, the way of life of the bulk of the population.

The predominant economy of eastern England was mixed agriculture, a combination of arable and animal farming to support the village community with meat and grain products, to provide dung to fertilize the fields, and to provide those surpluses which sustained kings, nobles, churchmen and towns. The inhabitants of the mid-Saxon (seventh- to ninth-century) village of Maxey, Northamptonshire, grew grain which they milled on quernstones and kept a variety of animals – cattle, goats and especially sheep and pigs.[17] The late Saxon communities in Huntingdonshire at Eaton Socon, Little Paxton and St Neots show a similar mix. When an overlord diverted the surplus of village agriculture he too was interested in the basics of subsistence which the villagers attempted to provide for themselves. When Wulfred leased land at Sempringham from the monastery at *Medeshamstede* (Peterborough) in 852, he agreed to make an annual render from the village produce of cattle for slaughter, loaves and ale.[18]

Animals were reared, but the most important food crops were grain and especially barley. A coarse, grain diet wore away the well-ground-down teeth of those buried at Loveden Hill in the sixth century, and left them with few caries.[19] Barley was sown in the spring together with oats, or with wheat and rye as autumn-sown crops. The two casks of clear ale and ten measures of Welsh ale provided by the villagers at Sempringham were probably brewed from barley; their 600 loaves may have been wheat, since they were intended for the lord, though barley is equally likely. No great estate could be set up or function without due emphasis on grain production. Among the gifts of Bishop Æthelwold to Peterborough were 350 acres of seed and 23 of clean wheat.[20]

The numbers of mills – grain-mills for the grinding of corn – recorded in Domesday testify to the significance of grain in the agriculture and diet of the region: 64 places are recorded as having a mill in Bedfordshire, 204 in Lincolnshire, 172 in Northamptonshire, 80 in Nottinghamshire.[21] Again the vagaries of Domesday, where so much is patchily recorded, make comparisons from county to county dangerous, but the distribution of mills may be some clue to the relative wealth and agricultural pattern. Derbyshire has only 52 places with mills, a mere 15 per cent of the total number of places recorded;

Nottinghamshire has 80 (27 per cent of the places recorded) whereas 45 per cent of the places mentioned in Bedfordshire have mills and 49 per cent of those in Northamptonshire. The greater importance of pastoral farming and of dispersed, small-scale settlement in Derbyshire and west Nottinghamshire contrasts with the rich arable and large villages of Bedfordshire and Northamptonshire.

A similar index of grain-farming is given by the Domesday ploughteams. The survey often records the number of ploughteams: in Wymeswold, Leicestershire, the landlords Robert and Serlo had two ploughs, the villagers

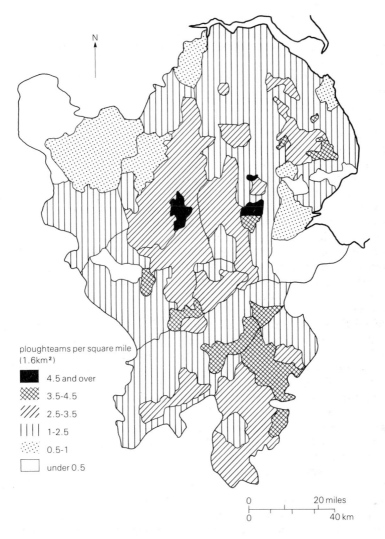

ploughteams per square mile
(1.6km²)

- 4.5 and over
- 3.5-4.5
- 2.5-3.5
- 1-2.5
- 0.5-1
- under 0.5

0   20 miles

0   40 km

Figure 9. Distribution of ploughteams recorded in Domesday (after H.C. Darby, *Domesday England*, 1977).

among them another ten;[22] at Bletsoe, Bedfordshire, the lord had one plough, the villagers three;[23] at Eyam, Derbyshire, the villagers had five ploughs.[24] The map of the distribution of ploughteams (fig. 9) again shows Northamptonshire and especially Bedfordshire as rich, arable areas, together with large parts of Leicestershire and Lincolnshire; Derbyshire is confirmed as relatively poor arable, though Nottinghamshire appears more like Leicestershire. It is on evidence such as this that the East Midlands appears at the end of the eleventh century as a prosperous agricultural area, though without the large areas of concentrated arable wealth apparent in for example East Anglia or the West Midlands.

Domesday concentrates on the dues of tenants and on arable wealth. It is certainly a distortion of the overall agrarian economy and of lifestyle, but it does show that late eleventh-century observers measured wealth primarily in these terms. The picture needs correction by an emphasis on animal husbandry, but not over-correction. Animals were of undoubted importance in the mixed economy of the region from the beginning. Objects fashioned from bone, often the bones of domestic animals, are a feature of the pagan Anglo-Saxon cemeteries. The excavations at Maxey showed a rough balance between cattle, sheep, goat and pig, though the tendency for pig bones to disintegrate more readily in the soil casts doubt on these proportions. The relative uses and values of these animals in the peasant economy is clear at Maxey. Two-thirds of the pigs had been killed before they were 18 months old, presumably for food. By contrast the cattle were two years old and more at death, many over three, whilst nearly half the horses were four to five years old or more;[25] these animals were more valuable, scarcer and used for draught rather than food. A large tenth-century monastic estate shows the same proportions and relative values of animals, though it should be remembered that such an estate, although primarily a subsistence unit writ large, may also have produced for the market. When the abbey of Thorney was set up, the monks of Ely sent supplies to aid in its establishment. Pigs predominated and were cheaper: 80 pigs were only worth £1 and a full-grown one 6d., whereas an unspecified number of mill oxen had to be purchased for 30 mancuses of gold.[26] Some of Ely's own herds are enumerated, including those at Hatfield which had 40 oxen, 250 sheep, 47 goats, 15 calves and 190 swine; Hatfield supplied Thorney with 13 breeding sows and 83 young pigs.

Domesday confirms the numerical importance of sheep and pigs in the agrarian economy as producers of wool, milk and meat. Pasture and woodland is often recorded not by total area but by the number of pigs or sheep it was estimated that it could support. Pasture seems to have been reserved for the valuable sheep, as at Langford (Bedfordshire) where there was pasture for 300 sheep,[27] whereas the pigs foraged in the woodland; the same village had woodland for 16 pigs. The Anglo-Saxon pig is believed to have been a dark-skinned, long-legged and hairy animal, small in size and ranging free in large herds.[28] The herds recorded in Bedfordshire, if they are not simply notional calculations of woodland, could be huge. At Easton there was wood for 100 pigs,[29] at Totternhoe for 150,[30] and on the huge royal manor of Luton for 2,000.[31]

It is when we move from the simple fact of mixed agriculture and its prevalence to an attempt to assess the importance of animal farming in the economy of the region or in particular parts of it that we encounter difficulty.

Within the domestic economy animals provided meat and wool. Few excavated domestic sites have not produced loom weights or even remnants of woollen textiles to testify to the weaving of cloth from local wool. The size of some of the herds already noted appear to be production for market rather than simply consumption, though the largest were on royal or ecclesiastical estates. A century or more later Lincolnshire would support huge commercial flocks of sheep, reared to produce wool for export,[32] and it has been suggested that the wealth of this area in the eleventh century, as recorded in Domesday values, was already partly derived from wool, whose production Domesday does not record.[33] Just outside this region at North Elmham, Norfolk, large flocks of wethers (castrated rams) were kept in Anglo-Saxon times, animals which produce a heavy fleece and which judging from their age at six years or so were kept primarily for wool.[34] Some commercial production especially on the large estates is likely, but the silence of Domesday on the size of livestock herds makes it impossible to check its importance in the overall economy.

Within an overall picture for the East Midlands of mixed farming with pockets of especial wealth in the rich arable areas of parts of Bedfordshire, of Northamptonshire, Leicestershire, Nottinghamshire and Lincolnshire, there is some significant regional variation. The Fenlands and its rivers had their own specific economies related especially to the opportunities provided by fishing and salt. The fenland abbeys kept boats on Whittlesey Mere: the abbot of Ramsey one, the abbot of Peterborough one and the abbot of Thorney two. The abbot of Ramsey's fisheries and meres in Huntingdonshire were worth £10 a year in the eleventh century.[35] Eels were the most important catch, and were bred in these ponds and weirs. Every year the fishermen of Wisbech rendered 37,010 eels to their lords, the abbots of Ely, Bury, Ramsey and Crowland and William of Warenne.[36] We hear most of fishing and fisheries in connection with the well-managed estates of great religious houses like Thorney, Ely or Peterborough. Eels could be caught inland in the mill ponds attached to grain mills, though here too the lord may have controlled this valuable asset as he controlled the mills themselves. On a river like the Trent fixed traps or weirs were set up, an obstruction which led to the protection of the Nottinghamshire Trent from anything which might hinder the passage of ships; this restriction probably lies behind the complaint in Domesday by the citizens of Nottingham that they were now forbidden to fish.[37]

The most important item of agricultural technology in the Anglo-Saxon period was the plough. Other equipment was certainly known and used; Tatwine has a riddle for the winnowing fork in the eighth century[38] and Thorney was provided with harrows for its estates at Newton, Yaxley and Stanground in the late tenth.[39] But it is the heavy plough drawn by a team of eight oxen which is the key to arable farming by the time of Domesday. It determined the pattern of fields, ploughing in long strips of ridge and furrow, and was a major determinant of the fertility of the soil and thus of agricultural yield, which largely depended in the absence of other means of fertilization on the availability of dung and the number of ploughings per year. It is clear that by the eleventh century the heavy plough and its associated field patterns were widely in use in eastern England. Charter bounds like that of Badby, Northamptonshire (fig. 7), occasionally describe the edges of open fields, charting the headlands and furrows which are a feature of this pattern of cultivation.

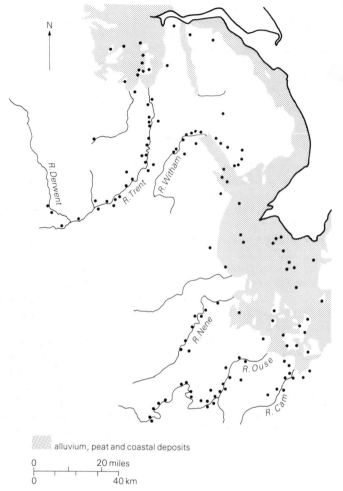

N

R. Derwent

R. Trent

R. Witham

R. Nene

R. Ouse

R. Cam

alluvium, peat and coastal deposits

| 0 | | | 20 miles |
| 0 | | | 40 km |

Figure 10. Fisheries recorded in Domesday (after H.C. Darby, *Domesday England*, 1977).

The same royal officials who were concerned with the obstruction of the Trent feared that the Nottingham to York road was in danger of being undermined or encroached by over-assiduous ploughing; no-one was to plough within two perches of it.[40] Domesday is full of references to ploughteams, a fact worthy of note in itself. An iron-clad plough drawn by eight oxen represented a significant capital outlay and when Domesday records, as it usually does, that the villagers held so many ploughs between them it means just that. Few peasant farmers, even the most prosperous, could afford such an investment. The sheer number of ploughteams recorded in areas like Bedfordshire and Northamptonshire (see fig. 9) is not merely an index of the arable wealth of these areas, but a reason for it. The advance of the plough and of the yield of arable farming went together.

Once again the earlier history of this technology and the consequent part it may have played in economic growth is obscure. The Romans had the use of a heavy plough, so that the technology itself is old.[41] But the extent of its early use is unknown. Ploughs like that found at St Neots[42] are not known from the archaeological record before the tenth century, and on this basis some scholars are inclined to keep an open mind on early techniques.[43] If it could be shown that the tenth and eleventh centuries showed considerable advance in the use of the heavy plough it would help to explain other apparent signs of economic growth in eastern England at this date. But the evidence is too negative to sustain the argument.

The villages which these fields served have been subjected to little study; settlement archaeology is still at an early stage. But many recent excavations have shown a tendency for village sites to 'drift' or move progressively over the centuries. The picture may be exaggerated because it is precisely where such drift has occurred that village sites are now available for excavation, whereas those which lie under modern settlements can rarely be investigated. At Maxey the Middle Saxon village lay between the present village and the isolated church;[44] at Salmonby, Lincolnshire, the early village was 750m west of the present one;[45] at Little Paxton the late Saxon site does not coincide with the modern village.[46] Such drift occurred within the Anglo-Saxon period as well as after it. The early place-name *Wīchām* represents a Romano-British settlement site; it is rarely found as a Saxon village name but often survives on the bounds of a settlement or as an outlying field name.[47] Such drift may indicate that new features, a church, road or similar, have attracted the village to them. At Salmonby a period of total desertion is possible. But it is also feasible that we are seeing the archaeological traces of an early Anglo-Saxon pattern of more dispersed settlement, such as that found in the Iron Age and later in parts of Northamptonshire,[48] which only gradually came to be focussed on a nucleated village centre. Church foundation is one possible factor in such a development; so too is the adoption of heavy plough agriculture and the consequent growth of large common fields and the need for more co-operative agriculture.

Great Estates

The peasant farmer, whether as unfree tenant, rent-payer or freeholder, was the basis of agricultural life, but his agrarian activity as opposed to his situation in society can rarely be glimpsed. It is the great estates, chiefly those in the hands of kings and churchmen, which are recorded most clearly in the documentary sources. The emphasis may appear regrettable but is not distorted. It was these accumulations of land in the hands of kings, nobles and churchmen which diverted, accumulated and distributed peasant surplus. As such they are a key to economic change, a factor in the life of peasant families, and underlie not only the social structure but also much of the religious and cultural history of the region. They are certainly not the only factor at work in these areas, but the story of their growth and consolidation is a prerequisite for the consideration of any of them.

The earliest estates were in the hands of kings, princes and other independent lords, products of a system of domination of peasant farmers already old in Europe by the sixth century.[49] They were less simple accumulations of land than of labour, services and renders to provide for the varied needs of the lord and his court. Townships, settlements and hamlets were organized around the lord's hall and their populations provided tribute and dues: hospitality to the lord and his followers, maintenance of his huntsmen and dogs, building works for the upkeep and repair of his house and various renders of cattle and provisions. The origins of this system lie back beyond the Anglo-Saxon period,[50] but by the time of our earliest documents estates of this sort are everywhere. A late seventh-century tribute list of the Mercian kings, the *Tribal Hidage*, describes the area around the Fens as a string of such estates, the *Widerigga* around Wittering in Northamptonshire, the *Gyrwe* around Peterborough, the *Gifle* in the Ivel valley of Bedfordshire.[51] Oundle was the centre of such a unit in Bede's time: he speaks of it as a *provincia* and it was later the centre of eight hundreds.[52] Many of the earliest English place-names describe either large estates of this nature or settlements within them. The names ending in *-ingas* mean 'the followers of/family of/more generally those in dependence on a person or place'. They often name the centre or chief settlement of an ancient estate, as Spalding of the *Spalda*, a group in the *Tribal Hidage*, whilst names ending in *-ington* or *-ingham* indicate settlements attached to that centre: thus Kettering and Ketteringham in Northamptonshire, and Nottingham, which was the *ham* or settlement of the *Snotingas*, dependants of an estate belonging to Snot. Such names are known to belong as early as the seventh and eighth centuries.[53]

Remnants of these estates are still there in Domesday and the survey gives some picture of their earlier nature. On the royal estates especially, Domesday records dues which go back in part to these earliest renders: the inhabitants of Leighton Buzzard provided the king annually not only with cash, but with half a day's provisions of wheat, honey and other things plus dues for the upkeep of the king's hunting dogs;[54] the royal lands in Northamptonshire paid the king the revenue of three nights every year (a sum notionally capable of the upkeep of the royal court for that period) as well as providing for hunting dogs, for hay, for a hawk and a hunting horse.[55]

In the eleventh century Lincolnshire, and especially the Pennine areas of Nottinghamshire and Derbyshire, contained huge estates known as sokes, 13 of them in Nottinghamshire alone.[56] These consisted of a central township to which outlying settlements were attached either as 'sokeland' or 'berewicks'. Berewicks were specialist home-farms where the lord's especial needs for food were met, sokelands were hamlets or villages occupied by men and women who owed services and tributes to the lord's court.[57] The pattern immediately recalls that of the old estates, and the very term 'soke' has its origin in the word for 'seeking', underlining the attachment of these villages to the estate centre. In the eleventh century places like Mansfield in Nottinghamshire (see fig. 11), Bolingbroke, Grantham and Kirton-in-Lindsey in Lincolnshire, and Ashford and Bakewell in Derbyshire were, along with many others, centres for such estates. By the eleventh century much may have happened to alter them; like all estates they were responsive to the changing needs and demands of lords, changes in land ownership and so on, and their precise nature and shape in Domesday is unlikely to be a simple continuation of that of the sixth and seventh centuries. But they preserve something of the structure of these

Figure 11. Mansfield and its sokeland and berewicks in 1086.

earliest estates both in their enormous geographical spread and in their pattern of dues and payments. The earliest and most continual demands of a lord were for material provision for himself and his followers, forced hospitality, provision for his hunting and the maintenance of the structures of his hall and court. From the beginning these huge estates were organized to meet these requirements.

They were originally in the hands of kings and great lords, two groups which were once not so clearly distinguishable.[58] The South Gyrwe was in the hands in the seventh century of a *princeps* (?prince) called Tondbert.[59] Another great lord, the *princeps* Frithuric, founded the monastery at Breedon and endowed it with such an estate, the *Hrepingas*.[60] Frithuric's gift shows how the Christian church, once it had entered the history of eastern England in the seventh century, was granted estates of this type. The original land-grant to Peterborough abbey (see fig. 12) was an entire tribute group named in the *Tribal Hidage*, the North Gyrwe, which straddled Lincolnshire, Cambridgeshire and

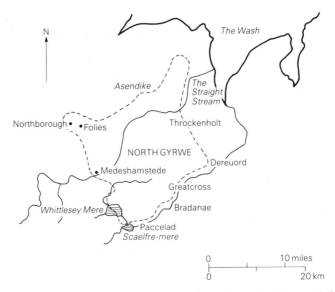

Figure 12. The original endowment of Peterborough abbey, probably the district of the North Gyrwe (after W.T. Potts, 'The pre-Danish estate of Peterborough Abbey, *Procs. Cambs. Antiquarian Soc.*, LXV, 1974).

Huntingdonshire.[61] In the hands of kings and sometimes churches these old units survived into the eleventh century. Rutland, the small and anomalous shire between Northamptonshire and Lincolnshire, may be just such a survival, fossilized by its use as the dower of Mercian and later queens.[62]

These estates were the prerequisite for the existence and lifestyle of the ruling elite of lay lords and churchmen. Their organized demands were the basis on which later and heavier services for many peasants would be built (see below, pp. 158–61). They diverted an enforced surplus from the peasant farmer, often producing a need for trade and exchange to fulfil the lord's demands. We shall see later that the centres of such estates were among the earliest markets and towns.

The transfer of these estates in large numbers by royal grants to the church in the seventh and eighth centuries is a sharp reminder that the conversion to Christianity had an economic as well as a cultural impact on the East Midlands. The church accumulated resources not only in land, but in a share of the loot of warfare and through the redirection of burial gifts from the bodies of the pagan dead to the Christian church.[63] It had new and staggeringly expensive needs: for buildings, ritual objects and, less obviously, for the resources to stock its libraries, the basis for its mission of the word. A book such as the Lichfield Gospels would have required the slaughter of 120 animals to provide the vellum alone;[64] the libraries of monasteries like Peterborough and Breedon required a massive investment of local resources.

Between the eighth and the eleventh centuries, and especially in the ninth and tenth, these ancient estates underwent a process of fragmentation. The end result of that process (or a stage in it) can be seen in Domesday. Noble and ecclesiastical estates were now made up not of one or two large units, but of large numbers of individual villages and settlements which Domesday lists separately and describes as 'manors'. The largest of these new estates might spread through several shires. Ulf Fenisc, that is Ulf the Fenman, held lands scattered especially through Lincolnshire and Nottinghamshire, whilst the house of Earl Leofric, that is Leofric's widow Godgifu and his grandsons Edwin and Morcar, held villages throughout the Midlands (see fig. 13). The abbot of

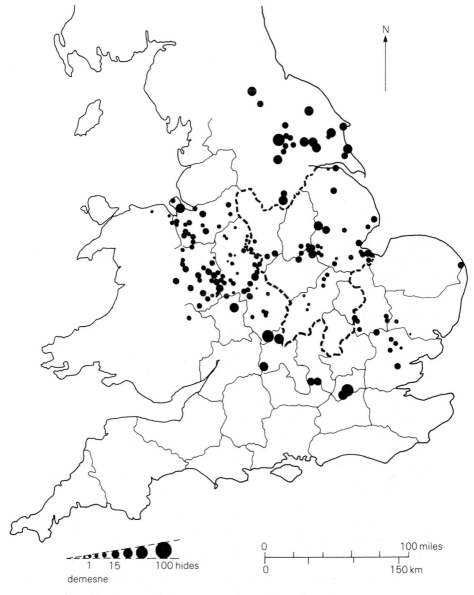

Figure 13. Lands of the Leofric family in Domesday (after D. Hill, *An Atlas of Anglo-Saxon England*, 1977).

Peterborough held extensive lands concentrated in Northamptonshire and along the Nene valley, but also manors scattered through south Lincolnshire, Leicestershire, Rutland and Yorkshire. On a smaller scale, a lesser nobleman like Ælfric son of Mergeat held nine manors in Leicestershire, and Ælfwold, seven villages in Bedfordshire. The size of some of these holdings is a result of political and religious changes especially during the tenth century, but their nature, consisting as they do of accumulations of individual villages or parts of villages, is a result of changes in the older estate patterns.

The story of these changes is linked to shifts in attitudes towards wealth and landholding. Land belonged originally not to the individual but to the family and the family's rights in it were inalienable. This idea was fundamental before the ninth century[65] and still tenacious at the end of the tenth; witness the problems caused by the monastic revival which challenged it on a large scale. The estates of the seventh and eighth centuries provided noble and royal families with their needs, and although land might be used to reward a follower temporarily, it did not permanently leave the family property. The earliest place-names emphasize this lack of a concept of individual ownership; they are group names as we have seen, and often geographical names describing land in terms of its location or function in an estate rather than in terms of ownership. Oundle, for example, was originally the name of a whole area, *Gifle* in Bedfordshire is a river name, the Ivel, used to describe a large unit.[66] Movable wealth, gold, silver, ornaments, horses, arms, were what normally passed between men; land by contrast was loaned not alienated. The intrusion of the church with its demands for land into such a society was potentially disruptive, but early ecclesiastical structures developed to fit social mores rather than vice versa. Family monasteries were founded on family land and family groups joined them. However, with the *idea* of alienation, the church had introduced a possible solvent into the system of landholding.

Gradually during the ninth and tenth centuries these views on inalienability were broken down and the primary agents of that change were kings. They now made permanent grants of land to their followers, perhaps especially quickly at times of political stress and change like the ninth-century Viking invasions and the tenth-century expansion of the English Kingdom. The Viking invasions and settlements were of especial significance in the East Midlands, and played their own part in the process, first by disrupting existing landholding as new landlords, a transfer into new ownership which necessarily breached older traditions, and secondly by stimulating a new market in land.[67] The monastic revival of the tenth century was most significant in the shires bordering the Fens. Like the Viking invasions it produced a massive transfer of property, now into church hands. Whereas earlier monasticism was assimilated to the social and landholding patterns of eastern England, the tenth-century revival with its emphasis on celibacy and on freedom from lay control was aimed precisely at breaking the hold of families over property granted to the church. As vigorous landlords the new abbots contributed to the growth of a market in land which again dissolved older ideas of inalienability. This long-term change in landholding cannot be fully chronicled and is only imperfectly understood. It was affected by fundamental economic questions. Fragmentation often occurred faster in lowland, arable areas where the surplus from an individual village was relatively large and the demands of the lord for labour or dues could be met on a small, local scale. In pastoral, upland areas small units of landholding were less viable, labour requirements were more dispersed and difficult to organize, the demands of transhumance and pasture created different needs.

The processes can rarely be seen at work, but on one Northamptonshire estate the process of division can be briefly glimpsed.[68] The old, large estate here was centred on Fawsley, which in Domesday still held soke over Farthingstone, Everdon, Braunston, Dodford and other villages; later in the Middle Ages it was the mother church for a wide area. Between 944 and 1023 several smaller manors were carved out of it by royal grant. Badby, Dodford and Everdon were granted to Bishop Ælfric,[69] and Newnham to the monk Æfic.[70] By Domesday Book the fragmentation was complete. Badby and Newnham were in church hands, Dodford and Everdon split among eight tenants. A similar process has been argued for Mansfield in Nottinghamshire on geographical and topographical grounds.[71] Mansfield was still a huge estate in 1086 with much attached sokeland. But it is probable that Sutton and Southwell, both granted to the church in the mid-tenth century, Bothamsall, in earl Tostig's hands by the eleventh, and possibly other lands had once formed part of a much larger and geographically compact royal estate of Mansfield. The disintegration of the Fawsley and Mansfield estates highlights the impact of royal grant and the motive of ecclesiastical patronage, as well as illustrating how rapidly disintegration could occur once the process was begun.

The estate patterns of the East Midlands by the eleventh century are the result of such interaction. The older units, represented by the sokes, survived especially in upland areas like Derbyshire and West Nottinghamshire, and also where continuous royal control had preserved them, as in Rutland. They survived patchily in areas little affected by the new ecclesiastical landholders of the tenth century, as in Lincolnshire. But overall they were rapidly disappearing, most completely in fertile lowland areas, especially where, as in Huntingdonshire, these were dominated by the new ecclesiastical estates, and in parts of Lincolnshire, Leicestershire and Nottinghamshire which had seen extensive Viking takeover. The place-names are witness to the changeover. Most names dated after c.A.D.900 indicate individual landownership. The East Midlands are covered by villages whose names record their tenth-century owners, names like Grimsby or Grimston, both of which mean the village (*by* or *ton*) of Grim. They are a record, often the only one, of the important shift in ownership which took place at this date.

This change both produced and was itself affected by the growth of new estates in the hands of new landlords. The most spectacular and the best documented are the new estates of the monastic houses reformed or refounded in the tenth century, especially those of Ramsey, Peterborough and Thorney. By the time of Domesday Ramsey abbey ranked tenth among the monastic estates in England, with an annual income of £358 5s. Peterborough followed close behind with £323, whilst Thorney and Crowland lagged in 36th and 38th places with £53 15s. and £52 6s.[72] In each case the estate had been built up since the late tenth century, with an original grant enlarged by purchase, gift and persuasion. Ramsey received a nucleus of land in Huntingdonshire from ealdorman Æthelwine and Archbishop Oswald; Oswald used lands acquired from his uncle Archbishop Oda, but purchased and exchanged lands himself. The village of Burwell, for example, was acquired in four separate, and strongly contested, transactions.[73] It had been acquired by Oda as a reward for his intercession with the king on behalf of a suitor in marriage; it was then claimed by Oda's brother, who had to be bought off, but more successfully by Wynsige, a relative of the original owner, who claimed hereditary right; Wynsige had to be placated by an exchange of lands. The tenacity of hereditary claims and the role of the monastic revival in loosening them is clear.

Figure 14. Domesday estates of Crowland and Thorney (after S. Raban, *The Estates of Thorney and Crowland*, Univ. of Cambridge Dept. of Land Economy, Occ Papers 7, 1977).

Thorney was set up with an original grant of Yaxley, Stanground, Woodston, Water Newton, Farcet, Barrow, land in Huntingdon and Whittlesey;[74] its sister house at Ely provided stock, harrows, ships and nets, mill oxen and iron, swineherds and a dairymaid as a slave, as well as money to purchase clothes for the monks and 2,000 herrings. The Thorney monks went on to purchase additional estate workers, including a smith. The setting up even of a medium-sized monastery involved a major capital accumulation in equipment and land. Equally significant is our first evidence for careful estate management; the astute Ely monks kept a detailed, written record of their loan. At Thorney the estate was exploited under a system of long leases, but with the lessee called to provide extra land when the lease reverted.[75]

It is at Peterborough that the scale of this concentration of resources can be seen at its most impressive. By the 980s Peterborough had acquired much land within the Soke of Peterborough and along the Nene valley. Bishop Æthelwold granted the abbey Peterborough itself, Oundle, *Anlafeston*, Kettering, 24 men at Farcet, half of Whittlesey Mere, the fens at Well, 350 acres of seed and 23 of wheat and the tithes of many villages;[76] to these the active abbots soon added places like Castor, acquired when Osgot was outlawed for murder, Maxey put together in five separate transactions, Wittering the subject of five purchases and so on. Between 985 and 1066 purchase and gift combined to create an estate extending into south Lincolnshire, on to the Northamptonshire/Leicestershire border, into Rutland and Yorkshire,[77] producing by the mid-eleventh century the staggering wealth of Abbot Leofric's 'Golden Borough'.

The growth of these monastic estates disrupted local landholding, challenged hereditary rights and contributed to the growth of the local land market. As large-scale and efficient landholders, keeping records and extracting dues, their presence was felt by the peasantry. Estates had always taken renders from the peasantry, as Peterborough did from Sempringham in the ninth century. But now with increasing needs for labour to till their vast lands, with the tenth-century emphasis on leisure for the performance of the liturgy, with the stimulus of the local markets (see Chapter 3) and the aid of written documentation, they built on older dues to create the pattern of manorialization familiar in the later Middle Ages. We shall return later to the question of serfdom, but the efficiency of the new landlords is obvious in a document like the Black Book of Peterborough. This dates within a generation of the Norman Conquest, and carefully records and defines the heavy labour services performed by the abbey's peasantry, a product of estate practice in the tenth and eleventh centuries.[78] This same efficiency created a surplus for sale, and equally the needs of the new monasteries for clothing and equipment, not to mention their building programmes, stimulated local demand. The crowds they gathered, whether to pay dues or to visit relics, attracted trade and town development at places like Peterborough. The monastic revival was one of a number of stimuli to economic growth, trade and town development in the East Midlands at the end of the Anglo-Saxon period. The Peterborough Black Book is also remarkable for its emphasis on cash payments by the peasantry, yet one more indication of how far money, sale and purchase were important at all levels of the local economy.

It has been estimated that during the monastic revival of the late tenth century and after, 50 per cent of the villages mentioned in Domesday Huntingdonshire changed hands;[79] by 1086 north Huntingdonshire, like parts of neighbouring Cambridgeshire and the Isle of Ely, was almost entirely in monastic hands. But the impact of the monasteries was greatest in those areas bordering the Fens. Bedfordshire, most of Lincolnshire, Nottinghamshire, much of Derbyshire and Leicestershire were less affected. Only ten manors in Derbyshire were in the hands of churchmen by 1086 and in Nottinghamshire the small quantity of church land was mostly in the hands of bishops. Lay estates were of wider importance but are ill-recorded and difficult to study. Many of the largest of them were fairly new, products of a combination of hereditary right and the new political opportunities of the tenth-century creation of a kingdom of all England. One large lay estate partly transferred into ecclesiastical hands c.A.D.1000 was that belonging to Wulfric Spott, founder of Burton-on-Trent abbey. It stretched north into Yorkshire and Lancashire and included extensive lands in Derbyshire, Nottinghamshire and Leicestershire. Some of it is hereditary holding and much passes on within Wulfric's own family. But a significant proportion was acquired during the tenth century, some by direct royal grant.[80] The house of Leofric was the greatest lay landowner in the Midlands by the eleventh century. Its rise to power was an eleventh-century phenomenon and its estate, at least on the scale it existed by 1066, is unlikely to be much older. Some land came via the fall of Wulfric Spott's family, perhaps through kinship between the two (see fig. 49).[81] But we are dealing less here with ideas of inalienable family land than with the manipulation of inheritance and claims to land through marriage and other strategies. Much of the land of Leofric's family came as a result of their holding of royal office in the enlarged kingdom of England, and this was the sole factor in the growth of the landed wealth of ealdorman Æthelwine and his family who founded Ramsey abbey. They were new to the East Midlands in the 930s, originating probably in Somerset, so that their extensive properties in East Anglia, Cambridgeshire, Huntingdonshire and elsewhere by c.990 had been built up during the tenth century.[82] Obviously new were the landholdings of Viking lords, seen in the tenth-century place-names of Viking origin throughout the region (see fig. 47), and in the new Danish settlers around the Fens after 1017.[83] In all these lay estates the tenth and eleventh centuries again appear as a period witnessing a virtual revolution in landholding throughout the East Midlands.

Although the lay estates represent significant new concentrations of wealth and change in landholding, their impact on the economy is difficult to gauge since we know little of their organization. Most consisted of a core of lands kept in the lord's hand and administered directly by him, plus a large number held by his tenants. The long lists of individual landholders in areas like Lincolnshire or Derbyshire in Domesday hides such under-tenancy.[84] It must be doubtful how effectively some scattered lay estates, and even the more outlying elements of ecclesiastical estates, functioned as part of an economic unit.

The lay holding of which we are best informed is neither a new creation of the tenth and eleventh centuries, nor a typical one. It is the royal lands which comprised many old centres, the remnants of earlier royal demesnes. There are fewer royal lands in the East Midlands than in southern England, virtually none at all in Lincolnshire by 1066. Those which exist bear the signs of ancient origin, but their functioning in the eleventh century was a result of active estate management by royal officials.[85] The simple survival of old forms of organization, such as the attaching of the services and dues of remote sokeland and sokemen to an estate centre, need not argue a great antiquity for the precise pattern as we see it in 1066. The tenth and eleventh-century disintegration of Mansfield has already been remarked; by Domesday the details of such an estate may be less straight survivals from the seventh and eighth centuries than the end product of tidying up and reorganization by recent estate managers. Nonetheless in Nottinghamshire and Derbyshire estates like Dunham, with attached lands at Drayton, Markham, Gringley, Ordsall, Headon, Upton and Normanton, like Arnold or Orston or Mansfield, all with similar structures, show that concentration of resources on a single centre, the combination of valley and upland which had characterized older estates. In Derbyshire a string of these centres at Newbold, Wirksworth, Matlock, Ashbourne, Parwich, Bakewell, Ashford, Hope and Longdendale together made up the vast royal 'Demesne of the Peak'. It was an area ideal for hunting[86] and wealthy in minerals. There were lead mines at Ashford and Bakewell, whilst Hope with its lands provided the king every year with five wagon loads of 50 lead sheets or blocks. This wealth in minerals and hunting, not to mention the strategic importance of this area on the north border of Mercia, had kept it firmly in royal hands and there is little sign here of estate division. In Bedfordshire the royal estate comprised three enormous manors at Leighton Buzzard, Luton and Houghton Regis,[87] which included large areas of surrounding land in their organization. Each one was managed so as to provide a cash income plus provisions in wheat, honey and other things. The peasantry who paid their dues in cash and kind had generated markets at Leighton Buzzard and Luton whose tolls contributed to royal income. In Leicestershire and Northamptonshire the royal manors had been organized by their sheriffs to provide similar dues, though the details are less clear.

The royal estates show how active management by sheriffs and other officials contributed to the efficiency of eleventh-century estates; but the royal lands consisted largely of old estate patterns, and are a reminder of the potential of these older structures for economic growth. Large new estates of the tenth century created conditions of surplus supply, demand and a need for cash to pay dues which all stimulated exchange. These new estates and the rapid division of older lands are one sign of the increasing importance of sale and purchase, of a land market and a cash economy, epitomized in Domesday Book where everything is expressed in cash values. A group of small-scale landowners, whose only record is that left in the place-names, gave concentrated attention to their new lands, their pride in them was expressed in building activity, in churches and in memorial building (see below, pp. 184–7), all of which again stimulated demand. Here are the agrarian bases of the economic upswing experienced by the East Midlands between the ninth and the eleventh centuries, seen at its clearest in urban growth and an explosion of the coinage.

3   Towns, Trade and Industry

The history of towns in the East Midlands effectively begins in the ninth century. Roman society, in this region as elsewhere, had been based on towns, but during the last stages of Roman Britain and in its aftermath they declined as truly urban centres. Early Anglo-Saxon England was an essentially rural society, though we shall see that this does not mean that no forms of trade and exchange or of industrial activity remained. But it is only in the ninth century that these activities assume a scale and nature which enable us to speak of an urban revival. The story of the revival of town life is that of the changing pattern of trade and economic development.

Towns and Trade: Fifth to Ninth Centuries

There had been many Roman towns in the East Midlands: Lincoln, Leicester, Ancaster, Horncastle, Towcester to name but a few. They were already in decline before the end of Roman Britain and owe their final demise not so much to the deliberate destruction of Anglo-Saxon invaders but to the loss of their raison d'être. The end of their administrative functions, the decline of trade and industry, the increasing importance of rural estates and centres sapped town life and new patterns of exchange replaced those located there. It must be doubted whether anything recognizable as town life continued at these places from Roman Britain into the Anglo-Saxon period. The Anglo-Saxons recognized and respected 'the work of giants' as they termed the Roman ruins; they carefully distinguished old Roman centres and English fortifications, calling them by different names, a Roman town like Leicester being a *civitas* or *chester*.[1] There is some evidence for continued use and occupation of urban sites. During the fifth and sixth centuries a Christian community in Lincoln was still using the site of the fourth-century ruined church of St Paul-in-the-Bail as a cemetery; they may represent continuity of some sort of occupation. In the seventh century Leicester and Lincoln were both chosen as ecclesiastical centres and a royal official was in control of Lincoln.[2]

Roman centres may still have been occupied, but this does not argue that they were any longer towns. A history of a continuous settlement of a site recognizable by its Roman remains does not imply the continuity of a true urban community.[3] Blæcca, the man in control in seventh-century Lincoln, and others like him may demonstrate no more than a recognition of the defensive potential of Roman buildings in troubled times, their occupation as strongholds by great lords. At Lincoln, as in so many other towns, archaeology suggests a positive break between Roman and late Saxon development. By the time that the pottery kilns of Leicester were constructed in the tenth and eleventh centuries the Roman street there was overlaid with soil and the

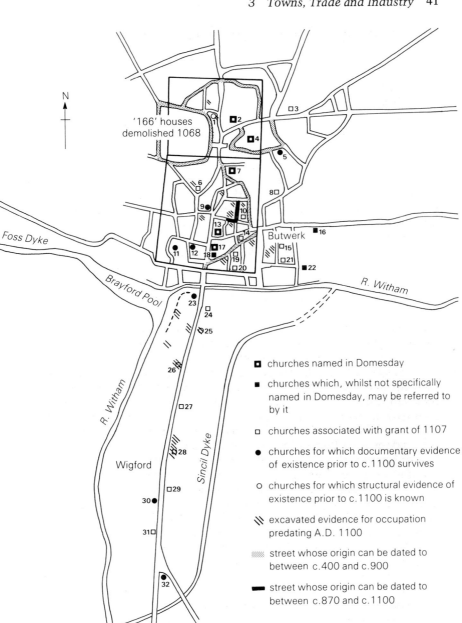

Figure 15. Street plan of eleventh-century Lincoln: street lines ignore the old Roman street plan (reproduced by permission of the Trust for Lincolnshire Archaeology).

surface of that street was cut into during the kiln's construction.[4] The massive, surviving walls of Roman Lincoln certainly defined the shape of the tenth-century town; they posed such an obstacle to building and communication. But the detailed layout of tenth-century properties shows that the Roman property divisions and street lines were by then irrelevant.[5] Towns like Nottingham and Derby flourished in the late Saxon period whilst their nearby Roman predecessors were in ruins. Nottingham shifted towards the Trent, and there is little continuity with the Roman fort at Margidum eight miles to the south. Derby, like Stamford, grew up at a river ford whose importance was the direct result of the decay of the Roman bridge at nearby Little Chester.[6]

A town is a community whose inhabitants' labour is specialized – as traders, craftsmen, administrators and so forth – unlike rural settlements where the needs of subsistence agriculture impose a common routine. Yet the Anglo-Saxon town often seems difficult to distinguish since all settlements, including towns, had agricultural aspects; the citizens of Nottingham at the time of Domesday owned meadow land and ploughs.[7] But concentrations of population, trading activity and, by the eleventh century, the special legal freedoms of town-dwellers to engage in trade are marks of urban life. It is these special characteristics which are absent from the East Midlands between the sixth and ninth centuries. Exchange of goods certainly occurred. The glass palm cups

Figure 16. Frankish bowl unearthed at Barton-on-Humber (reproduced by permission of the Kingston-upon-Hull City Museums and Art Galleries).

found in seventh-century graves in Derbyshire or Lincolnshire,[8] the Frankish material recently unearthed at Barton-on-Humber (see fig. 16),[9] many early grave-goods are all imports from the Continent. It is the nature of their distribution which is significant. The mechanics of exchange at this date were first warfare, in the pillaging and sharing out of loot and tribute, and second a limited trade which contributed rare goods to the loot distributed through the hands of kings, leaders and churchmen. The exchange of scarce commodities was through gift rather than trade. The abbess of Repton sent a lead coffin to house the body of the hermit Guthlac in the early eighth century,[10] a distribution of Peak District lead, but scarcely through mercantile activity. Early Anglo-Saxon society, especially by the seventh century, was unequal, with access to high-value goods and objects like weapons already restricted,[11] but that access was politically determined. Weapons, rings and luxury goods were acquired from kings and overlords whose power rested on them and whose courts were centres for their distribution.[12] As centres of gift and exchange, those courts attracted merchants and traders and the existence of a gift economy does not, of course, prove the non-existence of a money economy. But we do not have here the permanent population, the buying and selling, the activity of merchants and industry in fixed centres which are the bases for town growth.

The early history of the coinage confirms this picture. The import of Roman coin into Britain ceased in the early fifth century. A few Roman coins are found in early Anglo-Saxon graves at Sleaford, Stapenhill (Derbyshire), Dunstable Downs (Bedfordshire), and Martin St Lawrence (Northamptonshire), but they are the last remnants of circulation not signs of a money, trading, economy.[13] The Anglo-Saxon coinage began at the end of the seventh century with gold coins, followed by silver *sceattas*. These latter are found in the East Midlands, though not as yet in the quantities in which they have been discovered to the north and the south, and their major centres of production and use appear to have been south-east England where the trade revival was already marked. In the eighth century the regions which were witnessing the growth of a money economy barely included the East Midlands beyond Bedfordshire and Northamptonshire, though some doubt must hang over Lindsey. At least one group of *sceattas* may have been minted in the East Midlands, perhaps near Stamford.[14] Nonetheless the find-sites of most *sceattas*, along the Chilterns and south in an arc from the Wash,[15] do suggest that the trade which was reviving at this date was still peripheral to the East Midlands.

Yet at a different level the collection of food rents and dues at royal and ecclesiastical centres was encouraging a more formal distribution network in these centuries. The payment of dues and the provisioning of a court or monastery forced some exchange. The word *wic*, normally associated in the Middle Saxon period with a trading centre, survives in the name of the Lincoln suburb of Wigford (known in the twelfth century as *Wikeford*),[16] and seventh-century Lincoln was a centre of royal administration (see below, p. 98). It is at such centres, such old-established estates, that many flourishing towns are later found; at Oundle, the administrative centre for eight hundreds and the site of bishop Wilfrid's minster in the seventh century,[17] or at Melton Mowbray on the prehistoric Jurassic Way, an old minster church where ecclesiastical dues were gathered.[18] Such places had urban features by Domesday; Melton Mowbray, for example, already had a market worth 20s. a year. All the evidence for urban activity in these so-called 'primary towns' comes from the tenth and eleventh centuries. Their important positions on old routeways or as centres for royal and ecclesiastical payments made them natural candidates for growth when economic development did occur.[19] However, it is doubtful how much town growth had taken place there before the ninth century.

Coinage and Mints

From the ninth century onwards evidence for growth is overwhelming. The coinage is a litmus test for the development of trade and exchange; its burgeoning and location is a sure sign of the urban focus of trade by the tenth century. The coinage of Anglo-Saxon England was not supplied by a central mint issuing to the whole kingdom. Minting was decentralized, carried out in many places. Coin was produced as and where it was used, by moneyers who coined silver for merchants in the process of trade or for those paying royal dues. This decentralization probably reflects origins in a non-monetary economy, where coin did not circulate commonly but was produced to need. It certainly argues an original distrust of coin. Silver was melted down and reminted so that traders could be certain of a coin's value, and the practice of testing and weighing coins rather than simply counting them survived at the time of Domesday, though now for special reasons.[20] Whatever its rationale, such a decentralized system should reflect very closely the economic pattern of an area.

In the early ninth century Canterbury and more debateably London were still the major mints, Rochester was also striking coin, and another mint operated in East Anglia.[21] During the second half of the century an extensive coinage with a debased silver content was being struck in the name of Burgred of Mercia (deposed 874). This circulated more widely than any of its predecessors, throughout Mercia and to the north.[22] The volume and spread of this enigmatic coinage may indicate the need for tribute to pay the Vikings, but it may also be a token of the growing demand for coin consequent on the stimulation of economic activity. By the end of the ninth century coins were being struck at several places in the East Midlands which may thus qualify as urban centres. By c.A.D.900 imitations of the coins of Alfred were produced at Lincoln, bearing the Lincoln monogram (see fig. 17),[23] and by the 920s Lincoln

Figure 17. Lincoln coin of the moneyer Ercener (reproduced by permission of the British Museum).

was minting coins bearing the sword and name of St Martin on one face, and a cross and the town name on the other (see fig. 45).[24] The early tenth century seems to have been a period of expanding minting activity, though the attribution of coins to mints before the enforcement of mint-signatures in 973 often poses severe problems. From roughly the early tenth century, certainly by the reign of Athelstan, mints were working at Derby and probably at Leicester, Nottingham and Bedford.[25] Derby stands out from the other East Midlands mints at this date, its links being with the important mint of Chester rather than eastwards. By Athelstan's reign Derby was the major North Midlands mint after Chester.[26] With the same due degree of caution, Huntingdon, Northampton and Stamford can be added to the list of mints by the mid-tenth century, if not before.

The East Midlands mints in the first half of the tenth century proved resistant to thorough-going control by southern kings. They struck coins in the names of such kings, like Athelstan who doubtless received his proportion of the profits of minting, but unlike the West Saxon mints they did not strike coins bearing the king's head; indeed they resisted such coins until Edgar's great reorganization of the coinage in 973. Many blundered and irregular coins were produced here in Athelstan's reign,[27] and Derby briefly struck coins in the name of the Viking king Olaf c.A.D.940.[28] The coinage of the Danelaw in the early tenth century demonstrates not only the economic vigour but also the political separatism of the area.

For much of the tenth century the major Mercian mint in terms of output was Chester, with Derby locally pre-eminent in Athelstan's reign. By the eleventh century the situation had altered radically; Lincoln and Stamford now stand out.[29] At the height of its output in the 1040s Lincoln was apparently striking as much as 16 per cent of the English coinage. But this figure is distorted by the over-representation of Lincoln coins in Scandinavia,[30] an area with which the town had especial trading links and where major collections of Anglo-Saxon coins now exist for study. Figures for about the year 1000, which are subject to less distortion, suggest that Lincoln was producing about 10–11 per cent of the English coinage, with the total output of the Five Boroughs (here defined as Lincoln and the Lincolnshire mints, Derby, Leicester, Nottingham, Newark, Stamford and Peterborough) around 15 per cent.[31] But by this date the heyday of the East Midlands mints was in some ways passing. It was during the tenth century that the Mercian mints produced the bulk of the English coinage;[32] by A.D.1000 Nottingham and Derby were striking very little, Leicester's output was declining and neither Huntingdon, Bedford nor Northampton was of great importance.[33] During the earlier tenth century these East Midlands mints had grown rapidly, reflecting a general economic burgeoning in the area and its importance on the frontiers of trade with the Viking world. By the end of that century the dominance of a few large mints like Lincoln, and to a lesser extent Stamford, was established. This does not necessarily imply the decline of other towns, but rather the concentration of minting activity at the major points of entry of foreign silver and the existence by this date of a circulation of coin so rapid as to reduce the need for constant minting in other towns.

In 973 King Edgar reformed the English coinage.[34] His aim was undoubtedly to maximize royal profits from the rapidly expanding coinage, to tap the growth of trade for the royal coffers. Much of his 'reform' was designed to facilitate this. No old or foreign coin was to circulate; all silver was to be reminted and to bear the king's head. The design of the coinage was to be regularly changed and the new designs like that of the abortive Agnus Dei coins of Æthelred (see fig. 18) enforced, thus compelling merchants to remint

Figure 18. A 'reform' coin of Edgar from the Leicester mint and an 'Agnus Dei' coin of Æthelred II struck at Derby c.1009 (reproduced by permission of the British Museum).

their coins and raising royal profit. To enable checks on the system to operate, all coins were to bear the name of the moneyer who struck them and of the mint. After 973 the coinage itself and its conformity to these regulations is witness to the efficiency of the reform. Edgar's reform is testimony to the growing importance of coinage and trade in the tenth-century economy. It also makes the study of the coinage, towns and trade easier. New mints seem to have opened largely to facilitate the exchange of coin. After 973 coins were occasionally struck at places such as Aylesbury, Torksey, Caistor and Horncastle. These minor mints operated only intermittently: Torksey, Caistor, Louth and Horncastle only briefly in the 970s and 980s with moneyers on temporary loan from Lincoln.[35] The predominance of mints like Lincoln was not shaken by the reform, but the brief appearance of these other centres marks their urban and trading functions by the end of the tenth century.

The pattern of minting activity does not bear a simple and straightforward relationship to economic activity. Coins were minted not only where trade occurred and dues were paid, but where foreign silver and coinage entered England. The growth and dominance of the Danelaw mints in the tenth century indicates not merely their importance as towns (and in Derby's case the significance of the mining area to its north), but as frontier towns with the Viking world to the north.[36] Occasionally mint output reflects temporary needs and distortions. The payments, or Danegelds, made to the Vikings in the 990s and 1000s produced sudden demands for large quantities of coin and called temporary though very minor mints like Aylesbury into action.[37] But such arguments should not be pressed too far. If quantities of foreign silver were turned into English coins in the Danelaw towns of Derby, Leicester, Lincoln or Stamford in the tenth century it was because that silver flowed there as a result of trade with the Viking and northern world. If coin had to be produced to pay gelds or royal dues, goods had to be bought and sold to generate it. Moreover, the coinage tells a story not only of external trade but of vigorous systems of internal circulation.[38] Hoards of coin found in late tenth-century England are well mixed in their composition, containing coins from a wide geographical range of mints. They indicate buoyant trading activity. In eastern England as elsewhere the tenth-century coinage points to foreign, local and internal trade and to the sheer growth of economic activity.

Towns and Trade: Late Ninth to Eleventh Centuries

Town growth mirrors the picture painted by the coins, if more patchily. Recent excavators have described the 'dramatic intensification of occupation' in late ninth and early tenth-century Northampton,[39] or how Stamford 'burst into prominence in the second half of the ninth century'.[40] In the case of Stamford there is no evidence for any substantial occupation during the Middle Saxon period. At Northampton occupation stretches back to the fifth and sixth centuries, with a large seventh-century timber hall and later church complex showing its continuity, but nothing which could be described as urban. In both cases the existence of a royal and ecclesiastical centre may have provided a focus for a market before the late ninth century; both may well qualify as those 'primary towns' already discussed. But here the archaeological record provides important and positive proof that such primary functions did not necessarily entail any significant urban development in the early Saxon period. Stamford and Northampton as urban centres are products of the period from the late ninth century onwards. The most obvious signs of late ninth- and early tenth-century urban growth are written references in the *Anglo-Saxon Chronicle* to the building of fortifications, *burhs* (boroughs) by Viking armies or English rulers. Such fortified sites were constructed at Buckingham, Bedford, Towcester, Nottingham and Stamford, and at Leicester and Derby where Viking fortifications were surrendered to the southern English. Traces of early fortification on some of these sites remain. At Nottingham parallel lines of streets around the hill on which St Mary's church stands represent the defensive streets inside and outside an old earthwork, whilst the defences to the south of the city were provided by the natural cliff, marked now by Cliff Road.[41] The borough ditch here was already obsolete by the time of Domesday when 23 houses are recorded as built in it;[42] suburban growth had already occurred. At Bedford the rectilinear street plan may represent the town as laid out by Edward the Elder in 915,[43] whilst the southern *burh* which he constructed here to block the passage of the Ouse appears to have been surrounded by a dyke later known as the King's Ditch.[44]

The military fortifications which the Viking wars, especially the wars of internal conquest of the early tenth century, brought into being undoubtedly proved foci for the later development of urban centres. The defended sites they provided attracted trade and there were deliberate attempts by tenth-century kings like Athelstan to attract trade into such fortifications, in order both to oversee the trade and to ensure the maintenance of fortification.[45] The new fortifications normally encompassed older sites or marked a significant stage in their rejuvenation; Nottingham, Derby and Bedford for example were all pre-existing settlements. But real growth, especially at Nottingham and Bedford, postdates the Viking period. At Lincoln and Leicester old sites were chosen precisely because of surviving Roman fortifications which could be re-used. But as we shall see at Lincoln, the tenth century still marked a new departure in urban life and no simple continuity.

The Viking invasions and their aftermath stimulated the construction of defended sites and in this respect mark a turning point in urban development. The desire to maintain fortifications against the possibility of renewed attack led to positive attempts to stimulate trading communities in these centres. But the military contribution to town growth must not be stressed at the expense of the wider economic context. The large-scale defences covering huge areas at Nottingham are usually assumed to belong to the Viking period, i.e. to the late ninth and early tenth centuries, but there is little positive proof. Indeed at Nottingham a smaller defensive site has been discovered within the larger defences and may represent the original Viking fortification.[46] At Derby no traces of early defences have been found, although the *Anglo-Saxon Chronicle* records the fall of the army of Derby in 917 with a description of fighting inside the gates of a fortification.[47] The fortification used by the Viking army in 917 may have been, as at Nottingham, a small site within the later town but not yet discovered, or, as recently suggested, even the nearby Roman fort of Little Chester.[48] Here as at Lincoln the existing defences could have been re-used as an easy and quickly defended site, though this is difficult to

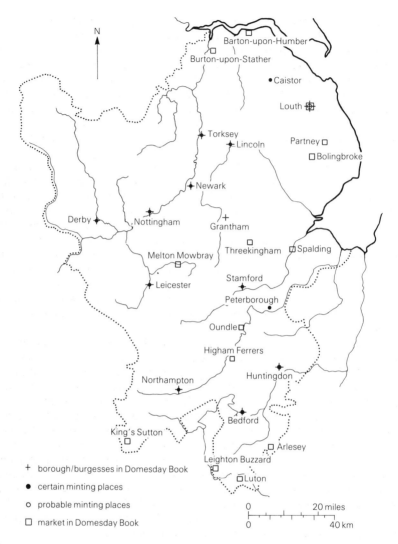

Figure 19. East Midland towns in the tenth and eleventh centuries.

square with the specific reference to *Derby* in the Chronicle. Such small, temporary refuges were constructed elsewhere during the Viking wars, like that built by the armies of Northampton and Huntingdon at Tempsford in 917, a fortification soon abandoned, proving no focus for later urban development and now difficult to locate. It must remain debatable whether the large, defended towns which archaeology shows existed during the tenth century at Nottingham, Derby and elsewhere represent simply the Viking or anti-Viking defences of the early tenth century. They may rather be the product of subsequent growth on such sites, fortified or refortified later in the century.

The late ninth and tenth centuries certainly saw the burgeoning of these towns. At Lincoln the excavations at Flaxengate and Grantham Street have shown the importance of the decades c.860/70–900, when a new street pattern was laid out, at least in this part of the city, and new property boundaries were established.[49] If Lincoln lacked the extreme regularity found at, for example, contemporary Winchester, there is nonetheless some evidence of a planned development, even possibly of the use of a standard measure for urban properties.[50] The new development was truly urban, housing craftsmen as well as merchants: Islamic sherds of Syrian origin have been found in these ninth-century houses[51] and there is evidence of crafts such as antler- and metalworking. Tenth-century Northampton provides similar evidence, on a lesser scale, of industrial activity.[52]

In the case of Stamford the Danish borough stood to the east of the existing small settlement around St Peter's church, whilst Edward the Elder's fortification was to the south of the river. Both date to the decades either side of the year 900. The Stamford pottery industry emerges at the same time; the first datable kiln within the town belongs roughly to the date of the origin of the Viking borough.[53] Here as elsewhere the Vikings were apparently the all-important fillip to urban development on an old centre, providing the stimulus of new settlement, the demands which fortification construction must have placed on the area and the added bonus of improved communications centred on Stamford when a bridge was constructed between the two boroughs on either side of the river. Yet the planning of the central nucleus of Stamford may be as late as the early eleventh century.

A Viking stimulus to town growth in the East Midlands is likely. The Vikings brought loot and contacts from their European raiding. It has been suggested that features of the Stamford pottery industry argue the arrival of European potters, perhaps in the Viking baggage train.[54] But the pottery trade and industry place the Viking stimulus in perspective. However far the Vikings may have stimulated it, the significant development of the pottery industry was already under way in eastern England before their arrival and the market it supplied was essentially a local one. The ninth and tenth centuries were times of urban expansion in England even outside the areas of Viking influence.[55] At York the Vikings did not create a flourishing urban community, but found one in a rapid state of development and merely contributed to that growth. The same may apply in the East Midlands, though only further excavation will prove it. The region was likely to experience a rate of growth more rapid than most, given its excellent communications.

The development of tenth- and eleventh-century Lincoln, as shown in the admittedly limited area of Flaxengate, supports a picture of a Viking contribution, but of sustained growth largely postdating Viking settlement. If the area received an initial boost in the late ninth century, contemporary with Viking arrival, its real boom as an industrial centre belongs almost a century later, to the period c.960/70–1060/70 and especially c.960–1010. It was then that glass- and copper alloy-working assumed something like industrial proportions, with specialized workshops and an expansion of the Flaxengate site into Grantham Street.[56] In at least this area of Lincoln the peak of prosperity was achieved at this date, with some possible decline setting in by the later eleventh century. It is dangerous to argue from a single site within Lincoln, but the correlation with the growth and decline of the Lincoln mint is worth noting. By the eleventh century coins found in Lincoln are drawn widely from the rest of southern England.[57] This is undoubtedly a sign of the vigour of the English economy in general by this date, but it also emphasizes that Lincoln belongs within that economy. It contrasts with the greater isolation and separation shown in the York coin evidence, and stresses the importance of the Humber as a political line in late Saxon England. Lincoln and other East Midlands towns may have benefited economically from their greater integration into the kingdom of England by the late tenth century; they were certainly profiting from the more general economic growth of that century.

The general economic upswing and the stimulation of local trade and markets was no mere Viking creation. The pottery trade indicates the nature of tenth-century growth and its contrast with the previous situation, and provides some clue to the forces behind it. Before the ninth century most pottery in general use was domestically produced, coarse and handmade. The pottery found at Maxey is typical. The shapes are old, typical of the Iron Age, and similar pottery is found in excavations of Lincolnshire villages between the seventh and ninth centuries.[58] They have every appearance of being local village products.

From the end of the ninth century in the towns of the East Midlands the industrial production of pottery on a fast wheel grew rapidly (see below, 'Industry'). By the tenth century there were numerous production centres: Leicester, Stamford, Lincoln, Torksey, Northampton and so on. The new production was urban-based, the product a mass-produced, basic pottery. Cooking pots and domestic utensils account for the bulk of output, though larger industrial centres like Stamford produced a wide range of specialized pottery.

The pattern of trade and supply was local. Late Saxon settlements at Eaton Socon, Little Paxton and St Neots used largely cheap, locally-produced St Neots ware.[59] Even a major centre like Stamford drew its strength primarily from the supply of a local Lincolnshire market. High quality, expensive Stamford glazed ware might be produced largely for long-distance trade, and is found not so much around Stamford itself but at the end of far-flung trade routes at Aberdeen, Dublin or in Sweden.[60] Fine tableware, pitchers and jugs were exported far afield, but the bulk of Stamford production was of cooking pots distributed largely in south Lincolnshire. The pottery industry, the best example of industrial production in the tenth-century East Midlands, was a basic industry sustained by a local market which was growing at a rapid enough rate to support an upsurge of production, a shift away from hand-made village wares to specialized industry.

The pottery trade parallels the evidence of the coinage. Long-range export, especially of expensive, high quality goods, was important, and follows the network of North Sea contacts reinforced and utilized by the Vikings, i.e. to Scandinavia, Scotland and Viking Dublin and within England to York. We are reminded of the significance of the Danelaw mints as points of entry for foreign silver from the Viking world. But only the expansion of the home market sustained the scale of growth witnessed; even Stamford depended on sales within a limited geographical radius. Vigorous internal trade was the story told also by the coinage, though it told of the range of merchant contacts throughout England. Growth fed by burgeoning home demand seems an accurate view of the East Midlands economy in the tenth century.

The development of trade, exchange and demand fostered the rise of markets. By 1086 markets were recorded at Leighton Buzzard, Luton, Aylesbury, Newport Pagnell, Huntingdon, Melton Mowbray, Barton-on-Humber, Grantham, Louth and elsewhere. Domesday is an incomplete record on this score, and here freezes a mere stage in a process of growth, yet by this date there were markets in Lindsey alone at Barton-on-Humber, Thealby, Darby, Burton-upon-Stather, Louth, Bolingbroke, Spalding, Partney and Threakingham.[61] The ferries which carried basic commodities across the Humber, and the attempts of Norman landlords to profit from them (see above, pp. 14–15), reinforce a picture of local trade on a large scale as the key to tenth- and eleventh-century growth.

The take-off dates from the late ninth century. To this period and a little later belongs, for example, the rise of the industrial quarter of Lincoln in Flaxengate. At a roughly similar date an increase of economic activity occurred at Northampton; a change in local pottery styles and the start of urban production, a complex sequence of timber structures suggesting the building and rapid rebuilding of the city's streets, the industrial production of iron, horn-working, the import of Northern French wares all bear witness to this.[62] The quantity of church fabric datable to the late Saxon period, let alone that associated with the tenth-century monastic revival which has mostly gone, is part of the same boom and stimulus to demand. It lies behind the expansion of stone-quarrying and the export of fine Barnack and Ancaster stone widely throughout the region.[63] Barnack stone is found as far afield as Hertfordshire and Essex, its quality making it ideal for decorative architectural features like the pilaster strips which adorn the towers of Earls Barton and Barnack churches (see figs. 20 and 59).

Trade was no longer an intermittent or insignificant activity. A pot pedlar was so familiar a feature of the countryside that legend has it that Hereward the Wake posed as one, hoping thus to melt into anonymity before his Norman pursuers.[64] In the late eleventh century a Lincolnshire saint, Godric of Finchale, illustrated the opportunities and rewards of enterprise when he passed from beachcomber to pedlar before joining with a group of merchants to engage in trade between England, Scotland, Denmark and the Low Countries.[65] Such a story of 'local boy made good' could easily be dismissed as twelfth-century elaborations. But the Archbishop of York writing c.A.D.1000 could speak of the trader who prospered so that he three times crossed the open sea at his own expense, and could already record it as a long-established state of affairs.[66] The wide distribution of a great variety of Stamford ware suggests the existence of specialist pottery merchants.[67]

By the time of Domesday the towns of eastern England were flourishing. The way in which the Domesday survey presents its statistics makes comparisons between towns, even assessments of their total population, difficult. All the problems of allowance for wives, children, other household dependants, servants and so on must be tackled for urban as for rural populations in 1086. But for the towns there are deep inconsistencies of record. In many towns it lists a number of *burgenses* (burgesses), plus other groups. At Huntingdon there were 256 *burgenses*, 100 bordars and three fishermen.[68] Not all the inhabitants of towns enjoyed the full privileges of burgess status. But how are we to compare this mixed population of Huntingdon with that of Derby, which

Figure 20. Pilaster strips and architectural sculpture on the tower of Barnack church.

included 'little burgesses',[69] and why does Domesday list 65 burgesses for Leicester but 318 houses,[70] and only inhabited plots, over 900, at Lincoln?[71] The survey has obviously made distinctions of status and record or simple omissions whose rationale is now difficult to interpret.

Judicious use of these figures has produced some estimates of size. Lincoln was the largest town by a wide margin, followed by Stamford, and then perhaps Leicester, Northampton and Huntingdon. Stamford's population in Domesday has been put at around 3,000,[72] which would make Lincoln 6,000 plus. Derby and Nottingham were not large; neither was much bigger than Torksey or Grantham. These population rankings show an interesting correspondence with those which emerged from mint outputs; again Lincoln was the largest, followed by Stamford and Leicester, Northampton, Huntingdon and Bedford. Nottingham and Derby appeared less significant as mints by c.A.D.1000, Derby especially having fallen from its tenth-century pre-eminence. Lincoln-shire in 1086 had a number of prospering towns, not only in Lincoln and Stamford, but at Grantham, Torksey and Louth. The sheer size of the shire accounts in part for this, but it may also be a result of the agrarian changes which the place-name transformations here in the tenth and eleventh century indicate. With 10 per cent or so of the population living in towns, eleventh-century England was highly urbanized by contemporary standards. But 90 per cent of the population still lived on the land. Towns and their growth must be seen in the framework of agrarian change, however obscure that may be.

Industry

Industry on any scale largely disappeared with the end of Roman Britain. Specialized craft production survived, and its products can be seen in the high quality weapons and jewellery of the early and mid-Saxon period. But such craftsmanship was largely confined to the courts of kings and great leaders or to the entourages of high ecclesiastics. Its products were highly prized status goods, dispensed in largesse rather than bought and sold in the market place. It was not until the late ninth century that industrial production even on a small scale revived.

The grave-goods of cemeteries, plentiful as they are, provide little evidence for industrial production. It is possible that jewellery, the saucer-shaped brooches, pendants and bullae, was still being produced on a large scale in the fifth century, though the centre of production was outside eastern England.[73] But trade and industry were in decay. Even funerary ware, the ubiquitous urns which contained the ashes in cremation cemeteries, do not seem to have been mass-produced. Their linear and stamped decoration may argue for specialized craftsmen, but so far no centre of production comparable with the 'Lackford potter' in East Anglia has been identified in the East Midlands. With the decline of the economic and urban structures of Roman Britain went the decay of the Nene valley potteries.

Two levels of activity replaced it, neither 'industrial' in any accepted sense. At a local level most needs were met at a subsistence standard with hand-made, largely village-made goods. Textiles were produced in most homes; scarcely an excavation has failed to turn up a set of loom weights which once held taut the warp threads of a tensioned or horizontal loom. Pottery too was hand-made. The art of throwing on a fast wheel and large-scale kiln production was lost in the fifth century. Most domestic pottery between the fifth and ninth century was like that at Maxey, built up, for example, by coiling on a flat base and fired in single-clamp kilns, and was occasionally tempered with grass.[74] Iron objects are rare and valuable in mid-Saxon settlement sites, and what has been found was largely locally produced. At Maxey slag was discovered, the residue of small-scale smelting, and at St Neots local smelting was still carried out at the end of the Saxon period.[75] By 1086 there were more specialized ironworks at Stow and Castle and Little Bytham (Lincolnshire), Corby and Gretton (Northamptonshire), and Cranfield and Wilshamstead (Bedfordshire).[76]

Whilst village and domestic production met most needs, specialized and skilled craftsmen at the court of kings or in religious houses turned out goods as close to art as to industry. They produced objects like the seventh-century necklace of gold and garnet found at Desborough, Northamptonshire (see fig. 21), the helmet worn by the lord buried at Benty Grange (see fig. 57), the swords of the early cemeteries. So highly prized were such craftsmen that a king like Alfred ranked them among the key workers at his court and made provision for them in his will.[77]

Figure 21. The Desborough necklace (reproduced by permission of the British Museum).

Figure 22. A Saxon mortar mixer of the ninth century from Northampton (reproduced by permission of Northampton Development Corporation).

Occasionally rare evidence indicates activity on a larger scale, significantly associated with building and the church. Recent excavation at Northampton discovered three Saxon mortar mixers in St Peter Street (see fig. 22).[78] They consisted of shallow bowls cut into the bedrock, some 2–3m in diameter, with a wooden paddle suspended from a beam and rotated. They date from the early ninth century. Far from suggesting the development of permanent industry in mid-Saxon Northampton, they are the relic of a spate of building activity most probably associated with the church. Evidence of iron and glass-working at the side of Repton church in the ninth century confirms a close correlation between ecclesiastical and industrial activity in the early period.[79] Ecclesiastical and royal stimulus lay behind building and the growth of connected industries. The oolitic limestone belt running south from the Humber was a source of excellent building stone, quarried during the Saxon period at Ancaster and Barnack.[80] The quarries often lay on royal or monastic land; Ramsey and Peterborough were disputing the ownership of a stone quarry in the mid-eleventh century.[81] The Barnack and Ancaster quarries were in use by c.A.D.800; Barnack stone was used, for example, for the Hedda stone at Peterborough and for many of the early Breedon sculptures, whilst Ancaster stone is the material used in the South Kyme sculpture; all probably date to the early ninth century.

By the tenth century, when as we have seen church building was undergoing a boom, the Barnack quarries produced stone exported far afield; St Peter's church at Bedford uses it. Again it is from the late Saxon period that the best evidence of production on something approaching industrial scale and for sale comes. By the tenth century the Barnack quarry appears to have mass produced grave slabs, like that at Milton Bryan and the numerous others scattered through Bedfordshire, Cambridgeshire and Northamptonshire. Before this, building activity and sculpture were produced under the aegis of the church. It is only in the tenth and eleventh centuries that a wider lay market – even lay production of stone sculpture – can be suggested.[82] It is the sheer quantity, and perhaps also the poor quality, of the crosses, grave slabs and funerary monuments of the Danelaw shires in the tenth and eleventh centuries that argue for mass production for a lay market. No longer is stone sculpture tied to the ecclesiastical centres, the monastic communities which produced the Breedon sculptures, the Bakewell or Hedda stone reliquaries, the Eyam cross. The lay market and production to meet its tastes and requirements is yet another sign of the rich and expanding secular economy of the East Midlands at this date. It was wealthy laymen who wished to commemorate their death in stone who stood behind the late Saxon boom in parish church building (see below, pp. 184–7).

Large-scale mineral extraction may have remained mostly in royal hands. Lead was mined in the Peak district in Roman times, and still in the early eighth century when the abbess of Repton despatched her gift of a lead coffin to St Guthlac. In 835 abbess Cynewaru made arrangements for an annual render of lead from Wirksworth to Canterbury.[83] Repton was a royal monastery, the later mausoleum of Mercian kings, and the lead mines of Derbyshire were royal land in Domesday. There were *plumbariae* (lead mines) at Matlock Bridge, Bakewell, Ashford and Crich, and three at Wirksworth.[84] Before 1066 Hope, Ashford and Bakewell made annual renders to the king which included five wagon loads of 50 lead slabs. Silver production is suggested by the Domesday entry for the royal manors of Matlock Bridge, Ashbourne, Parwich, Wirksworth and Darley, which were rendering in 1086 £40 of 'pure silver'.[85] The term pure silver is used elsewhere in Domesday without connotations of silver mining, but its use in Derbyshire is rare; the production of silver associated with lead mining is likely. The mineral wealth of the Peak goes far to explain why so much of this area remained in royal hands in the late eleventh century. Kings would have been loath to alienate such important assets.

As the instance of sculpture showed, the contrast between craftsman production and more industrial methods aimed at a market was a contrast between the mid and late Saxon periods. The shift is observable elsewhere. Ironworking, hitherto on a small village scale, became a town industry also, though it would be wrong to believe that this ended or replaced village production. Iron was worked at Northampton, Stamford and Lincoln. Metalworking was an important feature of the Flaxengate site in Lincoln; crucibles, heating trays and moulds made out of stone or clay, ingots, wire and beaten metal, like the half-made garment hooks found here, point to the importance of copper alloy working.[86] Other crucibles found at Flaxengate had been used for glass smelting, for the manufacture of yellow and green beads and finger rings, and jet was used for jewellery (fig. 23).[87] Bone and horn were carved and worked at Northampton and Lincoln. From Flaxengate came a bone combcase

Figure 23. Glass-making at Flaxengate: glass beads, rings and crucible fragments (reproduced by permission of the Trust for Lincolnshire Archaeology).

Figure 24. Bone comb, instrument mouthpiece, handle and pin from Flaxengate (reproduced by permission of the Trust for Lincolnshire Archaeology).

with the inscription 'Thorfast made a good comb', a rare glimpse of the craftsman's pride. Bone and antler working at Lincoln were on a small scale, and may even have involved itinerant rather than resident craftsmen.[88] The products of much of this industry were small, semi-luxury objects: copper pins and garment hooks for securing clothing, beads and ornaments, decorated combs and cases (fig. 24). It is the specialization and the urban concentration which is significant. The moulds are testimony to mass production; the urban location brought the craftsman's product straight to the market place. Again the stimulus is the growing home market of the East Midlands. It was thegns and prosperous farmers who bought the new-fangled clothing hooks, the beads and trinkets, just as the wealthiest among them were celebrating their wealth and underlining their status with tomb monuments or even churches.

The Flaxengate excavations have yielded both local Lincoln sandyware pottery and Stamford pots. Pottery was also produced within the town at Northampton, at Stamford (where the earliest kiln is datable c.A.D.900[89]), at Torksey and at Leicester, where a kiln was cut into the old Roman street during the tenth century.[90] Before the ninth century any demand for high quality, wheel-thrown pottery had been met by imports from the Rhineland or Northern France. The slow wheel may have been in use in England as early as the end of the seventh century, but only at a few centres like Ipswich. Ipswich ware was turned on a slow wheel but was well fired in large, controlled-temperature kilns. It was traded in eastern England, travelling especially along the Wash river routes, and is found at Castor, Northamptonshire, and Brixworth.[91] But as we have seen most pottery found on early domestic sites was locally handmade. By the mid-ninth century the fast wheel was introduced into England and by c.A.D.900 and later was in use at Stamford, Lincoln and other towns of the East Midlands. Production can be proved where kilns and wasters (i.e. pots discarded because spoilt during the production process) have been discovered; we can thus be certain that Stamford, Leicester, Northampton, Lincoln and Torksey had working potteries during the tenth century. The identification of particular local types of pot suggest other production centres in the region of Lincoln, Nottingham, Derby and St Neots.

Production normally involved the use of local clays. The excellence of Stamford ware derives in part from the local estuarine clay found along the Fen margins, which does not require additives for plasticity. At Torksey the fabric was rougher because of the occurrence of sandy, quartz crystals in the local clay. At St Neots the fabric was tempered with crushed shells. The pots were turned on a fast wheel and often bear the wire marks of removal or signs of knife trimming. Glazing was relatively uncommon. Only the finer Stamford wares were glazed with pale green, pale yellow or orange glazes; some others were splashed with glaze as in the case of the so-called 'splashed wares' of Lincoln or Nottingham. Decoration was added by thumbing, incising, combing, stabbing or by the application of strips, stamped motifs or rouletting; it is less common on cooking pots than on other wares. The pots were usually fired in single-flue kilns; the earliest kiln at Stamford was long, narrow and straight-sided, cut directly into the ground. Around A.D.1000 a clay-lined, circular kiln was in use at Stamford, again dug into the limestone, with a sloping chamber to channel hot air, a stoking chamber and exhaust vent.[92] At Flaxengate the wasters have a metallic finish suggesting firing at a very high temperature, and

1   cooking pot
2,3   red-painted storage vessels
4   cooking pot
1-4   from Stamford Castle kiln, late ninth-century
5   cooking pot 'Tesco' site, pre-Conquest
6,7   2 cups from Stamford Castle, pre-Conquest

Figure 25. Pre-Conquest Stamford ware from sites in Stamford (photograph Tony Story, reproduced by permission of the Trust for Lincolnshire Archaeology).

urban potters must have faced the problem of acquiring the large quantities of wood necessary to such firing. Controlled, high-temperature firing of this type is not characteristic of all centres of production. St Neots ware especially is a soft, soapy-textured pottery fired at a low temperature, with wide colour variations on individual pots. A firing process which allowed little control over cooling is the likely explanation, probably bonfire-firing. Two deep firepits found in the St Neots excavation may be such simple kilns.[93]

The East Midlands pottery industry in the tenth century bears the hallmarks of an industry which grew up to meet the demand of large-scale local trade. The volume of its production and the number of centres involved point to this conclusion. Cheap, poor quality pots, like those produced at St Neots or Leicester, predominate. Stamford potters turned out two distinct types; a very fine, off-white glazed ware, usually bowls and spouted pitchers, which was widely traded, and coarser, sandy pink-white cooking pots containing fossils from the local estuarine clay which were traded largely in the immediate environs of Stamford.[94] The great variety of forms and fabric indicate the scale of the industry (see fig. 25). At Stamford 25 major forms of pot, with hundreds of sub-types, have been distinguished, 6 different fabrics in use contemporaneously or consecutively in the late Saxon period have been identified, and 4 types of glaze and 77 patterns of surface ornament or modification:[95] we are not dealing with a single craftsman turning out a few pots in a back room. And if cooking pots were the staple of the industry, a wide variety of other vessels were turned out from the major centres like Stamford and Torksey, including storage jars, crucibles, lamps, pitchers and jugs.

The East Midlands in the tenth and eleventh centuries was in the midst of an economic upswing. The signs of growth are everywhere. New stone churches were built in parish after parish; a prosperous and confident laity were not only endowing these churches but aping ecclesiastical fashions in a new wave of funerary monuments. Towns were springing up and growing, and places like Lincoln or Stamford were taking on substantially the internal shape and street plan they were to keep into the Middle Ages. These new towns were filled with churches and parishes betokening not only the piety but also the wealth of their citizens. By the mid-eleventh century a town like Lincoln was at the height of its prosperity, whilst its decline in the late eleventh century was only temporary. These towns harboured thriving trade, both local and international, fed by the burgeoning output of coin from their mints, mints often unknown before the late ninth century but proliferating during the tenth. In many cases industrial production grew up again for the first time since Roman days, most notably in the pottery industry, but also demonstrated in the products of industrial quarters at Lincoln, or at Northampton.

In the countryside the picture is less clear, but points in the same direction. Rapid parish formation went hand in hand with the fragmentation of older land-holding patterns revealed in place-name changes; these are signs of social and political change, but perhaps also of increasing agricultural potential. New great estates were formed, especially around the monastic houses of the tenth-century revival, and these were managed and exploited more efficiently. The charter bounds show a well-cleared landscape, and population densities by the time of Domesday compare in the Lowlands with much of England and already show important concentrations. Social development and peculiarities bear out this picture (see below, pp. 158–61). The free peasantry so important in this region may be linked with a Celtic past, but their survival here is due not to economic backwardness, but at least in part to the economic possibilities opened up by growth, always a factor in preserving and enhancing peasant freedom.

The problem is to explain the economic surge already well under way in the first half of the tenth century. The Viking impact cannot be dismissed. The pottery revolution in eastern England was closely based on French products of the Pas de Calais and Normandy regions; glazed ware seems to have been introduced at Stamford and briefly at Lincoln after the Viking settlement. Normal trade contacts could have stimulated these changes, but these were prime areas of Viking activity on the Continent and there is positive evidence for contact between them and the East Midlands Danelaw via the Vikings.[96] Outside its local base the pattern of Stamford trade is a Viking pattern, though it must be remembered that the Vikings themselves used existing North Sea routes in their westward expansion. Lincoln's overseas trade was largely with the Scandinavian world and north-east Europe, its coinage massively represented in the Baltic; Baltic amber and ivory have been found in Flaxengate and the Syrian ware there suggests contact with the Islamic world through the Viking trade routes across Continental Russia. The pattern of Lincoln's growth and decline might be seen as a Viking pattern. As a mint and industrial centre Lincoln grew during the tenth century, replacing Chester as the major Mercian mint by 979. The peak of its importance came during and after the establishment of a Scandinavian North Sea Empire by Cnut, and its temporary decline set in when the Norman Conquest shifted English political horizons; the shake-up of the city following the Conquest was radical:[97] no pre-Conquest moneyer survived the traumatic years 1066 to 1071.

The Vikings provided an indirect stimulus to urban growth both in the defended sites which they set up, and perhaps more importantly in those constructed and maintained against them by tenth-century kings. They created and reinforced overseas trading contacts and may have contributed largely to the land market and changes in landownership which were a factor in agricultural growth. But the Vikings cannot be used as a simple *deus ex machina* to explain all changes. The towns of the East Midlands during the tenth century betray a vigour which transcended their defensive origins. Their function as frontier towns trading with a Viking world may have helped Derby or Lincoln, but industrial and internal growth argues a firm basis in local, not long-distance, trade. The potteries of Leicester or St Neots, even those of Stamford, the metalworkers of Flaxengate, the stone quarries of Barnack, were by the late tenth century largely supplying a prosperous local market.

A large part in the explanation of this growth should be played by the agrarian and social developments which created and supplied this market. Alas, this is the least understood area of the late Saxon economy. The political changes which we shall discuss in the following chapters were responsible for some of the changes in great estates, whether lay or ecclesiastical, and the invigorating of local royal courts may have had a much greater impact on the growth of a land market than at first sight appears. The fragmentation of estates, perhaps partly spurred by the Viking settlers, may be important, especially if it located individual landlords in villages, efficiently exploiting their local demesnes and creating surpluses. The new estates of, for example, the Monastic Revival created demand for goods and services, their building programmes stimulated the economy and their size and needs led to an increased build-up and transfer of agricultural surpluses, as new demands for cash and service fell upon the peasantry. By the early eleventh century, if not before, royal taxation was adding to the cash demands which landlords were increasingly making on the peasantry, spreading ever wider the cash economy and the consequent need to produce and market agricultural surplus. The lack of figures on population growth makes it difficult to know how far this contributed increased demand and labour input, and in any case it is unclear whether population growth fuels or follows economic expansion. There are imperceptible factors to allow for, like the increased soil fertility which constant ploughing brings, even the possible increased use of the heavy plough. And there are unknown quantities. Large areas of Lincolnshire, for example, are ideally suited to wool production, and this was later to prove a feature of the local economy, but thanks to the omissions of Domesday evidence for the eleventh century is almost completely lacking.

Economic growth is an elusive, but also a cumulative and interacting process. It would be foolish to ignore the general picture of the tenth century in western Europe as a period of economic development, but wise to remember that England, and in some respects eastern England especially, were precocious by these same standards. We must look, for example, as far afield as the Rhineland and Italy to match and surpass the urban revival in this area. Given the fragmentary state of the evidence our answers to the why of such change may never be firm, particularly since economic historians find difficulty in identifying and agreeing on the earliest stages and causes of economic growth in any period. What we can be certain of is the reality of that growth and its likely effects on the lives of those who lived in the East Midlands at the end of the Anglo-Saxon period.

Part Two

INVASION, SETTLEMENT AND POLITICS

In the early fifth century the East Midlands were still in the control of the Britons; by the ninth they were an integral part of the Anglo-Saxon kingdom of Mercia; in the early tenth century they were incorporated in the new and enlarged kingdom of the English ruled by the royal dynasty of Wessex. During these same centuries the area was twice invaded, its invaders in each case affecting the political and social and more debatably the settlement history of the region. In the fifth and sixth centuries the invaders were Germanic people from north-western Europe, the Angles and Saxons; in the ninth, tenth and again at the turn of the tenth and eleventh centuries they were the Vikings from Scandinavia. The stages of these transformations and many of their details are obscure, especially before the seventh century and even as late as the tenth and eleventh. Debate has centred on the nature of British rule in the fifth and sixth centuries, the extent of British survival into Anglo-Saxon England and the closely related questions of the timing, nature and size of the Anglo-Saxon settlements. Again, historians have been concerned to measure the extent of Viking influence on the region in the ninth and tenth centuries, to ask whether Vikings came and settled in such numbers as to swamp local populations and alter the pattern of settlement, or whether they came not as settlers at all but as a group of new overlords, taking over control of land and people with results which may be no less significant. It is largely the nature and obscurity of the sources which has left these questions so open, though the way in which the questions have been thought about and posed has played its own part in the debate. Two factors remain constant throughout. The role of kings and leaders in all these transformations was crucial. It is a role highlighted in the sources, but it is unlikely that they distort the significance of their contribution at this level of political and settlement history. And the church and churchmen, as landholders and as the recorders of information, are woven as a theme through the whole story.

4 Sources and Problems

Written Sources

The problems of reconstructing a political and settlement history of the East Midlands before the eleventh century stem from the sources, especially from the lack of them. Written material for this region is sparse, more so than for many other areas of early England. The greatness of a king like Offa, for example, who ruled the whole of the Midlands by the end of the eighth century, has had to be painstakingly recovered from a study of land grants and chance references,[1] usually in sources produced outside the area. Both the dearth and patchiness of the sources are to be explained partly in terms of the ecclesiastical history of the region, but they are also the product of a different attitude towards the written word. What written material does survive is of a particular type, largely concerned with kings and churchmen and almost exclusively produced by ecclesiastics, facts which introduce their own problems of interpretation and distortion.

Churchmen were the literate elite of Anglo-Saxon England. They dominated both the production and preservation of documents, so that the history of the church in the region is the basis of a history of its sources. Between the seventh and ninth centuries a number of great religious centres were founded, overwhelmingly monastic in character. Places like Peterborough, Breedon-on-the-Hill and Repton were flourishing religious establishments and many of them had *scriptoria* or writing houses where the monks produced records of land transactions, lives of saints and so on. Many of these houses suffered hard in the late ninth century at the hands of Viking attackers. Peterborough, for example, ceased to exist as an organized community, and very little from its early archives or library existed by the late tenth century.[2] Changes or decline in the monastic life between the eighth and tenth centuries may have played their own role in the loss or dispersion of what early documents may once have existed.

In the mid-tenth century a new religious movement was under way in England, a movement for monastic reform and revival which led to the foundation or re-vitalization of monastic communities at centres like Burton-on-Trent, Peterborough and Ramsey by c.A.D.1000. The archives of these revived abbeys enable us to build a much fuller picture by the late tenth century, not only of religious change, but of landholding, local political structures, estate management and local administration. The archive of charters of Burton,[3] the twelfth-century chronicles of Ramsey and Peterborough which drew on tenth- and eleventh-century records, the Book of Ely[4] and many other documents allow us to build up a picture of the endowment of these abbeys, their activities and impact within the local economy and society and their own concerns for the acquisition of relics and so on. Their records of legal cases and land transactions help flesh out the story of local political relationships, of local families and their wealth and influence, showing how

East Midlands society worked in the late Anglo-Saxon period and the interactions of its great men with the king. This welcome oasis of evidence will prove important throughout the narrative and beyond.

But the patchiness of ecclesiastical sources in time and geographical space is a constant problem. Even in the late tenth century what we know is still very partial, still produced by a handful of religious houses concentrated in only part of the region. Throughout, the particular concerns of churchmen will shape our picture and the questions we can ask. Saints' Lives like the early eighth-century life of St Guthlac[5] or the later one of Wigstan[6] provide much insight into political and religious history both from their major themes and incidental details, but they are primarily evidence of the religious concerns and attitudes of their day. Whilst it is true that in Anglo-Saxon England the gap between the outlook of churchmen and of lay nobles was often narrow or non-existent,[7] it is nonetheless a picture of only part of that outlook that such documents give. They are, however, a salutary reminder of the dominance of religious ideas and values in this early society. If they distort by leaving many areas of life impenetrable, many questions unaskable, they accurately reflect what mattered most to their authors and their audience and we must accept that those areas and questions were not among their priorities. The lives of heroic saints, the acquisition of land and the activities of kings were prime concerns.

The dominance of kings in our narrative is a dominance dictated by the sources. Even our early saints are often royal, Guthlac a member of the Mercian ruling house, Wigstan a murdered king. Such sources as survive centre on the royal dynasties and include not only such 'lives' but king-lists and genealogies of kings, celebrating their ancestry and proving their claims to the throne, like that which survived to prove the existence of the early kingdom of Lindsey (see fig. 31).[8] Again, our picture is distorted in favour of kings, but more insidiously in favour of those royal dynasties which proved ultimately successful. These latter took care not only to preserve their own memories but often to expunge systematically those of others. What we know is often what the successful rulers of the eighth, ninth and tenth centuries wanted us to know, what the religious houses closely bound to those dynasties chose to record and preserve. Such a process of selection may even have affected the charters and records of land grants which eke out eighth- and ninth-century history with information of where kings granted land and to whom. Not only are these affected by all the problems of destruction and survival, of the patchiness of ecclesiastical geography and thus of record already considered; even where churchmen did record and preserve land grants they may only have bothered to keep those associated with great kings and dynasties. Ours is a political picture focussed on ultimate success.

But destruction, partiality, the concerns of churchmen are far from a complete answer to the question of why the history of the invasion, settlement and politics of the East Midlands is so difficult to reconstruct. The production of written material was itself much less common in the early Middle Ages than in subsequent periods. Our emphasis on written documentation was not theirs; our ancestors lived in an oral society.[9] Churchmen certainly recorded some land grants and accounts of the kings they admired and relied on, but much less often than we would now imagine. The rituals accompanying the transfer of land, and the presence of responsible witnesses at these rituals, were still equally if not more important than the written record. When King Æthelred of Mercia granted land to Peterborough in the late seventh century he placed a turf from the land on a gospel book in the sight of many witnesses 'as a confirmation and evidence of his gift'.[10] As late as the tenth century property rights and changes in them were still as likely to be proved in court on oral evidence, by reference to collective local memory. When Bluntisham, Huntingdonshire, was disputed in the 970s, the case turned on events occurring before 920, when Edward the Elder had conquered the area from the Danes. The issue was decided by the witness of the 'old and wise of the province, who well remembered the time when jarl Toli was killed at Tempsford'.[11] The equation of the old and the wise, the venerable position of the old is, incidentally, a natural corollary of a society thus based on memory and oral tradition.

The dearth of records from the East Midlands before the late tenth century is not a simple question of loss, nor is the absence of adequate narrative sources. There were only a few centres of the writing of history and annals in particular in Anglo-Saxon England before the eleventh century and the East Midlands did not contain one of them. In the early eighth century Bede with his influential *Ecclesiastical History of the English People* created the basis of such a tradition in Northumbria, and annals were kept there sporadically until the mid-tenth century. In the ninth century the royal house of Wessex stimulated a concern to write up their own history and origins, which is the basis of the so-called *Anglo-Saxon Chronicle*. This stimulus was especially lively under king Alfred in the late ninth century and it was one which his children continued into the early tenth. One of these children, his eldest daughter Æthelflæd, became ruler of Mercia at this date and is the inspiration of the only set of annals we know to have been produced within Mercia, the *Mercian Register*, a record of her military exploits incorporated into some manuscripts of the *Anglo-Saxon Chronicle* (see fig. 26). For the Northumbrian and West Saxon chronicles of the eighth and ninth century the East Midlands as part of Mercia was very peripheral to their concerns. They mention the area infrequently and always from a perspective centred outside, at a foreign court or religious house. A tradition of annal or history writing probably never developed within Mercia; it was a West Saxon princess who stimulated the brief record of early tenth-century resistance to the Danes here. So faltering was the tradition of annal-writing anywhere in early England that it almost dries up in the tenth century after the deaths of Alfred's children, and its halting revival in the early and mid-eleventh century was again at centres outside the East Midlands.

With written sources thin, royally obsessed, mirroring the vagaries of ecclesiastical history and often consisting of the chance comments of outsiders like Bede, a political narrative of the East Midlands is especially difficult to reconstruct. But ideally we would wish to have a combined political narrative and settlement history, a story which told how invaders or churchmen took over the land, of their impact on its settlement as well as their shaping of its political framework. The written sources provide only hints at most of settlement changes, though those odd remarks must be the starting point. The only blanket coverage of the area which can be used to answer these questions is Domesday Book. This great survey will play a crucial role in the

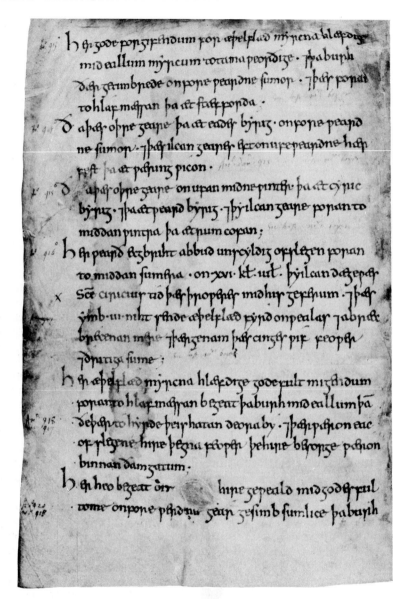

Figure 26. An extract from the Mercian Register in MS B of the *Anglo-Saxon Chronicle*. Translation of marked section: 'In this year (917) Æthelflæd, lady of the Mercians, with the help of God, before Lammas obtained the borough which is called Derby, with all that belongs to it; and there also four of her thegns, who were dear to her, were killed within the gates' (reproduced by permission of the British Library).

reconstruction, but two important caveats must govern its use. As a record of settlement it is late. It gives a picture of the East Midlands at the end of the eleventh century and only careful interpretation can make it yield any information on the Viking settlements of c.A.D.900; it must be doubted whether it can tell much of the Anglo-Saxon settlements of the fifth or sixth centuries. And Domesday is not a record of settlement at all, even for the eleventh century. It is, as we have seen, a record of tenants and dues compiled for the king and certainly omits many villages and settlements.[12] The combined picture will never be compiled from the written sources alone. The evidence of archaeology and place-names will always be essential to the reconstruction.

Archaeology

For the arrival of the Anglo-Saxons especially the evidence of archaeology has been crucial. Its limitations must thus be firmly established.

Historians often use archaeological distribution maps, like the maps of early Anglo-Saxon cemeteries in the East Midlands given in fig. 30, to answer such questions as where the earliest Anglo-Saxon settlements were and how and when they spread. But such maps distort reality because the gaps on them may have no significance. A blank on such a map need not indicate lack of early Anglo-Saxon presence, but merely lack of archaeological excavation of the area. England has never been subjected to total excavation and is unlikely to be so. The features which *are* recorded on such maps are significant; the gaps may not be. This limitation becomes doubly important when place-name scholars use such archaeological maps to date names and then go on to use such dating to argue for changing settlement patterns (see below, pp. 74–5). Names are now often dated by reference to archaeology, for example, to ask whether -*ingas* names like Spalding correlate with cremation cemeteries which are pagan and early, and so to argue for the approximate date at which such names were given. However, if all cemeteries are not known, the correlations or absence of them may be spurious.

Even where excavation has occurred it has often been of a very inadequate nature and the utility of its finds consequently impaired. Only a tiny proportion of the Anglo-Saxon cemeteries which are our major evidence for the earliest stages of Anglo-Saxon settlement have been excavated under rigorous modern archaeological conditions. Most of them were discovered randomly in the eighteenth and nineteenth centuries during activities like ploughing or railway construction. They were recorded, if at all, perfunctorily, their grave-goods scattered, with little attention paid to anything not of immediate and obvious value. The cemetery at Toddington, Bedfordshire, for example, was discovered in 1819.[13] Only hearsay recorded a large quantity of bones, gold-plated copper brooches, armour, spearheads, helmets, buckles, rings, beads and small pots filled with little bones. The site is known only from an anonymous author of the *History of Dunstable* who reported verbal estimates of 'a person daily on the spot'. The bones crumbled to dust and the grave-goods were scattered. Toddington must be counted as an Anglo-Saxon cemetery but little more can be said about it. Some nineteenth-century excavation attempted to be more systematic. Thomas Bateman, who opened most of the Derbyshire barrow burials, set himself high standards,[14] but Bateman often arrived only after labourers had accidentally opened a barrow and he had none of the techniques of scientific archaeology to record what he found and to preserve the more fragile material.

Even in the twentieth century few cemeteries have been totally excavated, so that important questions hang over the size of most of them, and we know less than we should about their overall layout and use. Where controlled modern excavation has been undertaken, as at Loveden Hill (Hough-on-the-Hill, Lincolnshire), it has transformed our view. Interwar estimates of the size of this cemetery, for example, were in hundreds, but have now been raised to c.2000.[15] With so few cemeteries excavated under these conditions it is impossible to know whether some of the smaller finds of five or fewer graves recorded in Audrey Meaney's *Gazetteer* indicate isolated burials or the edge of larger cemeteries, to decide how many large cemeteries existed and what their average size was, or to date their use precisely. Painstaking reconstruction based on museum collections and nineteenth-century records is beginning to reassemble fragmented material[16], but such work still does not cover the whole region and will never recover all that was lost.

Dating is crucial whether archaeology is to be used alone or to be married to written evidence to reconstruct changes such as settlement expansion. Archaeologists use stratification as a major dating method; that is, they date finds in relation to other clearly datable objects, for example, coins found in the same excavation layer. However, this method depends on the ability to date some objects precisely and in the period between the fourth and eighth centuries coins, the best dating objects, are very rare. Typology then becomes a major method. Here a sequence of, for example, brooch or pottery styles is established. Ideally this is done from a single site, where a sequence of styles can be constructed from younger (found in the topmost excavation layers) to older (found below). These objects are then used to date the layers in which they are found, and other material in those layers elsewhere in the excavation. Even here there are problems of establishing beginning and end dates for the sequences and when a typology established for one site is used to date objects in another excavation entirely other questions are raised of whether a particular style of pot or brooch is necessarily of the same date wherever it is found. In some cases a sequence is constructed without the firm basis of strata in a particular site to control it. Immediately subjective questions enter the construction and interpretation. How do styles develop? Is the sequence often suggested from simplest=oldest, to most complex=most recent, correct? Do styles necessarily evolve towards greater complexity rather than from complex to simple? Are different styles necessarily an indication of different dates, or of the use of different styles at the same date by different social groups? Are there backwaters where apparently 'old' styles continue to be made and used long after their disappearance elsewhere? How old were the goods when they were lost or deposited in a grave to become the object of later archaeological excavation? Given the influences of fashion and social status, the possible lifetime of an object before deposit, the likelihood of areas out of the mainstream of change, it becomes hazardous to construct typologies and even more so to argue that an object apparently indicating a mid sixth-century date in one place indicates the same date when found in another. Archaeologists are well aware of these problems and assign dates tentatively; we must be ready to accept their caution.

A final general problem which limits the archaeological record is that of survival. Not all materials survive in all soil conditions. Pot, metal and glass survive much better than wood or textiles which in most soil conditions disappear to leave meagre traces which until recently were rarely recovered. This is an especial problem when constructing the material culture, but it is one more complication when trying to distinguish Briton and Anglo-Saxon in the sixth century on the basis of that material culture.

There are specific pitfalls in using archaeological evidence to write the story of the coming of the Anglo-Saxons into eastern England. This is usually mapped by the finding of 'Anglo-Saxon' material in graves – pots, brooches, weapons of a 'Germanic' style. But to argue from material culture to ethnic origin in this way is dubious. If a body is found interred with a brooch bearing Germanic ornament, is it the body of an Anglo-Saxon? Or of a native Briton who has adopted Germanic tastes, now fashionable? Or of some quadroon, octroon or similar product of intermarriage between the races?[17] Fashions change and after the earliest Anglo-Saxon arrivals Germanic styles may have had a disproportionate impact, especially when they became the new ruling group. Aristocracies and rulers have a disproportionate influence on style.

Germanic style may itself be elusive, and inferences about its date and development may distort the picture of the earliest Anglo-Saxon settlements. Two classes of allegedly Germanic material have been extensively used in discussion of those settlements. A series of buckles and belt fittings have been identified as Germanic, military and early,[18] and examples of them found at places like Leicester, Duston, Sleaford, Lincoln, Clipsham and so on have been cited to suggest a Germanic military/mercenary presence in the East Midlands from as early as the fourth century. Yet it has been very difficult to prove that such belts and their fittings were either Germanic, military or even exclusively male wear.[19] Even if exclusively military and male they are likely to have been widely issued within the Roman army, and may thus indicate the presence of Roman troops but not necessarily of Germanic ones; and whatever their ethnic origin the assumption of a continuity or link between their presence and the later arrival of Anglo-Saxon settlers is unjustified.

Like the belt fittings, Romano-Saxon pots such as that from Great Casterton (fig. 27) have been taken to indicate the presence of Germanic mercenaries in eastern England in the fourth century; such pots are seen as products of fourth-century Roman potteries manufactured to suit Germanic tastes.[20] But the dimpled decoration taken to be a sign of Germanic style is unknown from purely Germanic areas before the late fourth century,[21] and is probably rather a Roman style which itself affected Germanic taste around the year A.D.400. Romano-Saxon pots cannot thus have been produced to appeal to a Germanic taste which had not yet developed.

Changes other than a numerically large settlement of Anglo-Saxons may leave a disproportionate effect on the archaeological record. The disruption of old centres of artistic and industrial production, often the result of invasion and attack, take on a magnified significance. The end of the Roman pottery industry in eastern England in the fourth century, for example, can too easily

Figure 27. Romano-Saxon pot from Great Casterton (reproduced by permission of Leicestershire Museums, Art Galleries and Records Service).

appear as the end of the inhabitants of Roman Britain. The return to crude, local pottery production, handmade wares where 'British' and 'Anglo-Saxon' cannot be distinguished, makes the transition from one to the other very difficult to chart. Indeed a major problem is that 'British' material culture is poorly identified and may have been very similar to that of the incoming Anglo-Saxons. Changes in church organization after the late ninth century in eastern England affected the production and development of, for example, sculptural styles, a change which can too easily be interpreted as indicating massive new Viking presence in the area. The eclipse of one aristocratic group and its replacement by another can easily look like the disappearance of a native population when so many recorded archaeological finds are of high-status goods produced under the patronage of that aristocracy.

For all such reasons, crude arguments based on a superficial reading of a map of Anglo-Saxon cemeteries or of their contents are risky. Archaeology is at its most effective in the reconstruction of the circumstances of daily life, of technology, even of religious beliefs. It is most limited where historians seek to use it to answer questions of the where, when and how many of Anglo-Saxon or Viking settlement.

Place-names and Language

Unlike archaeological excavations, place-names give a total coverage of any area, made increasingly available and accessible through the publications of the English Place-Name Society. Whereas written sources, artistic products, brooches and metalwork, even pottery, are the creations of specialists, place-names are the spontaneous products of the local people. A place-name records the description of a settlement or landscape feature in the language of those who lived around about at the time when the name was given. It ought thus to be possible to study the language and speech habits of the area at that date, and perhaps on that basis discuss the ethnic composition of the local population. Thus the fact that we speak English, a Low Germanic language, and not Welsh, and that the overwhelming proportion of our place-names were given in English, appears to indicate a massive Anglo-Saxon settlement, displacing the native British population. Similarly the large number of Viking place-names in the East Midlands would testify to a second large-scale settlement of Danish-speaking people in this area in the ninth and tenth centuries. At the same time the identification of the oldest layers of English place-names, like the *-inghams* and others, then the dating of subsequent groups, like the *-tons*, could show the earliest Anglo-Saxon settlements, and help chart the stages and dates of English advance, and the progressive stages of new settlement and land clearance. The days, however, when such straightforward deductions could be made are long past.

If place-names are to be used in settlement history they must be dated.[22] Some broad dates are readily established. English place-names can be no earlier than the late fourth century when the first English settlers of whatever type were arriving; Viking/Danish place-names can be no earlier than the late ninth century when the first known Viking settlements in the East Midlands were made. It is when we turn to more detailed questions that difficulties arise. Which are the earliest English place-names, perhaps indicating the earliest phase of settlement? Can a group of names indicating settlement up to c.A.D.700 be identified, and those later than this? Can the numerous Viking place-names ending in *-by* (e.g. Ashby) all be dated to the early stages of Viking settlement, say c.875–900, and thus be used as evidence of dramatic changes in landholding, settlement and perhaps as an indication of the scale of these arrivals, or were they given more gradually during the tenth and eleventh centuries, with a very different significance.

The appearance of a name in written sources is an apparently reliable dating method, and has been used successfully to demonstrate what are apparently the earliest group of names, those in use before c.A.D.700.[23] But written sources, especially before the tenth century, are very sparse, and although this method may establish that some names are definitely early it cannot exclude those which do *not* appear in the fragmentary sources as not early. The majority of English place-names are first recorded in Domesday Book in 1086, although most are clearly older than this. But even Domesday is an inaccurate record of all names then in use. An old and important place such as Breedon in Leicestershire, first recorded in the early eighth century, is missing from Domesday. With such unreliable written evidence it cannot be argued that a place-name is only as old as its first written record, and place-name scholars are increasingly turning to other methods of dating.

Correlation with dated archaeological evidence is much favoured. For example, those names regularly associated with pagan cremation cemeteries are argued to be early. On this basis the view that the -*ingas* names are the oldest in the East Midlands has been challenged, the -*ham* names now being seen as the oldest stratum because of their association with this early archaeological evidence.[24] But archaeological finds are random in distribution, as we have seen. Use of such correlation must also be strictly controlled: similar finds should not frequently appear *not* associated with the relevant

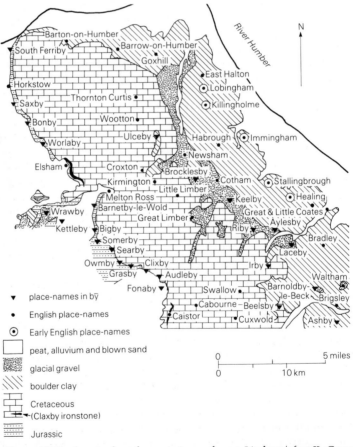

Figure 28. Geology and settlements in north-east Lindsey (after K. Cameron, 'Scandinavian settlement in the territory of the Five Boroughs: the place-name evidence', in *Place-Name Evidence for the Anglo-Saxon Invasions and the Scandinavian Settlements*, 1977).

place-name, and there must be 'real coincidence of locality', the name and the finds closely coinciding;[25] these are rigorous criteria which are rarely met.

Mapping place-names on a geological drift map is a frequent method (see fig. 28). The assumption is that better soils like the boulder clays will be settled and cleared first, poorer soils like the glacial gravels only later. Thus names regularly found on the best soils are argued to be older as a type than those regularly found on poorer soil.[26] Early attempts at these methods may have ignored other important factors governing choice (and date) of settlement sites, such as water availability, proximity to communications, the influence of existing settlement and the lack of necessary correlation between soil fertility and the underlying geological drift (it is geological, not soil, maps which are usually used in such exercises). The latest applications of these methods have been very sophisticated,[27] but significantly they have also blurred any easy conclusions about dating different types of place-name.

A range of other methods use the later history of the village to indicate its likely date of origin. If, for example, a village was deserted in the later Middle Ages it is assumed that the site was always marginal and thus the settlement and the name late.[28] Not only does this ignore the great variety of factors which led to village desertion, it returns to the assumption that poorer soil=later settlement and later naming. The administrative importance or tax assessment of a village later in the Middle Ages is used to argue that those wealthiest and largest at a later date are the oldest settlements, or that those villages important enough to become parishes in the tenth and eleventh centuries represent the oldest settlements and that their place-names are of a similar age. There may be some broad truth in all of this, but the date for this evidence for parishes, village size and so on is eleventh-, usually twelfth-century at the earliest. Much apart from the simple question of age of settlement could have combined to influence the development and size of villages by this late date. Domesday tax assessments, often used for this purpose, often include unnamed surrounding settlements under a named village. Nor do such arguments always take into account relationships with other settlements. In an already densely settled area such as the Wash river valleys, new villages may have been established from a very early date on poor soil, and their chances of growing large were always limited.

Attempts to assign dates to particular groups of place-names are usually part of attempts to assign dates to stages of land clearance and new settlements. Thus if, for the sake of argument, all -*hams* are sixth-century, all -*bys* late ninth/early tenth, by plotting these on a map the gradual extension of settlement and clearance will emerge. But even if broad dates can be assigned to name elements like -*ham* or -*by*, it does not follow that the village was founded when the name was given. Place-names can and do change. Bede, for example, mentions some places whose names he knew in the early eighth century, which had not changed by the eleventh century or even later. Barrow, Partney (Bede's *Baruae*, *Peartaneu*[29]) have changed over the centuries only in their pronunciation, the sort of change which has affected the whole language since Anglo-Saxon times. But he names *Tiowulfingcæstir* on the River Trent,[30] which seems to be the later Littleborough. Such changes are not simply because of cataclysms like Viking invasion. Physical transformation can change a name: Bede's *Medeshamstede* became *Burch* (Borough) and then

Peterborough because of its growth into an important town by the eleventh century.[31] Many villages with Viking names are so identical in every way to English-named villages that they are probably old villages renamed after the Viking settlement.[32] Some villages still had alternative English and Danish names in the eleventh century, indicating such a change which had failed to stabilize.[33] Many place-names, including those used to measure Viking settlement in the East Midlands, record a change of ownership rather than a new village foundation. In southern England, where tenth-century documents are fuller, it is clear that some places were called after their tenth-century owner,[34] not because he founded the settlement, but because he acquired it in the course of the break-up of some larger unit.

Place-names cannot be used to chart settlement history or to speculate on changes in ethnic composition of the local population until the reasons why they do (or as often, do not) change are fully understood. Throughout England, for example, a disproportionate number of river names are pre-English. In Derbyshire the river Dove has a name of British origin, from *dubo* ('the dark river'?). The survival of such British names certainly proves a period of contact between Romano-British and Anglo-Saxon during which the latter could learn these names from the former. They also indicate that such a physical feature, known to large numbers of people and not subject to individual ownership, may change their names rarely, i.e. they emphasize the impact both of currency and of ownership on name changes. At the other end of the spectrum, field names known only within a village may be very volatile. At a time when landownership was in the hands of a small ruling group, the village names of eastern England will inevitably reflect changes in that owning group, whether at the Anglo-Saxon invasion, the Viking conquest, or the great transformation of landholding during the late Saxon period already discussed. Many place-names, like Colston (Kolr's *ton*) or Barkby (Bjokr's *by*), indicate the first individual owner to make a mark on the village, to acquire it, to make a home in it;[35] the great shift in the nature of landholding between the eighth and tenth centuries probably marks one of the major changes in place-names. In view of such facts it is unwise to argue from place-name changes to the overwhelming of local populations by hordes of incoming settlers, or to an Anglo-Saxon or Viking influx which transformed the settlement pattern of the East Midlands.

Place-names have a further use as part of the evidence for language change and what that can indicate of changes in the ethnic composition of the population. The fact, for example, that in the tenth century the surrounding people could call a village Fotherby (Lincolnshire), using the Viking word -*by* for a village and not the English word -*ton*, and that they used a Scandinavian genitive ending in -*ar*, rather than the English genitive ending in -*es*, must suggest that at that date the local people were speaking a language or dialect heavily influenced by Scandinavian speech. The problem arises when we go on from there to argue about how large a Scandinavian settlement was necessary to bring about such a change, or how large an Anglo-Saxon settlement was needed in the fifth and sixth centuries to ensure that the people of the East Midlands spoke English by the eleventh century. Once again the difficulty lies in understanding how languages do change and interact, and whether such change and interaction is simply a question of numbers, or of time-scale and the nature of the incoming community.

Aristocracies may certainly influence language out of all proportion to their numbers. If the language of the local court is English or Danish, many Britons or English will learn enough of that language to get by there, and the language of the new aristocracy will certainly affect legal terminology as Danish did in the East Midlands, an area long known as the Danelaw. If two languages are fairly close, as old English and old Danish were, bilingualism may easily develop, and a large bilingual group in any population can cause changes in the native tongue.[36] These arguments for changes resulting merely from the intrusion of a new aristocracy have been countered by pointing to the Norman Conquest.[37] This can be used as a sort of 'controlled experiment' since it is known to have been an aristocratic settlement by a mere few thousand overlords. The impact of the Norman Conquest on English place-names was minimal, though the long-term impact on the language was more significant. Using the Norman Conquest as a control to show the influence of a small aristocracy on language and names would make the Viking settlement fairly extensive, but not overwhelming, since English place-names survive it as a majority and English remained the dominant speech of the area, but the Anglo-Saxon invasions overwhelming, resulting in a total transformation of place-names and language.

But if the Norman Conquest is to be used as a controlling experiment, the other variables in that experiment must be carefully considered. Place-names have been seen to have some fluidity, but especially during periods which saw the transformation of the very nature of landholding. One such change had already occurred before the Norman Conquest, and had coincided in the East Midlands with the Viking settlements, producing a disproportionate number of Viking names. A major factor in fixing place-names was the impact of the written record. The widespread use of writing, especially for administrative and taxation purposes, affects all oral development and especially names. The Domesday record and the variety of lost administrative documents which preceded and followed it[38] were part of the process by which English place-names came to be fixed. The Norman Conquest occurred during, albeit near the beginning of, the transformation of English culture and language which was the result of transition from an oral to a written culture. Its impact on place-names might thus be much less than, for example, the Anglo-Saxon or Viking invasions now appear to have been. By contrast, the major landholding changes of the tenth century have left such a large record in English place-names partly because they were the last great change before the development of that fixity of names.

Time-scale is the other unknown quantity. If two groups interact, inter-marry, communicate over a long period, the chances of linguistic change are greater and the impact of the politically dominant language ramifies. We know little of the immediate results in language and place-names of the Anglo-Saxon invasions. The earliest written records date from c.A.D.700, over 200 years later than the earliest movements. Although these records are in Latin, they do contain some vernacular words, mostly place-names, which are usually in English. However, these records are invariably the products of the Anglo-Saxon ruling elite; they give no indication of the language spoken by the majority of the inhabitants of eastern England by c.A.D.700 and even if they did suggest the prevalence of English by this date they are too far removed from the original invasions to prove whether that was the result of a cataclysmic overwhelming of the Britons by the Anglo-Saxons. The Viking invaders did apparently preserve their own language and grammatical usages at first,[39] but that language quickly disappeared[40] and has left little impact on the dialects of the East Midlands.[41] Place-name changes need not mean an immediate change of language with either invasion, nor need such language change argue the overwhelming of local populations. But arguments from language especially remain the strongest of those used to suggest that the settlements of Vikings and particularly Anglo-Saxons were on a relatively large scale.

The Influence of Models

Such caveats and cautions about the use and interpretation of place-name and archaeological evidence are necessary precisely because they are and always will be a major source for settlement history. The tentative nature of conclusions based on their careful use requires emphasis. But their most dangerous limitation may be one which the historian shares. However neutral their evidence in terms of lack of bias in its original production, place-name scholars and archaeologists interpret that evidence within the prevailing model of settlement history. Historians themselves have provided such a framework and have been guilty of thinking within it without awareness of its existence.

The prevailing model or framework of views which held the stage until recently was largely that developed by nineteenth-century historians. It saw the history of English settlement as a story of gradual extension, from the coming of the Anglo-Saxons if not before. It posited a landscape still largely unexploited at the end of Roman Britain, and saw the fifth century onwards as a time of constant battle against forest and fen to found new villages and clear new sites. The arrival of the Anglo-Saxons and later of the Vikings were momentous events in that story, folk movements, especially in the first case, of ethnic groups of Angles, Saxons and Jutes under their tribal leaders or as bands of pioneers, undertaking massive new land clearance. The new groups brought with them new (and Germanic) forms of social, political and economic organization and their numerical importance submerged the existing population.

This model affected the way that place-name scholars interpreted their names. If place-names could be dated, their chronology would show that same steady march of human endeavour, as -*hams* were followed by -*inghams*, -*ings*, -*tons* and so on. It affected archaeological interpretations which approached the cemeteries of eastern England seeking evidence of mass migration. It affected assumptions about political, administrative and estate structures: our Anglo-Saxon ancestors drew new bounds through largely uncharted land. It affected the role assigned to Anglo-Saxons and Vikings in the history of settlement; both were in the true sense colonizers and settlers.

Now, thanks to the work of Jones, Barrow and Sawyer,[42] this old view is changing. The land appears never, at least in historical times, to have been as empty and unexploited as the old view suggested. Its bounds and estates go back to Celtic times if not before. Place-names and documentary evidence record less the relentless extension of settlement than the changes in land organization and ownership which occurred over the early medieval period. It is typical of this new atmosphere that two recent interpretations of Viking settlement, whatever their detailed reliability, emphasize the military and colonial nature of the Viking settlement of the East Midlands.[43] In one case we are offered a picture of soldier colonists settled by a military aristocracy; in the other Danelaw peculiarities are presented as the rational legal system of a military, colonial society. The new emphasis on aristocratic organizations and re-organizations of society is in keeping with the new approach of Jones, Barrow and Sawyer.

The old model was in part a product of the paradigms of progress and the pioneering spirit current in the nineteenth century. It was coloured by prevailing interests in racial origins and a passion in some intellectual circles for all things Germanic. At a deeper level the new model may show dissatisfaction with such ideas and a post-colonial ability to see the mechanics of empire. Enthusiasm for the 'folk' and its spontaneous organizations has been supplanted by a recognition of the controlling powers of ruling groups. The new model has certainly shown up the unproven preconceptions of the old, even if its own remain to be identified.

5   The End of Roman Britain and the Coming of the Anglo-Saxons

In A.D.410 the Emperor Honorius wrote to the cities of Britain urging them to undertake their own defence. Bede, writing in the early eighth century, tells how in 449 the Angles and Saxons were invited by Vortigern, a British ruler, to settle in eastern England in order to defend it.[1] When so few documents survive, such random letters and references can take on a mesmeric power, and dates like 410 and 449 have become lodged in the historical record as significant stages in the end of Roman Britain and the coming of the Anglo-Saxons. Yet the transformation from Roman Britain to Anglo-Saxon England was a drawn-out process in which British survival is now seen to have played an important part.

Although Bede does not always stick to the year 449, he clearly felt that the 440s, that is the mid-fifth century, were a significant turning point.[2] Bede bases his picture on Gildas, a mid-sixth-century Welsh monk, who fleshes out the gory and commonly accepted scenario of the Anglo-Saxon invasion. Barbarian attacks had prompted the Romano-Britons to employ mercenaries of Germanic origin who 'first fixed their talons in the eastern part of the island'.[3] They were provided with supplies by the British, but became dissatisfied and rose in revolt against their masters. Gildas wrote early in the sixth century, during the uneasy peace which followed the suppression of that revolt. The picture he gives of the Anglo-Saxon invasions and their course is cataclysmic and it is well to remember that he was a preacher using recent history to castigate the morals of his society and its kings, scarcely a perspective which would have led him to underplay the violence of events. He is also a geographically remote commentator whose information on eastern England was at best fragmentary. Both Bede and Gildas agree in seeing eastern England as one of the earliest areas of settlement; both picture the earliest stages as a settlement of mercenaries, of defenders who went on rapidly to take over the lands of their masters, and Bede sees the mid-fifth-century as a crucial period. But the problems involved in using both sources, and Bede's dependence on Gildas, mean that their picture must not be allowed to dominate the archaeological record.

As early as the fourth century the Roman towns of eastern England were defended by new or increased fortifications[4] and garrisons against the threat of Pictish attack. The presence of mercenaries and their Germanic origins has been argued from the belt buckles and fittings found at places like Leicester, Sleaford, Lincoln and so on,[5] and allegedly Romano-Saxon pottery. But the interpretation of both of these types of evidence has been seriously challenged (see above, p. 71), and although some Germanic presence is likely in the fourth century it was probably as an integral part of the Roman army and its material traces are elusive. By the late fourth century the Romans were settling mercenaries within the Empire as *foederati*, groups under a leader with whom the Roman rulers had a treaty or *foedus*. Such organized groups should have retained their own way of life and culture and should show up more clearly in the archaeological record (always allowing that fourth-century Germanic material culture *can* be readily distinguished). The ambiguity of the fourth-century evidence is against the presence of such organized groups in the East Midlands.

Gildas's story suggests that it was such larger groups of Germanic mercenaries who settled in eastern England, whose rebellion and reinforcement led to the eventual Anglo-Saxon take-over, and whose presence therefore can be linked to later, large-scale settlement. This movement belongs to the fifth century. From the first half of the fifth century there is some evidence to suggest that Germanic groups were defending important routes such as the Humber and the Ancaster Gap, and associated with important Romano-British sites. At Great Casterton, Rutland, a group of pagan burials has been found in the bank of the Roman town;[6] at Ancaster a pagan cremation cemetery lies just outside the south face of the Roman defences;[7] in north Lincolnshire a cemetery like Kirton-in-Lindsey may date in its origins pre-450.[8] The siting of such burials suggests deliberate employment by the Romano-British, though there is room for doubt. The mere proximity of Anglo-Saxon and Romano-British occupation need not argue coexistence or deliberate employment. At Vernemetum early Saxon burials overlie Roman buildings, arguing a time-lag between the two.[9]

What may have started as a controlled movement of mercenaries in the employ of the Britons had apparently passed out of their hands by the late fifth century. The very earliest Anglo-Saxon cemeteries like Kirton-in-Lindsey show a dramatic increase in size in the later fifth century and the early sixth, though their continuity with the early fifth century is equally significant. The phase of rapid expansion of the Anglo-Saxon presence is marked by cemeteries like those at Elkington, Fonaby and West Keal.[10] At the same time cemeteries lose their early correlation with Roman sites and centre rather along the North Sea routes and the major river valleys. To this stage belong the settlements marked by cemeteries such as that at Kempston in the Ouse valley,[11] Duston[12] and Kettering in the valleys of the Welland and Nene. This picture of a major shift of settlement in the late fifth century fits well with the picture of north Germanic movements on the Continent: in the fourth and early fifth centuries these seem chiefly to have been southwards towards Gaul, but in the later fifth century the direction seems to change towards Britain (see fig. 29).[13]

Seventh-century tradition already attached particular importance to the decades around A.D.500. In the twelfth century a local chronicler, Henry of Huntingdon, wrote a history of the English which included the earliest Anglo-Saxon period. Although a late author, he appears to have had access to lost material, probably of a seventh-century date.[14] His sources recorded the arrival of Anglo-Saxons in the area around the Wash under the year 527; 'At that time many came from Germany, on many occasions, and they occupied *Eastangle* and *Merce*; but as yet they were not brought under one King. Many leaders [*proceres*] occupied these regions, whence innumerable wars arose. The names of the leaders, since they were so many, are unknown.' Gildas's picture of the

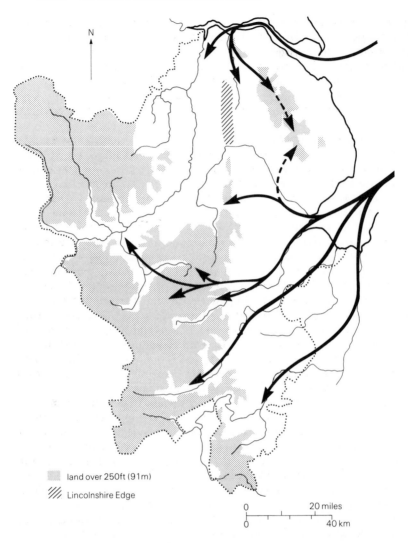

N

land over 250ft (91m)

Lincolnshire Edge

0   20 miles
0   40 km

Figure 29. The probable routes of Anglo-Saxon immigration into the East Midlands in the fifth and sixth centuries.

Anglo-Saxon arrival passing out of Romano-British control is apparently confirmed. But these late fifth- and early sixth-century arrivals may still have been of mercenary groups, of *foederati* under their leaders. The shift away from the Romano-British centres may not simply indicate the Anglo-Saxons now penetrating along the river routes, but also a shift away from those centres by the Romano-Britons themselves.

It is certainly not the case that these Anglo-Saxon incomers were now searching out virgin land for settlement. In the valleys of Ouse, Welland and Nene the Anglo-Saxons were moving into areas already densely settled; the gravel terraces of these river valleys had supported a high population since prehistoric times. There is little evidence for any significant change in the settlement pattern; if anything the fundamental pattern which underlay that of Roman occupation reasserted itself. A line of early village names in Lindsey, at Cammeringham, Corringham and so on, is not associated with the artificial line of the Roman road from Lincoln, the Ermine Street, but with the prehistoric track and the spring-line sites favoured by earlier settlers. Take-over and continuity rather than new settlement and fundamental reorganization were the rule.

A similar pattern emerges in the Trent valley where the Anglo-Saxon arrival was rather later, belonging to the sixth century rather than the earliest stages of settlement. Movement into the valley of the Trent and its major tributaries was in two directions; some penetration may have been from the north down the Trent itself, so that Newark would be an outpost of the Humber movements;[15] but most, if not all, of the thrust came from the east via the Wash rivers like the Welland into Rutland and east Leicestershire, into the valley of the Soar and especially the plateau around Tilton,[16] and thence into the middle Trent valley. Most of the pagan Anglo-Saxon cemeteries (see fig. 30) are east of the Soar, at places like Empingham, Rothley, Market Overton, North Luffenham, or in the lower Trent valley, with the significant exception of the earliest group of all associated with Roman Leicester. Early place-names like Empingham, Beckingham, Collingham, Walkeringham, Nottingham have a similar pattern. Again these are largely areas of existing settlement: the plateau around Tilton, for example, was a nucleus of pre-Roman settlement. A picture of pioneering Anglo-Saxons rowing up the rivers to find desirable virgin land gives way to one of settlers drawn from the beginning to existing areas of settlement, already established on the most fertile soil.

Derbyshire, in spite of the existence of important Roman sites like Buxton, appears on archaeological evidence to be an area of very late Saxon appearance; there is little or nothing before the rich seventh-century barrows like Benty Grange, Borrowash or Cow Low, near Buxton.[17] At the same time evidence for Celtic survival, especially in the north, is strong, with Celtic place- and hill-names like Crich, Chevin and Mam Tor. What pagan cemeteries there are, are in the Trent basin at King's Newton and Stapenhill, extensions of the Trent valley settlement already discussed. All this suggests later Anglo-Saxon movement into a remote and inhospitable region, and there is an interesting parallel in the lack of Derbyshire evidence for Viking influence. It is assumed that in these late seventh-century rich barrow burials in Derbyshire we are seeing the late establishment of powerful Anglo-Saxon overlords rather than the mass migrations into areas further east, but many problems lie in the way of this interpretation. Overlordship of the native population rather than mass migration may be the pattern of Anglo-Saxon settlement everywhere, and even where it is clearly a minority overlordship it is as likely to be early as late in date, witness the case of Bernicia in Northumbria.[18] Rich mineral deposits and Roman exploitation of them should have attracted the Anglo-Saxons here earlier, and barrows like Benty Grange, Hurdlow or Galley Low are significantly close to the Derby/Buxton Roman road. The wealthy barrow-burials of Derbyshire are well recorded precisely because of their wealth, and the graves of humbler folk may have gone unrecorded; almost all the Derbyshire archaeological record dates from poor nineteenth-century excavation. By the late

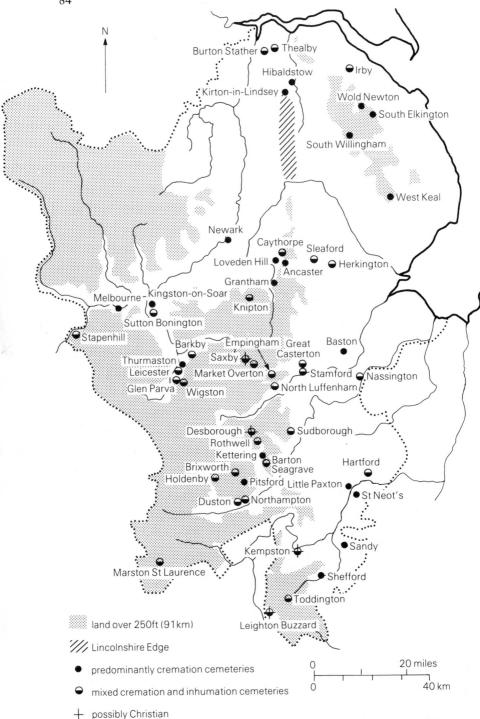

N

Burton Stather • ◐ Thealby
Hibaldstow
◐ Irby
Kirton-in-Lindsey
Wold Newton
● South Elkington
South Willingham
● West Keal

Newark
Caythorpe
Sleaford
Loveden Hill ◐ Herkington
Ancaster
Grantham
Melbourne Kingston-on-Soar
Knipton
Sutton Bonington
◐ Stapenhill
Barkby Empingham Great Baston
Thurmaston Saxby Casterton
Leicester Market Overton Stamford
Glen Parva North Luffenham Nassington
Wigston
Desborough Sudborough
Rothwell
Kettering Hartford
Brixworth Barton
Holdenby Seagrave
Pitsford Little Paxton
Duston Northampton ● St Neot's

Kempston ● Sandy
Marston St Laurence ● Shefford
Toddington
Leighton Buzzard

land over 250ft (91km)

Lincolnshire Edge

● predominantly cremation cemeteries

◐ mixed cremation and inhumation cemeteries

+ possibly Christian

0   20 miles
0   40 km

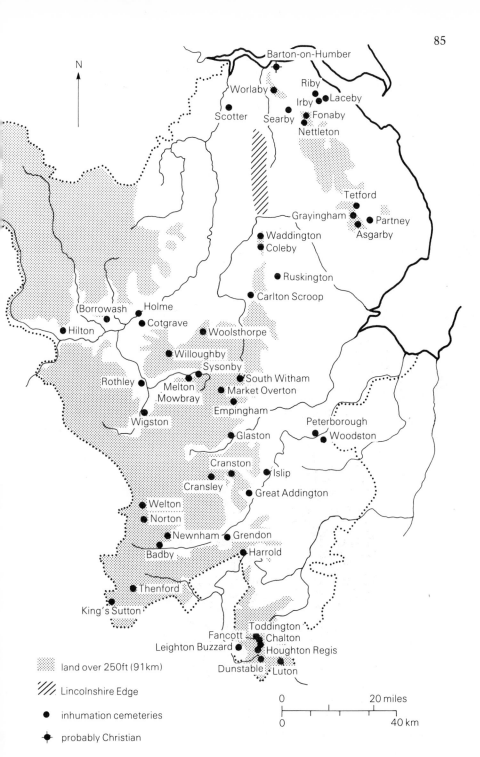

Figure 30. Early Anglo-Saxon cemeteries of the fifth to seventh centuries. Cremation cemeteries and most inhumation ones belong to the pagan period.

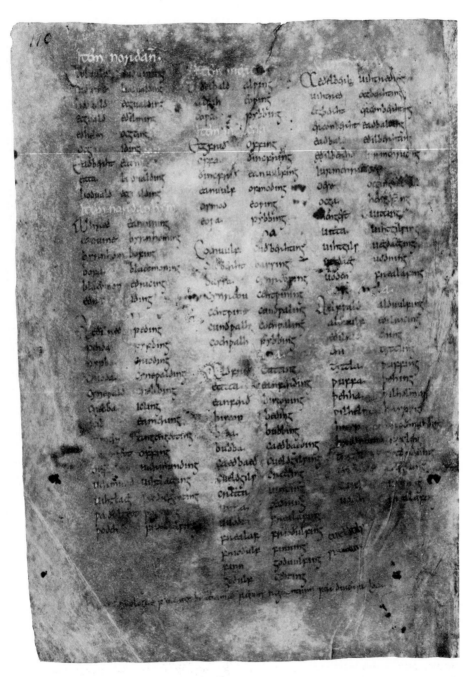

Figure 31. The genealogy of Aldfrith, king of Lindsey [centre columns, bottom list] (BL Vespasian B6, reproduced by permission of the British Library).

seventh century such rich barrow burials are found not only in Derbyshire but in old-established cemeteries like Loveden Hill in Lincolnshire,[19] and testify to important social, economic and political changes. Their high profile should not mislead us into thinking that they indicate the earliest Anglo-Saxon presence in Derbyshire. In the absence of the large pagan cremation cemeteries of the eastern part of the region or the Trent valley Derbyshire cannot be shown as an area of early Anglo-Saxon settlement, but at the moment the question of the date of the arrival here of Anglo-Saxons should remain open.

Anglo-Saxon presence in the East Midlands begins c.A.D.400 and was extensive by the early sixth century. The fate of the native population and their contribution to the making of the region is problematic. Gildas in the sixth century wrote his diatribe for British kings ruling British kingdoms in northern and western Britain. As late as the end of the sixth century parts of the south Midlands were still under British political control. In 571 the West Saxon King Cuthwulf fought a battle against the Britons at *Biedcanford*,[20] not Bedford, but somewhere on the Bedfordshire/Buckinghamshire border.[21] As a result Cuthwulf captured Limbury, a fort on the river Lea in Bedfordshire, and Aylesbury in Buckinghamshire, hitherto in British control. As late as the early seventh century an organized British kingdom still existed just to the north of Derbyshire, Elmet in the Aire valley. But from the East Midlands themselves there is little evidence of such political survival. Anglo-Saxon settlement here was certainly very early, its military leadership and organization around the Wash evident from the beginning of the sixth century. This early settlement could have extinguished the political organization of the Britons here. But the Thames valley was similarly an area of early settlement, yet saw the survival of that British organization well into the sixth century. It may be the absence of written material which makes the transition from Roman Britain to Anglo-Saxon England in the East Midlands appear so cataclysmic. Shreds of evidence point to more prolonged contact and continuity even at the level of political organization. A genealogy of the eighth-century king of Lindsey, Aldfrith (fig. 31), includes a British name, Cædbæd, an anglicization of Catuboduos,[22] who would have lived in the sixth century. Such lists are dubious documents often tampered with for political reasons,[23] but there could be little reason for the later fabrication of a Celtic ancestor. Cædbæd is evidence at the very least of contact, even intermarriage between Briton and Anglo-Saxon at the highest social levels in sixth-century Lindsey. Recent reinterpretation of the church of St Paul-in-the-Bail, Lincoln, suggests that a Christian and thus possibly British community still existed there in the fifth and sixth centuries. As fig. 32 shows, they buried their dead on the site of the then-ruined fourth-century church.[24] As late as 627 Lincoln was still an important political centre where Paulinus consecrated Honorius as Archbishop of Canterbury and where the provincial ruler of the Northumbrian kings had his home.[25] At Leicester the original seventh-century church of St Nicholas was joined to the façade of the old Roman basilica, now the Jewry Wall, deliberately incorporating the older Roman fabric. Such ecclesiastical evidence may argue no more than the passion of seventh-century missionaries for all things Roman. But at Lincoln especially the evidence for some sort of continuity, and thus for an Anglo-Saxon take-over of existing political organizations, is strong. Its very name is a Romano-British survival, still recorded in its British form *Lindocolina* by Bede

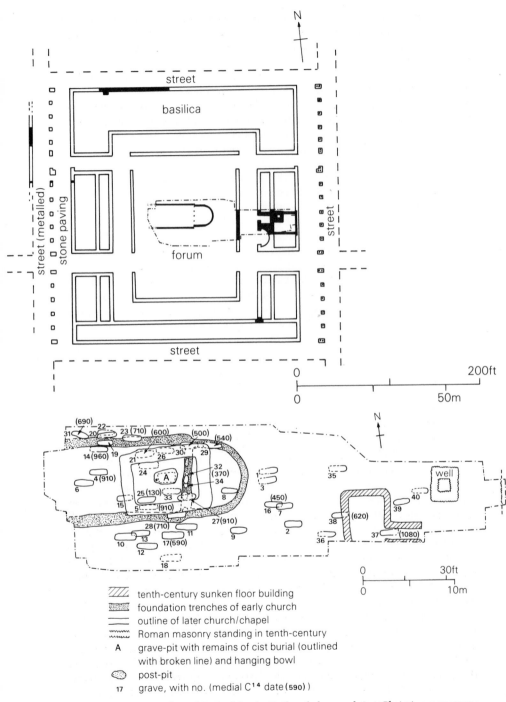

Figure 32. Plan of St Paul-in-the Bail and the overlying Christian cemetery (reproduced by permission of the Trust for Lincolnshire Archaeology).

in the early eighth century.[26] Given what we now know of the continuity of older estate patterns in early Anglo-Saxon England, take-over rather than destruction of much of the political and administrative framework of the Britons is likely.

Continuity at the level of political organization may be difficult to prove, but contact on a wider basis between Briton and Anglo-Saxon is clear. A 'fire and sword' picture of the destruction of the British population is untenable. Two place-names, *eccles* and *wīchām*, undermine such a view (see fig. 33). *Eccles* is

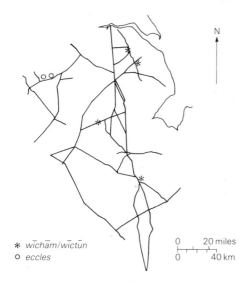

N

* *wīchām/wīctūn*
o *eccles*

0   20 miles
0   40 km

Figure 33. Distribution of *eccles* and *wīchām* place-names in the East Midlands in relation to the Roman road system (after K. Cameron, '*Eccles* in English place-names', in *idem* (ed.), *Place-Name Evidence for the Anglo-Saxon Invasions and Scandinavian Settlements*, 1977; and M. Gelling, 'English place-names derived from the compound *wīchām*', *ibid.*)

a borrowing into English of the British word for a church;[27] *wīchām* is an Anglo-Saxon word, but used to describe a surviving Roman *vicus* or small town.[28] Their use by English speakers is evidence both for contact with British population to transfer the word, and of the survival of flourishing and recognizable British institutions. Another borrowing, *ceaster* (as in Ancaster, Brancaster, Little Chester, Leicester), is of the Latin *castrum*, used to describe Roman towns, though here the word may have passed into early Germanic usage on the Continent long before the arrival in England.

The *eccles* names are chiefly evidence for Celtic survival in the Derbyshire Pennines, where there are many other Celtic names like Mellor, Dinting, Tintwistle, Crich, Mam Tor and so on. But Celtic place-names are not confined to such upland regions, and Celtic river names especially are found throughout. It remains a fact that the overwhelming majority of our place-names are English, and the few surviving Celtic names may indicate pockets of surviving Britons.[29] But the problem of assessing both linguistic and place-name change has been discussed (see above, pp. 73–8), and no simple deduction can be made that the disappearance of so many of their names meant the disappearance of the Britons.

Many Anglo-Saxon religious sites occupy earlier ones. At Maxey in Northamptonshire the church stands on a prehistoric mound and the churchyard is circular like those in Celtic Britain;[30] Breedon-on-the-Hill stands within the rampart and ditch of an Iron Age camp (see fig. 34), and the earliest site of Peterborough abbey was between two tumuli.[31] The continued veneration of holy sites is a common phenomenon, though the sense of holiness may have been transmitted by an indigenous population. Against this probability of large-scale continuity must be set the lack of archaeological evidence to confirm it. The excavated villa sites of eastern England provide no evidence for continuity of settlement.[32] At Southwell in Nottinghamshire the Saxons moved in after the Romano-British had abandoned the site, whilst at Denton the villa was used for Anglo-Saxon burial, one grave cut in the very centre of a late Roman mosaic. The archaeological record is far from complete; moreover, both Romano-Britons and Anglo-Saxons may have moved away from villa sites. Settlement sites and patterns, as opposed to villa occupation, show no sharp break in the fifth and sixth centuries. Fieldwalking in the parish of Brixworth, Northamptonshire, shows Saxon settlement there following the same dispersed pattern as in Roman times and before,[33] indeed continuity with

Figure 34. Aerial photo of the site of Breedon-on-the-Hill (reproduced by permission of J.G.G. Shields).

Iron Age patterns of settlement and agriculture is evident elsewhere in Northamptonshire, traditionally seen as an 'Anglo-Saxon' area.[34] This may be no more than the obvious re-use of prime sites, a spurious picture of continuity which merely reveals how far the land and landscape determine all human agrarian and settlement activity. The problem of Celtic survival is a quagmire of fragmentary and contentious evidence, but central to it must be the question of motivation. Why should the incoming Anglo-Saxons have destroyed and exterminated? If they came as new lords and conquerors, why alter existing methods of taxation, administration, dues-collecting, especially if as *foederati* they had already been maintained by those methods? Why not retain older methods of diverting the surplus of peasant groups, of family units[35] still Celtic in origin? The only motive for widespread change would have been if the Anglo-Saxons arrived in such numbers that not only did they take over the land as overlords and settle some of it as prosperous farmers, but required the mass displacement of the native population to allow their settlement. The nature and size of the incoming Anglo-Saxon communities are crucial questions.

The 'Angles' and 'Saxons' who arrived in the East Midlands in the fifth and sixth centuries came largely from north Germany and Frisia. On the Continent 'Angles' and 'Saxons' may once have been distinct groups, recognizable by their material culture, the Angles preferring bow or cruciform brooches and sets of miniature objects, the Saxons round brooches and narrow-necked pots decorated in a baroque profusion of ornament. But any such original distinctions, which are in any case cultural rather than ethnic, had disappeared by the time of the Frisian Continental cemeteries like Issendorf, which are contemporary with the English settlements. The cemeteries of eastern England show such a mixture of styles, whether of pottery or other artefacts, that it is clear that the settlers had already passed through the cultural melting pot of Frisia before their arrival[36] and that they certainly do not fall into clear groups of Angles or Saxons.

It is through their cemeteries that these settlers can most readily be studied. Well over 1,000 cemeteries have been recorded in England, a majority of them in the east. There are concentrations of Anglo-Saxon cemeteries in Lincolnshire, Northamptonshire, Leicestershire and Rutland. The first impression is thus of a large-scale population movement into eastern England, an impression which fits in geography if not scale with the evidence of Gildas and Henry of Huntingdon. These cemeteries are evidence of Anglo-Saxon communities and cannot be argued away as containing large numbers of Britons, all ethnic differences wiped out in death. Cemeteries like Loveden Hill, Elsham, Newark, South Elkington, Sleaford and Thurmaston were cremation cemeteries in the sixth century and before (see fig. 35). There is little evidence for the survival of British or Christian burial rites, as found in the early Anglo-Saxon cemeteries of Yorkshire.[37] In life and in death the inhabitants of these cemeteries were non-Christians, a new religious group. If, as seems likely, a British population survived here, it was buried in separate cemeteries, or was so totally dominated by the new Anglo-Saxon culture as to have changed its most fundamental religious and social habits. The Anglo-Saxon communities retained their own pagan culture long after their first arrival.

This need not argue for large numbers. Settlements of *foederati* or similar

Figure 35. Cremation urns from Thurmaston cemetery (reproduced by permission of Leicestershire Museums, Art Galleries and Records Service).

dominant groups may have deliberately retained their culture as a distinguishing characteristic, may have achieved greater coherence and definition in relation to surrounding communities. But the Anglo-Saxon settlers cannot be seen merely as a new and small aristocratic group. There is certainly little in the East Midlands to match the size of the 'migration period' cemeteries across the North Sea, cemeteries like Westerwanna with over 4,000 burials. An estimate of the total size of Loveden Hill would place it at about 2,000,[38] well short of the Continental ones, but no small group of overlords; incomplete excavation makes it difficult to know the real size of others like Elsham with c.600 urns, or Newark with about 200.[39] A cemetery like Loveden Hill was in continual use for over 200 years and may have served several communities; it was placed away from the settlements on high land overlooking the Witham valley between Grantham and Newark. But estimates of its size are largely for the early cremation section, and it is the nature of the inmates of such cemeteries which must argue most strongly against a simple aristocratic settlement. The earliest cremation cemeteries already suggest a contrast between a handful of wealthy individuals and a poorer majority (see below, pp. 152–6). Poverty of grave-goods may mean many things apart from material poverty in life, but it is difficult to see the bodies buried at Loveden Hill, their crushed bones bearing signs of heavy labour and premature ageing,[40] as those of an aristocratic group. The communal nature of these cemeteries and their use over a long period mean that they cannot be used to argue for the size of the local Anglo-Saxon settlements, and they certainly cannot tell us of those who may *not* have been buried there – the Britons. But they do indicate an Anglo-

Saxon settlement consisting of both aristocrats and peasant farmers. Parts of Lincolnshire, the Wash river valleys, east Leicestershire and parts of the Trent valley experienced a substantial, though not necessarily overwhelming, Anglo-Saxon settlement before the end of the sixth century.

The transition from Roman Britain to Anglo-Saxon England is a virtual blank in the written records. It is into such gaps that the unconscious preconceptions and models of historians most readily move. They in turn help determine how the fragmentary and difficult evidence of archaeology and place-names is interpreted. The Britons have disappeared from the historical record largely because no-one wished to remember them. Their memory served no purpose in the highly political documents of early Anglo-Saxon England. It is for this reason that every trace of them must now be carefully recovered. That effort may sometimes appear to distort the obvious truth, but that 'obvious truth' was in this case produced by and for Anglo-Saxon invaders. The Britons must be set alongside the Anglo-Saxons whose role in the making of the East Midlands emerges so clearly from the sources.

The East Midlands was a region where Anglo-Saxon settlement was both early and relatively extensive; in that sense it is a very 'English' part of England. Yet those settlements did little to alter a pattern of agricultural exploitation and settlement already very old. The eventual levels of linguistic influence exerted by the Anglo-Saxons was great; their language and their place-names were imposed, though over a long period of time and chiefly on those features of the land which could be owned and taken over. The incoming group were farmers as well as nobles; they assimilated and continued to exploit existing estate structures, but some of them must also have farmed the land and eventually been drawn into those structures. The swamping and replacement of the existing population is unlikely. Anglo-Saxon settlers were drawn to the best land to control it as new landlords, to fit into its possibilities. The destruction and cataclysm existed more in the political moralizing of Gildas than in fifth- and sixth-century reality.

6 Kings, Kingdoms and Churchmen, the Sixth to Ninth Centuries

Kings and Princes: the Sixth and Seventh Centuries

Henry of Huntingdon's annal pictured the arrival of the Anglo-Saxons under many different leaders, who fought amongst each other and presumably against British lords. By the end of the seventh century the political shape of the East Midlands looked different. The *Tribal Hidage*, a document probably drawn up about this date,[1] shows the area around the Wash still organized into a series of lordships and small administrative units, the *Gyrwe*, the *Wisse* around Wisbech and the river Wissey, the *Gifle* in the Ivel valley of Bedfordshire and so on. But already dwarfing these are the large kingdoms, like Wessex to the south, East Anglia to the east and in the East Midlands, Mercia and Lindsey. From the seventh century onwards these kingdoms engross the attention of historians, largely because they engrossed the attention of the original creators of the historical record.

That narrow focus certainly distorts the political shape of the region, especially in the sixth, seventh and early eighth centuries. When Penda King of Mercia marched against the Northumbrians in 655 he was accompanied by 30 royal lords (*duces regii*).[2] Many of them were lords and rulers of areas in the Midlands, not great and successful overlords like Penda, but princes like those who ruled the groups listed in the *Tribal Hidage*. They are reminiscent of the multitude of rulers of the settlement era, or of a prince (*princeps*) like Frithuric who founded Breedon abbey. Our sources, obsessed with the great dynasties and kingdoms, rarely mention them, but it was on their support that the greatness of warlords like Penda was built, and the politics of plunder, loot and tribute which are the story of these early centuries were fashioned by the need to attract and keep that loyalty.

The *Tribal Hidage* was a tribute list drawn up probably for Penda's son Wulfhere (657–674 A.D.). It listed the peoples subject to him in terms of hundreds or thousands of families: Lindsey and Hatfield were assessed at 7,000 hides, or family-lands, the *Gyrwe* in the Fenlands at 1,200 hides, the *Gifla* at 300 families and so on.[3] These were tax units rather than real families by the late seventh century. The *Tribal Hidage* is a political document and begins with the Mercians themselves, the land of 30,000 families, centred on the Trent valley; some doubt must remain over whether it is a true tribute list used for the actual assessment of tribute. But it is a timely reminder that the well-organized taking of dues and tribute is an old phenomenon in English history, certainly not new in the late seventh-century by which time the assessment units were already frozen. The resources which this tribute brought to an overlord like Wulfhere were a major object of the warfare of these centuries; to take control of kingdoms was literally to make them tributary. And as the *Tribal Hidage* suggests, the tribute which a successful overking might command was vast, a basis of his wealth and power. Success succeeds and

Figure 36. A suggested reconstruction of the political geography of the *Tribal Hidage* (after C.R. Hart, 'The Kingdom of Mercia', in *Mercian Studies*, ed. A. Dornier, 1977).

kingdoms like Mercia in the seventh century had grown and dominated their rivals and lesser rulers through the powers of warrior dynasties.

Mercia was largely the creation of a dynasty which emerged in the last decades of the sixth century.[4] Its original connections were with the Wash and East Anglia and Mercian royal exiles in the late seventh and early eighth centuries, men like Guthlac and Æthelbald, still returned to the eastern Fens.[5] The kingdom they created was known as the *Merce*, the Marcher or Border people; the 'border' in question is that with the Northumbrians to the north and the name belongs especially to the lower Trent valley.[6] The earliest Anglo-Saxons in the area, like their eventual kings, came from the east. The early cremation cemeteries in the Trent valley are to the south and east, especially along the southern tributaries, whilst the later focus of Mercia was in the upper valley of the Trent around Lichfield, Tamworth and Repton. North of the Trent Anglo-Saxon settlement was apparently later. There are no cremation cemeteries, which would indicate sixth-century and pagan settlement; instead we find only the later, seventh-century barrows. Bede in the early eighth century still saw the Trent as dividing the North and South Mercians.[7] Thus as the Anglo-Saxons extended their control westwards, North Mercia (Nottinghamshire and Derbyshire) may have been an area subject to prolonged raiding. It was from this very region that the Mercian rulers took the name of their kingdom, as it was from here that they derived the plunder on which it was built.

Nothing could indicate more clearly the importance of raiding and warfare in the emergence of kings and kingdoms in the sixth and seventh centuries. The loot and prestige of war and battle attracted noble followers, laid other groups under tribute. By the late seventh century the kingdoms which were emerging as dominant were not those in the heartland of earliest Anglo-Saxon settlements but on its fringes. It was probably in the north Trent valley, against Romano-British and Northumbrians, that the Mercian dynasty amassed the booty and reputation which laid the basis of their rule. Here was certainly the focus of military activity in the seventh century when the border between Mercia and Northumbria, still largely represented by the northern borders of Derbyshire and Nottinghamshire, was painfully defined in battle. In 616 the king of Northumbria fell in battle on the river Idle, his successor Edwin was killed fighting the Mercians in Hatfield Chase, possibly near Cuckney in Nottinghamshire;[8] in 655 Penda of Mercia lost a great battle on the river *Winwæd*, further north in the Aire marshes; and finally in 679 Æthelred of Mercia won the battle of the Trent against Ecgfrith of Northumbria. These battles were funnelled into that narrow stretch of land between the Trent/Humber marshes and the Pennines, along the Roman road to the Trent crossing. Geography had determined that the dynasties north and south of the Humber, the Northumbrians and Mercians, should centre their struggle here.

One object of that struggle was the plunder of battle. Before the battle of the *Winwæd* Penda had been offered 'incalculable and incredible store of royal treasures and gifts as the price of peace',[9] and plunder, including human plunder, was so normal a fruit of battle that as late as the tenth century the Blickling homilist could describe Christ's harrowing of Hell as a victory from which he returned with the spoils of battle (*here – hyhþ*), the freed souls of the just.[10] A closely related desire was the control of lands, people and tribute.

When Wulfhere of Mercia attacked Ecgfrith of Northumbria on the death of King Oswy it was 'not so much for the sake of warfare but to reduce him to tribute'.[11] The kingdom of Lindsey was the prize recovered. Assessed at 7,000 hides, it was a kingdom on a par with the South or East Saxons. In the seventh century its port of Barton-on-Humber may have been an important point of entry for Frankish trade.[12] Lindsey changed overlordship continually during the wars of Northumbria and Mercia. Sometimes the Northumbrians controlled it, as when Edwin sent his bishop Paulinus to preach and baptize there in 627,[13] at others Mercian kings, as when Wulfhere founded the monastery of Barrow-on-Humber in 658.[14] After the battle of the Trent in 679 Lindsey passed finally into Mercian lordship and its only recorded king appeared at the court of the Mercian king Offa at the end of the eighth century.[15]

Lindsey and its kings were under Mercian overlordship by c.A.D.700, but the term should not carry a heavy meaning of subordination and subjection. Bede writing only a generation or so later was still vague and hesitant on the meaning of words like 'king', 'underking', 'leader', 'prince',[16] and his problems of definition reveal a genuine difficulty of political and social classification. The rulers of Lindsey still looked like kings in many ways; the tribute they took in theory for overlords was probably largely diverted to their own use to maintain their all-important loyalty. Some 'subordinates' were more obviously the creations of overlords. The Middle Angles, in Leicestershire and Northamptonshire, may have been created by Penda as a sub-kingdom for his son Peada, to solve the problems of ruling a huge block of territory and to satisfy the political ambitions of his son.[17] But Peada followed his own ambitions and allied with the Northumbrians; the situation was still a fluid one and subordination is a strong word for such fragile bonds. Kingship was certainly not new in the seventh century, but extensive rule like that of the Mercian kings may have been. That novelty and the uncertainties it created were part of Bede's problem. But Bede and his ambiguities mark the arrival of a new element in the political landscape, and one which would have its own impact upon it: the Christian church.

Conversion to Christianity

When the Anglo-Saxons arrived in England they were pagan, judging from their burial rituals. Cremation, and later burial with grave-goods, continued into the seventh century, a witness to the continuing vigour of these pagan beliefs. Yet the British communities they encountered were Christian, and many of them continued to practise organized Christianity long after the coming of the Anglo-Saxons. The *eccles* place-names show Christian churches still in use after the Anglo-Saxon arrival, and the continuity of site and use from Roman temple to fourth-century Christian church to sixth-century cemetery at a place like St Paul's-in-the-Bail, Lincoln, may argue for Christian worship continuously practised at such places. The Britons do not appear to have attempted the large-scale conversion of the Anglo-Saxons, which awaited the activity of missionaries from Rome and Ireland. Admittedly such a statement is based on Bede, who is silent on the role of the native Britons in conversion. Bede's silence is loaded; he disapproved of the Britons and can be shown to have suppressed reference to their activities.[18] But his disapproval grew out of a disgust at the British failure to conduct a successful mission among the Anglo-Saxons, and the burnt and half-burnt bodies, the grave-goods providing for the afterlife in cemeteries as late as the early seventh century, bear him out. The political circumstances of conquest and settlement, the overlap with British rule in a framework of conflict and rivalry, could do little to encourage conversion. The only evidence of missionary activity by the Britons is in a context of political alliance.[19] British Christian communities may have maintained an existence in eastern England through the fifth and sixth centuries, so that the later conversion was that especially of the Anglo-Saxons. But their numbers were probably small, their social position would give them little impact, and their lack of organized political backing probably meant they were in decline.[20]

In its earliest stages the conversion was a political movement determined by kings. The first recorded missionary in the East Midlands was the Roman Paulinus, sent from the Northumbrian court of Edwin at a time when Lindsey was under the control of Northumbrian kings. Paulinus travelled from royal estate to estate preaching, converting Blæcca at Lincoln, baptizing many in the Trent at *Tiowulfingacæstir*, probably Littleborough where the Roman road crossed the Trent. The conversion of the rest of East Mercia begins in the mid-seventh century, and again the framework for the coming of Christianity was political alliance. Peada, son of Penda, then sub-king of the Middle Angles, married Alhflæd, daughter of King Oswy of Northumbria, and was baptized as a condition of the marriage.[21] Four priests Cedd, Adda, Betti and the Irish Diuma were sent to Peada. His conversion, like the accompanying marriage, expressed his alliance with, even dominance by Oswy; to accept overlordship was to accept the gods of the overlord. When Penda died Oswy himself took over Middle Anglia, extending his lordship south from Lindsey, whilst he gave his brother-in-law Peada rule of the South Mercians; he made Diuma the first bishop of Mercia and the Middle Angles.[22] The next two bishops, Ceollach and Trumhere, were similarly Northumbrian appointments. The church not only reflected overlordship but through control of appointments extended and underpinned it.

The political context of the first stages of conversion meant that it mirrored the directions and swings of political dominance. The Fenlands were converted not from Northumbria but from East Anglia: the early history of Peterborough shows no sign of that Ionan influence which would connect it with Northumbria, the centre of Irish Christian influence in the seventh century.[23] The area around the Wash was still as closely linked with East Anglia as with Mercia in the seventh century and remained a border territory between the two kingdoms. The church in Lindsey reflected the disputed nature of that area: Wulfhere of Mercia founded Barrow during his domination; when Ecgfrith of Northumbria took over (c. 673–5) he first gave it to his bishop Wilfrid, later creating a separate diocese in Lindsey for the Northumbrian Bishop Eadhæd.[24] Political allegiances and loyalties were expressed in religious terms. The nobleman Æthelwine who was bishop of Lindsey 680–692 had studied in Ireland,[25] almost certainly indicating Northumbrian loyalties at that stage of his career. Conversely at the end of the seventh century the monks of Bardney, a royal Mercian foundation in Lindsey, expressed their dislike of past

Northumbrian domination by refusing to accept under their roof the bones of the Northumbrian martyred king Oswald.[26]

The link between politics and religion is real and close but it must not be allowed to obscure the fact that Christianity brought new dimensions, new loyalties and wider horizons. Bishop Æthelwine studied in Ireland but by the end of the seventh century the Irish connections of the English church had been eclipsed by those of Rome. That eclipse was symbolized in East Mercia in 678 when Archbishop Theodore divided the area into the dioceses of the Middle Angles and Lindsey.[27] Theodore was a Greek, sent to Canterbury by the Pope, and anxious to impose Mediterranean patterns of diocesan organization on the English church. The Roman aspects of Christianity were to the fore by the late seventh century. The large church built at Brixworth at about this date was modelled on the Roman basilica plan and had a ring crypt like that of St Peter's in Rome (see fig. 37).[28] It was a statement in stone of *Romanitas*, not built in local Northamptonshire stone but with the re-use of much Romano-British material, especially in the tile arches.[29] At Leicester a similar large church (on the site of St Nicholas) may have been constructed in the seventh century in the centre of the Roman town, incorporating Roman material and structures.[30] The triumph of Roman Christianity brought eastern England remotely but firmly into the orbit of Mediterranean culture. A church like Brixworth was part of a European-wide revival based on East Mediterranean models.[31] Tatwine of Breedon, with his Anglo-Saxon riddles and his Latin grammar full of classical reference, typifies the resulting blend. BL MS Royal 2.A.XX, an eighth-century Mercian manuscript, contains a Mercian collection of private prayers but shows links with the liturgies of southern Italy and Greece.[32] Church dedications of the late seventh and early eighth centuries reflect Roman aspirations rather than local saints, St Paul's in Lincoln and St Andrew at Oundle.[33] The shape which Christianity was taking by the year 700 was not that of the Spartan Irish missionaries admired by Bede but rather the colourful career of Wilfrid, briefly bishop of Mercia, an amasser of churches and lands, founder of monasteries and follower of Rome, a bishop whose lifestyle rivalled and threatened that of kings.

Christianity had come to stay. In the early seventh century some kings had resisted the new religion. Penda had stuck doggedly and successfully to his old gods. By the end of that century few allowed political shifts to detach them from their powerful new god. In 657–9 the Christian, pro-Northumbrian Peada was murdered and his half-brother Wulfhere made king of Mercia by a group one of whose motives was opposition to Northumbrian control. But shaking off Northumbrian dominance no longer meant shaking off Christianity. Rather Wulfhere played a key role in the Christianization of the East Midlands, showing the liveliest appreciation of what the new religion meant for his kingship.

The beliefs, institutions, ideas and structures which Christianity brought to eastern England moulded society as much as they were assimilated by it. Monks like Bede underpinned kings with new ideals of Christian kingship and heroism, gave kings a place in the divine purpose. But by 700 the new church was wealthy and thus powerful in its own right, successfully laying claim to a share of tribute and the spoils of war as well as acquiring lands.[34] Its bishops lived in splendour and treated with kings on equal terms. Such a church could

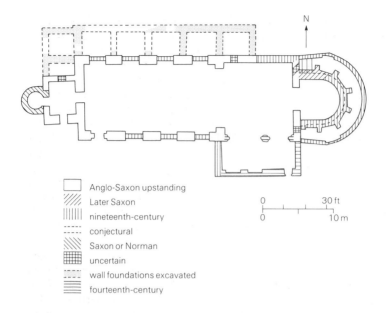

☐	Anglo-Saxon upstanding
▨	Later Saxon
▥	nineteenth-century
-----	conjectural
▧	Saxon or Norman
▦	uncertain
░░░	wall foundations excavated
≡	fourteenth-century

```
0                    30 ft
├──┬──┬──┤
0                    10 m
```

Figure 37. Plan of Brixworth church and photograph of the South Arcade (reproduced by permission of Brixworth Archaeological Research Committee).

not be neutral in its effect on a society based on warrior ideals and wealth. Its success was a measure of its appeal to the noble and royal families who generously endowed it. At the same time it whetted their desire to take over ecclesiastical positions. In the late seventh century the noble bishop Æthelwine of Lindsey had a sister who was an abbess and a brother who was abbot of Partney,[35] whilst the abbess of Repton was the daughter of a king.[36] These families were the patrons of churches, but took them over as family possessions. Those who failed to control it resented this wealth and power: the monastery which Wilfrid founded at Oundle was attacked and burnt by local nobles.[37] The church was diverting resources on a grand scale. In a political world based on the distribution and exchange of gifts, where men relied on their overlords to provide objects of status and loans of land, such a large-scale diversion of patronage was disruptive, and had to be adapted to social patterns.

The vehicle for that adaptation was monasticism. Monasticism fitted well into a kin-based society. A monastic house was a community, a *familia* – a word which can apply to any large household in the early Middle Ages. It looked like a family, could accommodate noble dowagers, hereditary abbots and abbesses, was endowed with family land. It could cater for the family's needs, especially in the world to come, providing for the burial and cult of the family dead. The daughters of Penda, Cyneburga and Cyneswith, founded Castor near Peterborough and were buried and remembered there;[38] their brother Æthelred retired to the monastery of Bardney in Lincolnshire of which he was a patron.[39] Monasticism offered all the appeal of withdrawal and asceticism, one of the great ideals of the early church; it captured the enthusiasm of the converts. And it offered that ideal in the shape of a community in the family's image, under its control and providing for its needs forever. Monasticism flourished. Partney, Peterborough, Oundle, Breedon were all monasteries. It was they rather than Theodore's dioceses which shaped the church. They became centres of conversion; it would be wrong to see them as self-absorbed centres of family cult. Peterborough may have played a part in the foundation of Brixworth, and certainly helped at Breedon with the provision of 'a priest of good repute to minister baptism and teaching to the people assigned to him'.[40] As centres of learning they trained the seventh- and eighth-century missionaries.

The royal dynasty was especially prominent as patrons of monasticism. The foundations of the children of Penda have already been mentioned, and those of his son Wulfhere should be added, Barrow in Lindsey and possibly Peterborough.[41] The royal dynasty was a family and monasticism suited its needs as it did others. Kings were the leaders of society and had to excel in all giving, including to the church. But the family here was *royal*, and the cult of its dead and its lordship of monasteries could not be divorced from their political implications. Royal saints were the spiritual counterpart of heroic warrior kings; both were increasingly necessary in a Christian, military society. Royal cult centres were a reminder of the power of the dynasty and spread its influence widely through their role in conversion. It may be no coincidence that some at least of the royal foundations were on the fringes of Mercian power, on the edges of the Fens at Peterborough, or in disputed Lindsey. It was the protean capacity of the new religion to enshrine so many ideals, to encompass such varied motives which was the secret of its rapid success. By c.A.D.700 the East Midlands was Christian, though as yet that Christianity may have been only nominal for most of its inhabitants.

Mercia in the Eighth and Ninth Centuries

Wulfhere was succeeded in 674 by his brother Æthelred, who retired to Bardney in 704, followed in rapid succession by his nephew Cenred, who retired to Rome in 709, and his son Ceolred, whose rule of alleged debauchery and adultery is said to have ended in an appropriate death in the midst of feasting in 716.[42] The instability of a rule based on giving and the impact of the new religion are both in evidence. From 716 to 796 Mercia was ruled by two men: Æthelbald from 716 until his murder at Seckington in 757, Offa from 757 to 796 – a lucky accident of two consecutive long reigns. The actions of Æthelbald and Offa, though obscure in the extreme, suggest a shift of attention west and south, to border warfare against the Welsh and to attempts to secure land in the Thames valley, especially to control London and Kent. Here were the new struggles for tribute and loot, attempts to gain trading centres where the status goods which kings distributed to their followers could be obtained and the profits of trade reaped. The Mercian heartland, however, remained that area which is now the Derbyshire/Staffordshire/Warwickshire/Leicestershire border. Ceolred was buried at Lichfield in 716,[43] Æthelbald was murdered at Seckington and buried at Repton,[44] and Offa attempted to make Lichfield a new archbishopric in the 780s. What little we know of the itinerary of the eighth- and ninth-century Mercian kings shows Tamworth as their favourite residence, with occasional meetings at Peterborough, Irthlingborough, Gumley and Glen.[45]

The death of Offa, or rather of his remote cousin Cenwulf in 821, ushered in a period of great instability on the Mercian throne, with at least two, possibly more, families disputing title (see fig. 38). For the East Midlands it was a story which ended in 874 with the abdication of King Burgred and the beginnings of Viking rule and settlement in this area.

The history of eighth- and ninth-century Mercia underlines the problems of early kingship. Between 716 and 874 it is doubtful whether more than one king was succeeded by his own son. The death of Ceolred in 716, for example, saw the throne pass to Æthelbald, a descendant of Eowa, brother and co-ruler with Ceolred's grandfather Penda in the early seventh century, and Æthelbald himself was succeeded by Offa, a remote cousin and descendant of Eowa through another line. Early kingship was a family affair in which claims to rule, as to family property, passed not simply in the eldest male line but through a wide range of male relatives. All might expect a share in the family property, especially if that property was extensive, and these expectations caused difficulty even at noble level. The fact that the kingship was both a rich prize and indivisible produced acute problems. Some kingdoms saw joint kingship, but Mercia was not often among their number, nor was the kingdom divided, though there were struggles for control of the whole kingdom. Sub-kingdoms occasionally satisfied sons, but the claims of male members of the royal family were extinguished only with great difficulty. Offa may well have

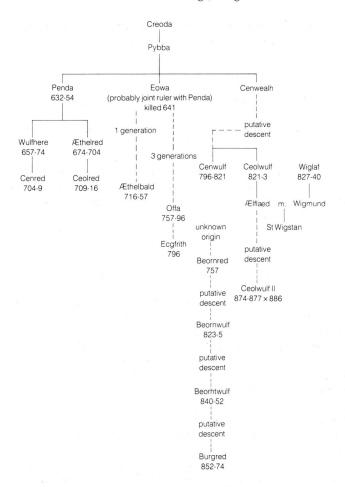

Figure 38. The succession to the Mercian throne.

destroyed them literally by murdering claimants who might rival his own son.[46]

Struggle over the kingship was the norm rather than the exception, enhanced by the development of the great kingships of the seventh century and by the question of suitability to rule. Overlordship on its seventh-century scale was novel. A greater prize sharpened the fight, and automatic rights to these new powers, even within a bloodline, may not have been well established. A strong king who succeeded in battle could survive the problems raised by wide claims to the throne; a weaker or more beleaguered one would find himself challenged. A king who failed to provide the military success and booty which were both the basis and the raison d'être of early kingship was soon in difficulty; he threatened the very good fortune of his followers which he was meant to guarantee. Challengers could always claim that a king or his potential successor was unfit to rule, a rallying cry for discontent and a platform for a bid to the throne. Rivals could recruit support amongst those dissatisfied with defeat, those galled by the limitations of opportunity, resentful of thwarted ambition, perhaps of patronage to the church. Wulfhere and his brother Æthelred, who established Christianity in Mercia, may have bequeathed a legacy of increased tension; Viking attacks in the ninth century certainly exacerbated the administrative and political tensions within the huge kingdom created by Offa and his predecessors. Whereas in earlier days such dissatisfied men might have decamped to another kingdom to seek their fortune, increasingly their landed commitment within a kingdom led them to back rival candidates to the throne.

A simple correlation could be made between these struggles for the throne and Mercia's defeat in the 870s by the Vikings. A correlation exists, though not an entirely straightforward one. Struggle over the throne is not necessarily weakening and is indeed a feature of most early kingship. But it does provide opportunities for enemies, internal and external, to exploit. Where external enemies are involved, as with the Vikings in the ninth century, the situation becomes more complex. Not only may such enemies exploit rivalries, as the Vikings apparently did that between Burgred and Ceolwulf in the 870s (see below, pp. 109–11), but defeat at the hands of the enemy increases internal criticism and dissatisfaction and fosters accusations of unfitness to rule. Challenges and rivalries are thus exacerbated, and the mounting of effective defence and warfare becomes increasingly difficult. This vicious circle took over in ninth-century Mercia and is no doubt one reason for the very rapid changes of king and dynasty which took place over these years.

Figure 39. Sculptural friezes from Breedon-on-the-Hill.

Figure 40. Sculptured figure from Castor, possibly part of a sarcophagus.

If the political and military history of the East Midlands as a part of ninth-century Mercia often seems bleak, it must be viewed beside other evidence which presents a picture of vitality up to the very eve of Viking defeat. The Continental links established at the court of Offa flowered into a great artistic development in East Mercia. The Coptic textiles and Avar treasures which Charlemagne sent to Offa inspired artists at Breedon-on-the-Hill to produce architectural sculpture of unparalleled quality and delicacy,[47] exotic birds, beasts and pelta ornament (see fig. 39), even a classical revival of sarcophagi based on antique models. Similar work was produced at Peterborough, Castor (see fig. 40), Fletton and Bakewell,[48] and all point not only to a vigorous artistic flowering, but also to the vigour of the monastic institutions which supported it and perhaps also to that economic strength which is often a prerequisite of such development. Mercian art in the ninth century influenced styles in northern England as far away as Hovingham and Masham.[49]

Such artistic influence suggests wider political and cultural contact between eastern England and Northumbria, contacts which worked both ways. At Bakewell, Eyam (fig. 41) and Bradbourne in Derbyshire, ninth-century crosses were raised in the finest Northumbrian traditions; the Peak was a border land between Mercia and Northumbria throughout the Anglo-Saxon period. Political contacts were still tense, though their traces are tantalizingly obscure. There are political dedications to Northumbrian royal saints in North Mercia,

Figure 41. The Eyam cross.

as at St Alkmund's Derby, often to Northumbrian royal exiles:[50] in A.D.800 Eardwulf of Northumbria had ordered the death of Alkmund, son of a previous king Alhred; Eardwulf's attack on Cenwulf of Mercia in 801 because he was harbouring enemies[51] makes it likely that Alkmund and men like him had taken refuge in Mercia. As late as the early 870s the Mercian court was still acting as a refuge for Northumbrian political exiles.[52] Artistic and religious development suggest a continuing vitality, and Mercia was still a great kingdom to be reckoned with.

The story of Repton and its monastery between the seventh and the ninth centuries is a microcosm of the political and religious changes in early Mercia.[53] A seventh-century cemetery is the first sign of Christianity on the site. But already by the late seventh or early eighth century a monastic community with close links with the dynasty had been established. Occupation deposits overlaying the earliest cemetery contain high-status material such as Continental vessels and window glass. Associations with the Mercian

royal line are clear. Merewalh, prince of the Mægonsætan (south Shropshire/
north Herefordshire), the third son of Penda and one of the first generation of
Mercian royal converts, was buried here c.686.[54] Abbess Ælfthryth, who
tonsured Guthlac at Repton before A.D.700, was a woman of royal blood;
Guthlac himself claimed descent from the same line as the later Mercian kings
Æthelbald and Offa; Æthelbald himself was buried at Repton in 757. The first
stages of the crypt, now under the chancel of Repton church, may be
Æthelbald's mausoleum; the two-celled mausoleum excavated to the west of
the church is another possible burial place, of Æthelbald, Merewalh, or some
other early Mercian prince.

From the seventh century Repton was thus a major dynastic centre, a
favoured royal burial place where royal women tended the cult of the royal
dead. The site was a significant choice. At this date the course of the Trent
came close to Repton, and monastery and mausolea stood on a bluff of
sandstone and gravel overlooking the river. The parallel with the siting of early
princely and royal burials like Taplow or Sutton Hoo is striking. By the late
seventh century the newly established dynasties were making clear their
association with the powerful new Christian god and emphasizing their pre-
eminence within society. That pre-eminence required demonstration because
it was novel and precarious; it could be demonstrated because the wealth
which supported it could be expressed in overt status symbols. By the seventh
century the Anglo-Saxon kings were mythologizing their own origins as the
origins of their kingdoms: a story of sea-kings who had led their followers in
the dangerous crossings of the North Sea and along the river systems of eastern
England. The fact that the Mercian dynasty and most of its followers had
probably arrived not along the Trent but from the east was no deterrent to a
symbolic placing of their burials above the most important Mercian river.

In the mid-ninth century two Mercian kings, Wiglaf and his grandson
Wigstan, joined Æthelbald in burial at Repton.[55] The royal mausoleum in the
crypt at Repton church (fig. 42) was remodelled extensively, not simply to
incorporate the bodies of the two kings but also to allow access for pilgrims. A
cult quickly developed around the relics of Wigstan, a king murdered in the
course of a struggle for the throne, and a life of the saint was written to
encourage it. This cult must surely have been fostered not only to discourage
the murder of kings, but especially in the interests of Wigstan's surviving
relatives and their continuing claims on the throne: a royal saint was always a
splendid weapon in the medieval political armoury. Ninth-century Repton, its
crypt and relics, its saint's life and its relic cult are an outgrowth of those very
political problems which it might be argued helped undermine Mercian
kingship in the ninth century, of political violence and its roots in dynastic
instability. Churchmen here wrote the life of a royal saint aimed in part at
those problems. The mausoleum itself, in its original conception and its
grandiose development, embodies the aspirations of the kings who built and
remodelled it. They took advantage of the opportunities Christianity offered
them to celebrate their power even in death. Repton had been a royal centre of
Christian worship since the late seventh century at least; throughout the
eighth and ninth it was closely involved in political changes. It was the burial
place of one of the greatest Mercian kings, and of another of his beleaguered
successors. It was no chance that the victorious Viking army encamped here in

the winter of 873–4, but a deliberate demonstration of the ineffectiveness of
the defences of the Mercian king who could not prevent such an outrage. Their
action toppled that king, Burgred, and began a process which was to end the
independent kingdom of Mercia.

Figure 42. Repton crypt probably originally built as a Mercian royal
mausoleum.

7   The Vikings and the Danelaw

In 874 Burgred of Mercia was driven out and fled to Rome where he later died. The occasion of his expulsion was the triumphant over-wintering of the great Viking army at Repton, a climax of earlier successes. Burgred had failed in the primary duty of kingship, the defence of his kingdom, and a rival claimant – Ceolwulf – now found sufficient support to oust him. Part of that support was an agreement with the Viking army itself. Ceolwulf became king with internal backing but also on the undertaking that he would provide tribute to the Vikings:

> and the same year they [the Viking army] gave the kingdom of the Mercians to be held by Ceolwulf . . . and he swore them oaths and gave hostages that it should be ready for them on whatever day they wished to have it, and he would be ready himself and all who would follow him at the enemy's service.[1]

The *Anglo-Saxon Chronicle* which made this statement is really a West Saxon Chronicle and some of the gloss which it puts on Ceolwulf's actions has to be seen in this light. Ceolwulf was doing what other ninth-century rulers, and would-be rulers, had done before him: coming to terms with the Vikings in a way which advanced his own interests but also provided the tribute which the Vikings sought, that tribute which had been the hallmark of political domination since the sixth century. Ceolwulf ruled the whole of Mercia for less than three years. In 877 the Viking army returned to Mercia and shared out some of it and gave some to Ceolwulf. Ceolwulf is an obscure figure, perhaps deliberately left so by the West Saxon chroniclers. His share of Mercia appears to have included some control over London and its mint and perhaps originally most of Mercia south of Watling Street. By c.880 that may have been reduced to the area north and west of London, the area 'not under subjection to the Danes' which King Alfred is alleged to have taken over after Ceolwulf's death.[2] In 877, if not before, the Vikings began their settlement of north-east Mercia and eastern England, of the area which was to become known as the Danelaw and the Five Boroughs, that is, Bedfordshire, Huntingdonshire, Northamptonshire, Leicestershire, Nottinghamshire, Derbyshire and Lincolnshire. This settlement and change of rule was to have effects on the area and its boundaries comparable to those of the political developments of the sixth and seventh centuries, though it is debatable how far the Vikings transformed eastern England.

The Viking attacks on western Europe had begun at the end of the eighth century. Before the 860s we hear of only one attack on eastern England, on Lindsey in 841, a reminder of the vulnerability of the eastern coast to Viking ships.[3] In southern England intermittent attacks are recorded throughout the mid-ninth century, but there was apparently little activity in Mercia. This may simply reflect the dearth of sources and the fact that our information derives from the West-Saxon-based *Anglo-Saxon Chronicle*. But it is significant that Northumbria, which did have a tradition of annal writing in the ninth century, also shows few attacks after the early part of the century. Before the 860s it looks as if other areas were bearing the brunt of the Vikings, namely western Frankia and the English Channel, and that eastern England was relatively unscathed. The continued architectural and artistic output from the monastic centres of the area (see above, pp. 105–6) goes some way to confirming this, and the military attentions of the Mercians seem still to have been directed against the Welsh,[4] though any such picture based on the silence of inadequate sources must be very tentative.

If there was such immunity, it was rudely broken in the 860s by the arrival in England in 865 of Ivar the Boneless and his brother Halfdan. Ivar's career prior to this had been acted out partly in Ireland, but in the mid-860s he and his brother brought to England a great Viking army from the Continent. York fell to it in 866/7, and in 867 it turned its attentions against Mercia; in 867 it was at Nottingham. Revolts in Northumbria diverted it in the early 870s, but at the same time it was reinforced by the arrival of a second Viking army under a Danish leader, Guthrum. It was the combined operations of Halfdan (Ivar had returned to Ireland) and Guthrum which brought about the political crisis in Mercia in 874. In the autumn of 872 they had taken up winter quarters at Torksey, within easy reach by water of Mercia and Northumbria.

In autumn 873 they made a winter camp at Repton itself. The reality behind that laconic statement has been dramatically demonstrated by the recent excavations at Repton.[5] A large, D-shaped fortress, covering some three and a half acres, was constructed for the winter camp of 873–4. The Trent itself formed part of its defences, the rest was surrounded by a bank and ditch into which the monastery church was incorporated as a strongpoint or gatehouse. Within this defended site a large dock, possibly a ship repair yard, was cut in the banks of the Trent. The winter fort may thus have been a defended ship base used to protect and repair the longships of the great army. It is ironic that the symbolic river-site, chosen by seventh-century Mercian kings near the limits of navigation on the Trent, should have consequently proved an ideal base for the Viking attacks which ended Mercia as a separate kingdom.

Not only was a fortress constructed, but the earliest of the mausolea, that to the west of the church, was re-used in the late ninth century. A high-status Viking burial, probably a cist grave with burial goods, was placed in the centre of the mausoleum; the disarticulated bones of some 250 individuals were stacked around this burial and the whole deposit covered with a low mound. Sacrificial deposits and grave goods suggest pagan rituals. Coin evidence dates the burials to the late ninth century, even closely associates them with the years 873–4, and it is tempting to interpret the burials in relation to the events of that winter. The bones appear to be largely male with signs of healed and unhealed wounds; the flesh had already gone from them before burial. Are they the mute testimony of the battle of that winter: the Mercian victims of the massacre, their bodies so long left unburied that they had been picked clean of carrion, or the dead of the Viking army killed in that same encounter? Is their association with a princely pagan Viking burial evidence that these are not Christian Mercians but pagan Vikings, or are the cist grave and other burials not contemporary? Was the high-ranking Viking a leader of the great army killed in 873–4, or is his burial slightly later showing the continuing importance of Repton, now as a Viking rather than a Mercian centre? Final interpretation of the Repton site must await complete analysis of the bones and the results of further excavation. But the fortress and perhaps the burials underline the importance of Repton and the events there in 873–4 in the last stages of the Mercian kingdom.

Repton was an important ninth-century Mercian royal site, saintly kings were buried here, and together with Tamworth and Lichfield formed a triangle which defined the political heart of Mercia. The camp at Repton was a gesture of defiance, a deliberate move to demonstrate the incapacity of Burgred's defence. It may have been designed to bring Burgred to tribute; in fact it allowed his rival Ceolwulf to profit from his discomfiture, a man emerging from the turmoil of defeat. In the early 870s the Viking leaders in England appear uncertain whether settlement or tribute through alliance and domination was their aim. After 875 direct tribute-taking through settlement was adopted. In that year part of the army under Halfdan settled in Northumbria; in 877 part of what remained settled in Mercia, probably to the north and east of the Watling Street.

The pattern of this earliest stage of Viking settlement in eastern England is obscure. In East Anglia and Northumbria Viking leaders took over kingdoms and presumably the organization of those kingdoms; in each area their rule was soon underpinned by the cooperation of local churchmen. In the East Midlands they did not take over an entire kingdom but a part of one, though in taking Lindsey they had taken over an area with a distinct political identity. The role of ecclesiastical authority in preserving continuity is unclear. The bishops of Lindsey and Leicester disappear in the 870s,[6] a disappearance confirmed by the gaps in tenth- and eleventh-century episcopal lists. By the early tenth century the bishopric of Leicester had been re-established at Dorchester-on-Thames; here there was definite change. In the case of Lindsey there can be no certainty. There were bishops there in the later tenth century[7] and there are reasons to believe that Lindsey may have followed a different road in the early tenth century from the rest of north-east Mercia. The bishops of Lindsey may have survived the Viking settlement, even played a part in the link with York (see below, p. 114). By c.910 the north-east Midlands and parts of eastern England were in the control of armies under jarls or leaders centred on fortified towns such as Leicester, Nottingham, Stamford and Bedford. But this need not have been the pattern of the settlement of the 870s and 880s but rather a deliberate military regrouping against the advances of the West Saxon king, Edward the Elder, and his sister Æthelflæd in the early tenth century. The crucial years between 877 and c.910 yield little information.

In 886 or thereabouts a line of demarcation had been drawn. The death of Ceolwulf and the take-over of London had brought Alfred of Wessex and Guthrum the Viking king of East Anglia into contact in the South Midlands. A treaty between them established a border between English and Danish Mercia, running up the river Lea to its source in Bedfordshire, from there to Bedford and up the Ouse to Watling Street.[8] The context of the treaty between these two kings meant that the definition of Danish power further north was unnecessary to either of them, but the Watling Street almost certainly continued to mark the boundary of that power almost as far north as Tamworth. The ancient road long marked the boundary of Warwickshire (English Mercia in the tenth century) and Leicestershire (Danish Mercia). By the early tenth century Tamworth was certainly a border town. The rulers of English Mercia, Æthelred and Æthelflæd, shifted to Gloucester and the Severn valley as their new political centre.[9] Derbyshire had become Danish territory and they were making efforts to extend their power by persuading English nobles to acquire land there.[10] However much we minimize the number of Danes in eastern England there can be no denying the political impact of their settlements which sliced clean through the heart of Old Mercia.

The nature of political authority north and east of Watling Street at this date remains dark. In 894 King Alfred sent an ambassador to the Viking capital of York to negotiate about large territories which the York Danes controlled to the west of Stamford, between the Welland and the thickets of Kesteven.[11] The West Saxons were probably interested because of Æthelflæd, a West Saxon princess married to the ruler of Mercia: the area in question is close to Rutland, part of the dowry of Mercian queens.[12] But the involvement of the York Vikings so far south is more surprising, and must lead to conjecture whether they revived Northumbrian claims to dominate south of the Humber. About the year 900 an otherwise unknown king, Halfdan, was ruling somewhere in the north-east Midlands and coins were being struck in his name at a mint or mints (see fig. 43),[13] and by 910 and later there were many military

Figure 43. Coin of Halfdan struck in the north-east Midlands (reproduced by permission of the British Museum).

rulers like Jarl Thurcytel at Bedford, Jarl Thurferth at Northampton and Jarl Toli at Huntingdon, who ruled the armies centred on these towns.[14] The most that can be said is that political authority was fragmented and shifting in Danish England and that there is little sign of any unified control within the Viking settlements. In the early tenth century we hear only of the activities of the armies of Northumbria and East Anglia; perhaps political authority in the north-east Midlands lay between these two.

The defeat of the Northumbrian army at Tettenhall in 910 altered this. The Vikings settled in the east and north-east Midlands faced the concerted advance of Edward King of Wessex and his sister Æthelflæd, Lady of the Mercians. They regrouped defensively around fortified towns at Stamford, Leicester, Derby, Lincoln, Nottingham, Northampton, Huntingdon and Bedford. The defences of these towns were probably not as extensive as they became later in the tenth century. At Derby, possibly Stamford and elsewhere, temporary small defences were thrown up and older Roman ones re-used.[15] By 913 the regrouped armies had themselves turned to aggression and looting, when those of Northampton and Leicester raided English Mercia and reached Hook Norton. These raids fuelled Æthelflæd's desire to recover the lost parts of Mercia. The events of the early tenth century are dynamic action and reaction on the parts of Viking and English leaders and not merely a simple picture of planned expansion or aggression.

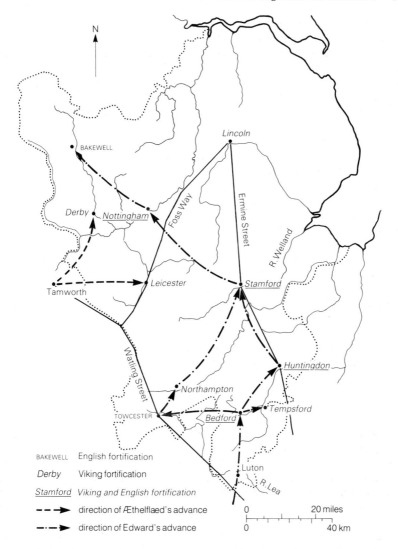

Figure 44. The campaigns against Danish Mercia, 913–21.

In 913 Æthelflæd built a fort at Tamworth; a year later Edward constructed a double borough at Buckingham on either side of the river. This produced the capitulation of Jarl Thurcytel and the great men of Bedford and of some of those who belonged to Northampton. In 915 Edward moved on to Bedford, took the borough and built a second fortification on the south side of the Ouse. These double boroughs, like the later ones at Northampton, Stamford and Nottingham, were a development of fortified bridges and were designed to block Viking access along the crucial waterways of eastern England. In 917 Edward fortified Towcester, seven miles south of Northampton. The Viking armies of the south-east Midlands now felt seriously threatened. The army of Northampton first retaliated with a raid on Aylesbury, then joined the armies of

East Anglia and Huntingdon to establish a fortification at Tempsford, from where they successfully attacked Bedford. This temporary realignment and hasty construction of a new fortification lends credence to the view that Viking borough construction and reorganization around them throughout the East Midlands was an early tenth-century response to the advances of Edward and Æthelflæd rather than the original pattern of the settlement. Late in 917 Edward built a stone wall around the fort of Towcester, the army of Huntingdon collapsed and that of Northampton as far as the Welland submitted. At the end of the tenth century old men still remembered the surrender of the army of Huntingdon and how all the local landowners had come to King Edward, recognized his lordship, and if that proved acceptable to him, received confirmation of their possessions from him.[16] We should be in no doubt that the conquest of the East Midlands by the southern king was a conquest and not a liberation, with all that that meant for the future rule of the area.

The campaign of 917 is well recorded in Edward's chronicle; those in which Æthelflæd gained control of Derby in 917 and Leicester in 918 are little known. Once again a hard campaign, now at Derby, seems to have produced a peaceful capitulation at Leicester. In 918 Edward completed the conquest by taking Stamford and Nottingham, bridging and fortifying the Trent crossing at Nottingham in 920. By now Æthelflæd was dead and Edward, ruler of Mercia and Wessex, came to Bakewell in the Peak, ordered a borough to be built there and received the allegiance of Viking and English rulers of Northumbria and of the Scottish kings.[17] 'Allegiance' may be too strong a word to describe the meeting of kings and rulers; it was the way Edward and his followers wished to present matters. But it is notable that the Peak still marked the northern boundary of Mercia in the Pennines, a boundary surviving the Viking settlement of the area.

The taking of Lincoln is not recorded, and the town is assumed to have fallen in 918–20. But Lindsey and Lincoln may have shared the fate not of the East Mercian towns and areas but of Northumbria in the early tenth century. Lindsey was apparently under the authority of the Vikings of York in the 890s and later. We have seen Alfred negotiating with the York Vikings about land in the south of Lincolnshire, and as late as the 920s the Lincoln mint was striking coins based on those of York (see fig. 45).[18] The archbishops of York would long

Figure 45. A St Martin coin of Lincoln and a York penny for comparison (reproduced by permission of the British Museum).

claim rights in Lincolnshire,[19] rights which may well go back to Northumbrian claims south of the Humber, but which may also have been reinforced by York control of Lindsey in the early tenth century. Lincoln and Lindsey need not have submitted to the kings of Wessex until the fall of Northumbria in 927.

By the 920s formal political control by the Vikings in the East Midlands was virtually over. But a brief flurry of events between 939 and 941 momentarily re-established it, and underlined some of the new boundaries which Viking rule had drawn. In 939 Olaf Guthfrithsson tried to establish his rule over the East

Midlands as far south as the Watling Street.[20] He was a member of the Viking family which ruled at Dublin and frequently at York in the early tenth century.[21] Olaf marched south with support from York and found a ready acceptance in Mercia east of Watling Street; Leicester became his base and at Derby coins were struck in his name (see fig. 46).[22] By 941 Olaf had acquired the

Figure 46. Penny of Olaf struck by the Derby moneyer Sigar (reproduced by permission of the British Museum).

Five Boroughs of Leicester, Derby, Nottingham, Stamford and Lincoln and these five towns are referred to for the first time as a group in this way. Only at Northampton did Olaf meet determined resistance from the garrison, and there was fierce fighting at Tamworth. The Watling Street now marked a line of division and was confirmed as a boundary in the peace negotiated at Leicester in 941.[23] Olaf's death immediately after reversed these successes; the southern English king Edmund recovered the Five Boroughs and 'overran Mercia as bounded by Dore, Whitwell gate and the broad stream, the river Humber',[24] that is the old boundary between Mercia and Northumbria. But Olaf's successes, and especially the bounds of his easy advance marked by the Watling Street, are a reminder that Viking rule and settlement had produced new divisions and loyalties in north-east Mercia, and in some cases perhaps reinforced old ones. His very attempt to make good a claim to authority as far south as this reinforces the possibility that all or part of this area may once have been under the York Vikings. There can be little doubt that the Vikings and their rule had affected the political development of this region during the tenth century, not only drawing it into the sphere of conquest of southern kings determined to expel the Vikings but also creating new loyalties among its land-holding elite. What remains open to debate is the wider impact of the Vikings, on settlement history and on social composition; how far the Vikings transformed eastern England. Once again the question is one of numbers.

Viking Settlement

From the eleventh century onwards many writers classified the East Midlands as part of the 'Danelaw'.[25] This was contrasted with areas of West Saxon and Mercian law, and in this definition the area took in the whole of the East Midlands, together with Yorkshire, East Anglia and the south-east Midlands as far as London. It corresponds with the area defined by Alfred's Treaty with Guthrum and with most of the areas which can be shown to have experienced *any* Viking domination in the ninth century. But the earliest of these documents, like the post-Conquest *Laws of Edward the Confessor*, follow tenth-century laws in suggesting a more restricted 'true' Danelaw, comprising Yorkshire, Nottinghamshire, Derbyshire, Leicestershire, Lincolnshire and some of Northamptonshire. In the late tenth century much of this was known

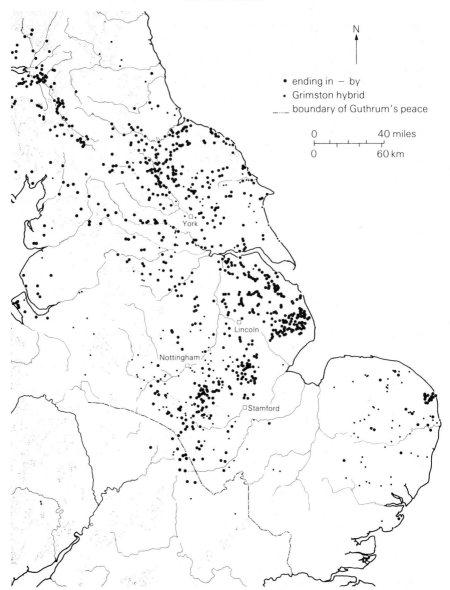

Figure 47. Scandinavian place-names of eastern England (reproduced by permission from D. Hill, *An Atlas of Anglo-Saxon England*, Basil Blackwell, 1981).

as the territory of the Five Boroughs, of Derby, Nottingham, Lincoln, Stamford and Leicester, which already had their own local court, administration and legal identity.[26] These areas looked distinctly Danish to southern kings by this date, and it was their legal differences which especially marked them out. But the perspective of tenth- and eleventh-century kings and administrators focusses on the highest social levels. Their interests were primarily in the nobility, and in the local courts where those nobles met. The legal peculiarities noted in the Danelaw, like the lawmen of Lincoln or Stamford, could have been the products of an aristocratic settlement of Vikings. They would be nonetheless significant, since such a transformation of the local nobility must have had wide repercussions, but they need say little of the ethnic composition of the region in the late tenth century,[27] or of the changes which a large-scale settlement of Vikings would have brought. The East Midlands became part of Danish England by the tenth century, but how 'Danish' was the Danelaw?

The first Viking settlers came as members of armies, like that which settled in 877. These armies were certainly large by the standards of the day but not to be numbered in tens of thousands. They attacked, looted and conquered prior to settlement and appear a classic group of new overlords established by battle. But this picture of the Viking settlement of the East Midlands is belied by the evidence of place-names and language. There are hundreds of place-names of Viking origin here, well over 300 in Lincolnshire alone.[28] As fig. 47 shows, the Watling Street is their clearly defined boundary, and in parts of Lincolnshire and Leicestershire they are the dominant form of local name. Yet as the same map demonstrates, their spread is patchy. Even without doubts over the interpretation of the names, their distribution raises questions about what they reveal of 'Danish England'.

The place-names are impressive evidence of the Viking presence. *By,* the Scandinavian word for a village or estate, passed into use throughout the region and is found in place-names like Laceby, Lincolnshire (Leifr's village/estate), Ashby, Leicestershire (Ash-tree village/estate), Kettleby, Leicestershire (Ketil's village/estate), and Derby (the village/estate of the deer). *Thorp,* meaning a secondary settlement, is widespread, often used alone as a name, as Thorpe near Newark, sometimes coupled with the name of an owner or other element, as Scunthorpe (Skuma's thorpe). A host of other names betray Scandinavian origin. From the Old Norse word *waŏ,* a ford, comes Waith in Lindsey; from *hliŏ,* a slope, Lyth in Nottinghamshire; from *lundr,* a grove, Lound in Nottinghamshire, Lindsey; from *flag,* a turf, Flagg in the High Peak. In parts of north Derbyshire the landscape is still described in Scandinavian terms: carr (marsh), holme (watermeadow, marsh), booth (hut) and so on. By the twelfth and thirteenth centuries many fields and features of villages bore Viking names, even in areas like Holland in Lincolnshire, otherwise poor in Scandinavian names.[29] By the date of Domesday changes had even occurred in the pronunciation of English names. Screveton (sheriff's *ton*) in Nottinghamshire would be Shreveton or some other, softer form in southern England; Charlton (the churls'/peasants' village/estate) is normally Carlton in the East Midlands. Add to this the wealth of Scandinavian personal names in Domesday, the Ketils, Leifrs, Fotrs, Ðorfroðrs which are preserved in place-names like Kettleby, Laceby, Foston, Thoroton, and the impression of a Viking take-over at all levels is strong for much of this region.

Although these place-names and changes occur throughout the East Midlands, there are marked concentrations and gaps. Bedfordshire has few Scandinavian names of any type, nor has Northamptonshire south of Watling Street. At the other end of the scale, the Wreake valley in Leicestershire has a concentration of Danish -*by* names at, for example, Asfordby, Dalby, Frisby, Rearsby, Gadelesby, Kettleby and, even more unusually, the river name itself has changed. Its upper reaches are still known by their original Old English name, the Eye, but the rest of the river is the Wreake, from the Scandinavian word *vreiðr*, meaning 'twisted'. Other concentrations of -*by* names are found in the North Riding of Lindsey, in parts of the South Riding, on the Lincolnshire Wolds, in south Kesteven, and east and north-east Leicestershire. In Nottinghamshire Scandinavian place-names are found less in the Trent valley than in its tributaries, especially in the less hospitable areas in the north of Sherwood forest. Derbyshire has very few -*by* names, and most of them around its border with Nottinghamshire and Leicestershire, at Blackfordby, Appleby and so on, but north Derbyshire shows many Scandinavian topographical terms in use to describe the landscape itself. Are we seeing in this geographical distribution of Viking place-names the original pattern of the Viking settlement – if not of the army of the 870s, then at least of the peasant farmers who moved in under their protection? Are the concentrations of place-names of Viking origin the indicators of the densest areas of that settlement? The written sources certainly do not refer to large-scale peasant settlement, but the written sources were usually West Saxon and remote from events, and produced close to the courts of kings whose major interests were in armies and battles. Many of these names seem to occur on poorer soils, on intractable boulder clay rather than easily-worked gravel terraces; they are close to river- and sea-borne routes of access, but out of the major river valleys, on tributaries.[30] Are these true Viking immigrants, not aristocratic overlords established in battle, but peasant colonizers?

Archaeology throws little light on this movement. The Anglo-Saxon settlers stood out in their large pagan graveyards, but the pagan Vikings have left virtually no trace. Two pagan burials at Nottingham, a cemetery with some 60 cremations at Ingleby near Repton, are a scant remnant of a mass migration.[31] The preference of the Anglo-Saxon settlers for exposed upland sites may have made their cemeteries easier to locate, but the conclusion is still unavoidable that the Vikings rapidly adopted English habits of burial, in Christian churchyards, without grave goods. A rapid conversion to Christianity occurred.[32] The evidence is not clear-cut. By the late ninth century Christianity in the East Midlands was culturally, socially and politically a coherent and organized religion in a strong position to absorb and convert pagan incomers. Even so, the large-scale influx of a politically dominant group should have withstood such pressure longer and arguably have left a clearer trace in the archaeological record.

The interpretation of the place-name and language evidence becomes doubly important. Attempts have been made to explain it away, largely using the general criticisms of such evidence outlined above.[33] Not every Viking place-name indicates a village full of Danish settlers. Ingleby (the -*by* of the English) in Derbyshire cannot be such a settlement, though it does suggest that a village owned by the English was of note in the area; the numerous Denbys (-*by* of the Danes) show Danes as owners, but similarly exceptional. Yet in both cases the settlements were termed -*by*, indicating in each case that the local inhabitants used a Scandinavian not an English word to describe a village. Field-names as a group are dubious; they are recorded late, long after the supposed Viking settlements, and indicate no more than the adoption into the East Midlands speech of a wealth of loan-words of Scandinavian origin.

The place of these Viking names within the longer-term trends of landown-ership and name-giving is the most crucial objection to a simplistic reading of them.[34] An overwhelming proportion, especially of *-by* names, indicate land ownership, individual lordship. At least 40 per cent of them are of the Barkby type, X's village.[35] They mirror exactly the pattern of contemporary place-names in Southern England, where the most common name at this date was X's *ton*, *-ton* being the contemporary English word for a village or estate. A group of Scandinavian place-names underlines the correlation. Some place-names combine a Scandinavian personal name with the Old English word for a village, *ton*: thus Foston, Derbyshire, Lincolnshire and Leicestershire (Fótr's ton); Thoroton, Nottinghamshire, and Thurvaston, Derbyshire (Ðorfroðr's ton) and Barkestone, Leicestershire (Barkr's ton). The Fostons, the *-bys*, the *-tons* all show that by the ninth and tenth centuries names indicate landown-ership, and a significant change in that ownership which had given individual nobles control of villages. The very number of *-bys* may show how rapidly this transformation was occurring in the East Midlands, and shows the tenth century as crucially important in the process. They may indicate the role of Vikings, as new lords purchasing or taking land, in that transformation. But they clearly do not simply indicate numbers and density of Viking settlement. They indicate not so much areas of migration as areas of the rapid break-up of older great estates into individual ownership,[36] a break-up which took place whilst Viking place-names were in use, and one which has thus artificially inflated the number of those names and helped determine their distribution.

This insight into the significance of Viking place-names makes sense of much of the evidence. The odd contrasts within Derbyshire of few Scan-dinavian place-names, but a wealth of descriptive topographical words of Scandinavian origin, merely indicates that the break-up of the older estates was not progressing here. We have already seen the survival into the eleventh century of the great sokes of the Pennines (see above, pp. 30–5). The distinction between this and the Wreake valley would be less a contrast of numbers of settlers than the fact that it was precisely in fertile arable lowlands that the break-up of estates went fastest. The Wreake valley never fitted easily into a picture of Danish peasants settling inhospitable lands since the soils here are not markedly less fertile or harder to work.[37] The place-names hide many more processes than simple settlement extension. But are we justified in dismissing them as evidence of a large-scale Viking influx?

Some aspects of the linguistic evidence remain intractable. A name like Foston (Fotr's ton) looks like no more than a new Viking lord or owner in an area still predominantly English. But when the population of the Wreake valley named the village owned by Ketil, Kettleby, they did not merely note a new Viking owner, they used a Viking word for village, *-by*; how had that word entered local speech? They went on to rename their river, using the Viking word for 'twisting', and rivers cannot be owned. The language of the inhabitants of the Wreake valley by the tenth century had been deeply affected by Scandinavian speech. If that change were confined to terms of landowner-ship or legal usage it could still be argued that a small aristocratic settlement was leaving its mark. But when rivers are re-named, or, as in Derbyshire, new words adopted to describe the landscape and its fields, or as throughout the region, new terms for fords and slopes, a much wider linguistic influence is argued. Some place-names show beyond any doubt that at the date when they were given at least, the local population were speaking a heavily-Scandinavianized language. At Fotherby in Lindsey, at Harby in Nottingham-shire, at Londonthorpe (*Lunderthorpe*) in Kesteven, the Scandinavian genitive in -*ar* is used to indicate possession, not the English genitive in -*es*, and there are many more examples of the Scandinavian genitive in -*s*.[38] Such changes in the grammar of speech itself cannot simply mean that a few words for village and so on have been borrowed from Old Norse into Old English; the language has been changed in its most fundamental aspect.

The view that concentrations of Viking place-names are proof of the use of Scandinavian speech in the area finds much to confirm it. A closer inspection of the geological background of place-names has broken down the simple distinction of -*bys* on poor soils, and -*tons*, or English villages, on rich, which underlay the view that Vikings came as new settlers to take up marginal land.[39] Scandinavian-named villages are found in geographical situations identical with English-named settlements. The factor which determines whether they are called Grimsby or Grimston is the general speech of the local population – was it a heavily Scandinavianized dialect, or still largely English? In Domesday, a handful of places are still called by two alternative names, one 'Viking' and one 'English'. Appleby, Leicestershire, is both *Aplebi* and *Apleberie* in Domesday; Dalbury near Derby is *Delbebi* and *Dellingeberie*, and there are some 15 other examples.[40] These apparently unstable place-names where the local population had two different names in use are all on the fringes of heavy concentrations of Viking names, in border areas between English and Scandinavian dialect. In certain parts of the Pennines, including north Der-byshire, the influence of Scandinavian language on dialect was notable within historical memory. Such influence in other parts of the East Midlands has been lost, though dialects here once contained a much larger Scandinavian element squeezed out by the advance of Standard English over the centuries.[41] The conclusion is inescapable that in the tenth century the inhabitants of parts of Lindsey, the Wreake valley, north Derbyshire and so on were speaking some hybrid dialect in which the Scandinavian element was prominent. It was sufficient not only to affect the naming of villages now passing into new ownership, but possibly to change the names of other existing settlements, and it affected the terminology which peasant farmers used to describe their landscape. A full understanding of this change, and the number of settlers required to bring it about, must await a fuller understanding of linguistic change in general. But it is hard to reconcile with a settlement consisting of no more than an aristocratic take-over.

This does not open the way to restore a picture of mass peasant migration. There is little to suggest a deep impression on settlement patterns. Viking names do not, in the overwhelming number of cases, represent new settle-ment. Fieldwalking west of the Car Dyke around Sleaford, an area of con-centrated Scandinavian place-names, has produced much evidence of pre-ninth-century settlement, that is suggesting a Scandinavian take-over rather than pioneering clearance, their absorption into an existing framework.[42] Many of the earliest Anglo-Saxon cemeteries of the fifth to seventh centuries are close to places with Viking names; in the Wreake valley, for example, there are such cemeteries near Melton Mowbray and at Sysonby, and it is beyond belief that this, some of the best agricultural land in Leicestershire, could have remained unexploited until the tenth century.[43]

The new picture of the Viking influence on the East Midlands has nothing of the compelling logic and tidiness of the old view of mass migrations of new settlers, clearing new land and naming new villages. But neatness is no sign of historical truth. A new Viking overlordship throughout the region, as far south as Bedfordshire and beyond, is clear from the narrative built up from written sources. The geography of the place-name and language evidence does not coincide with this overlordship, but suggests concentrations within the area north and east of Watling Street, already recognized as a Danelaw in the tenth century. Place-name concentrations are far from a simple chart of dense Viking settlement. They indicate in part areas of change in landownership, so that as well as over-emphasizing Viking settlement in some areas, they under-estimate it in regions like the Derbyshire Pennines where these changes were not under way. But changes in landownership would not have been recorded in Viking terms had not Viking speech had an impact on the local dialect, and place-name concentrations do indicate the prevalence of a Scandinavian element in local speech. Taken with the great variety of Scandinavian personal names in use by the eleventh century this indicates a sizeable and vigorous Danish community in parts of the East Midlands by the tenth century, though there is no way of putting a precise proportion on this Danish element.

If the linguistic and place-name evidence indicates a sizeable Viking presence, there is still nothing to suggest changes similar to those after the Anglo-Saxon settlements, whose size is again debatable. An area of Viking settlement such as the Isle of Man is a useful control. Here the transformation of society and language was almost total; a form of Scandinavian speech survived into the Middle Ages and only one pre-Viking place-name has survived.[44] The picture in the East Midlands is different. Only in small areas of Lincolnshire or the Wreake valley do Viking place-names represent 50 per cent or more of the surviving names. The majority of place-names throughout the region remained English. The existing population was too dense, the existing cultural, social and economic structures too coherent, the new settlements too small to produce major change. The Vikings left their mark on the language and accelerated processes of land division which were progressing throughout England. As farmers and settlers they were absorbed. But as new lords and landholders they did help to alter the political face of the East Midlands.

8 The Last Century of Anglo-Saxon Rule

By the mid-tenth century the East Midlands had been incorporated by conquest into the expanding kingdom of the English ruled by the kings of Wessex. The occasion and pretext for that conquest were the Viking settlements here which the West Saxon kings and their Mercian allies were determined to destroy as a threat to themselves. The last century of Anglo-Saxon rule is a story of increasing assimilation into the politics of the larger kingdom. That assimilation was complicated by the existence of local loyalties compounded of former Mercian independence, new Viking settlement and rule, and the ties of patronage and clientage which bound the local nobility together. At the same time a new religious movement was under way, whose effects were felt especially around the Fens. This was a movement of monastic reform and revival with obvious repercussions on landholding and within the church. In its close link with the southern court and in the involvement of the local nobility it played its own part in the politics of late Saxon England.

Separatism and Loyalty

The nobility of the East Midlands were involved in at least three of the political crises which bedevilled the last century of Anglo-Saxon England. All these crises centred on the succession to the throne, the burning political issue of the day which articulated all other grievances and concerns. In 975 the East Mercians of the Fenlands stood with their ealdorman Æthelwine against Ælfhere, ealdorman of the rest of Mercia (and thus of the rest of the East Midlands) in the struggle which followed the death of King Edgar.[1] Between 1013 and 1016 the region was deeply involved in the crisis at the end of Æthelred the Unready's reign, with Æthelred struggled against his own son and against a Viking invader, Swegn king of Denmark. Swegn received support in Lindsey and to the east of Watling Street;[2] his son Cnut married into a local great family in the north Midlands which had supported Edmund, son of Æthelred, against his father.[3] In 1035–7, on the death of Cnut, the East Midlands, along with the rest of Mercia, supported Cnut's son Harold Harefoot against Harthacnut, favoured by the Earl of Wessex;[4] once again that same north Midlands family, to which Harold's mother belonged, was involved. To uncover the reasons behind these actions would be to understand much of regional politics and their interaction with national ones and to achieve an analysis of local society which produced those politics.

Human motivation is the most intractable and the most fascinating of historical questions. It is a particularly difficult question not only because much of the material to answer it may be irrevocably lost, but because motives interact in a complex fashion, are rarely simple and single and because the motive of groups of people is more than an aggregate of those factors which impelled many diverse individuals. In the late Anglo-Saxon period we frequently find the 'Mercians', shorthand for the Mercian nobility, apparently acting as a group and often in opposition to the 'West Saxons'. Such was the case in 1035 for example, when the Mercians under their ealdorman Leofric supported Harold Harefoot against the West Saxons and Harthacnut. Such had been the case in 957, when the Mercians and Northumbrians chose Edgar as their king, and rejected his older brother Eadwig who was left as king merely of Wessex.[5] A first loyalty and motive might be identified as Mercian separatism, an attachment to the old independence of Mercia and a dislike of the remote rule of a West Saxon king whose presence in the area was very intermittent. Many things went into that nebulous concept of Mercian separatism and nationalist feeling may not have figured prominently. There were concrete problems of patronage and protection. The royal court was the chief fount of patronage, and if it was remote and West Saxon then so too would be most of the recipients of royal largesse. In such circumstances local centres of loyalty, in the form of great nobles and churchmen, bulked larger in men's lives and their actions swayed larger groups. The southern kings ruled Mercia through ealdormen, later known as earls. These provincial rulers helped keep alive the name, boundaries and memory of Mercia and its constituent elements for much of the tenth and eleventh centuries. When the Mercian nobles acted in 957, 975 and 1035 it was under the leadership of an ealdorman or earl of the whole of Mercia. Lindsey too retained an identity; it had an ealdorman of its own as late as 1016.[6] Feelings like those of separatism are not constants; they grow through expression, and the fraught politics of late Anglo-Saxon England provided ample opportunity for that expression. They are focussed at a religious level on the cults of local, especially political, saints, like St Wigstan at Repton.[7]

In creating an ealdormanry which covered the whole of Mercia, southern kings arguably played a part in keeping these feelings alive. They had little choice. As contemporary rulers they had to act within the constraints of contemporary allegiances and susceptibilities, and they needed to solve the problems of ruling the vast new kingdom of England. Attempts were made, not so much to break Mercian feeling, as to create new loyalties or shift existing ones. Relics were moved. When Cnut took those of St Wigstan from Repton to Evesham in the eleventh century it was not merely to provide a more fitting home.[8] Bishoprics were carefully controlled since noble bishops were potentially centres of separatist feeling. The bishopric of Leicester was moved to Dorchester-on-Thames in the course of the Viking invasions.[9] It was never moved north again before the Norman Conquest, but kept safely within the orbit of Wessex. The new monasteries of the tenth century revival, intensely pro-king in their orientation, proved new foci of loyalty. Ealdormen were potentially dangerous appointments. Their delegated powers of justice, of landholding and patronage made their courts surrogate for those of the king himself and they had wide opportunities to attract local loyalty. In the mid-tenth century two appointments were made, of Ælfhere to Mercia,[10] and of Æthelwold father of Æthelwine to East Anglia.[11] Both these families were West Saxon in origin and continued to possess lands in Wessex, facts which it was hoped would secure their allegiance to the king. Some existing noble families within the region were wooed, like that of Wulfric Spott in the north

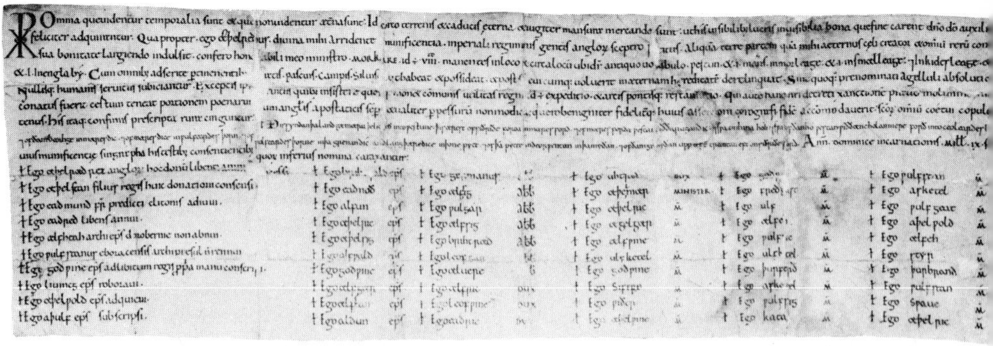

Figure 48. Royal charter of Æthelred II granting land at Weston-on-Trent, Morley Smalley, Kidsley, Crich and Ingleby to Morcar, A.D. 1009 (reproduced by permission of the William Salt Library, Stafford).

Midlands, with grants of land such as that of Weston to Morcar (fig. 48) and finally with the plums of royal office. But it is significant that when Wulfric's brother, Ælfhelm, received office, it was not in the Midlands, but at York.[12]

'Mercian separatism' is inadequate as a comprehensive explanation of the political reactions of the East Midlands nobility, though it was a factor in them all. In 975 and 1013–16 the region was divided in its allegiances, and other motives complicated action. If a sense of being Mercian was left from more than two centuries of the existence of the Mercian kingdom, was it now divided by a feeling of being Danish and Mercian in those areas north and east of the Watling Street? Judging from his tactics in 1013, the invading King Swegn of Denmark assessed the north-east Midlands as Danish and likely to support him. When he began his conquest of England in that year he came here first. After a brief attack on Kent, he sailed north into the Humber, along the Trent to Gainsborough, and there received the submission of the areas north and east of Watling Street: 'all the Northumbrians . . . all the people of Lindsey and then all the people belonging to the district of the Five Boroughs and quickly afterwards all the *here* [army] north of Watling Street'.[13]

Swegn then marched south, and did not begin his ravaging until he had crossed the Watling Street. The Anglo-Saxon, south-eastern English, chronicler who recorded these events gave prominence to this Danish connivance at Swegn's victory; Æthelred blamed them for siding with Cnut and ravaged Lindsey in 1016; the West Mercian version of the chronicle emphasized the Danish ancestry of the leaders of Lindsey who had fled before the Viking invaders of 993.[14] All these judgments were made at a time of external attack, when scapegoats for defeat were sought. Ethnic minorities are an identifiable target, and since the enemy was Danish, Viking men of Danish ancestry inevitably fell under suspicion.

That suspicion can only have deepened any sense of Danishness and separateness already existing, and in the late tenth century the distinctiveness of Danish England beyond the Watling Street was recognizable. When King Edgar issued a law code in 973 he allowed that only certain laws should apply throughout his kingdom; 'there should be in force among the Danes such good laws as they best decide on'.[15] Edgar's son Æthelred legislated specifically for the Five Boroughs in his third law code dated c.A.D.1000.[16] It is clear from this code that the Five Boroughs had a court of their own, whose meetings and actions constantly underlined separate and local loyalties. Perhaps especially in the stresses and strains of Æthelred's reign, when failure against external attack undermined all allegiance and Danes in England came under suspicion and were even persecuted,[17] such a sense of ethnic distinctiveness might be activated, even as far as support for a Danish king. Such action was easy in the absence of nationalist feeling or any deep loyalty to Wessex.

But the history of Late Anglo-Saxon England should not be rewritten along ethnic lines, with the Danish settlers as a destabilizing element or Mercian identity as a constant feature. The politics of the East Midlands were determined by the allegiances of its great families; it was their sense of belonging or not belonging to a wider English community which largely constrained the actions of the lesser nobility. Paramount for these great nobles was the idea of lordship and of loyalty to a good lord. By and large in the tenth and eleventh centuries the kings of England were seen to provide that good lordship, and it is significant that revolts and divisions in which allegedly separatist feeling showed itself normally came after a king's death (in the turmoil of succession dispute) or at times like the last years of Æthelred's reign when military defeat presented a king failing in the first duty of lordship. But even in times of peace and prosperity good lords are rarely as generous as their followers hope, and this was especially true of West Saxon kings towards their Mercian nobility. A feeling of disgruntlement was always there to be mobilized. By the late tenth century the pressure of royal demands on their nobility was also growing, and it is clear from the commitments required of him at the end of his reign that Æthelred II was seen to have contravened the canons of good lordship in many ways.[18] If such contravention legitimated grievance, Mercian separatism or Danish ancestry might mould it in the right circumstances. But such feelings of group identity were not constants. In the mid-tenth century the Mercian ealdormanry was recreated and with it regular meetings of the Mercian nobility.[19] Such an administrative change stimulated the regrowth of local feeling, if indeed it was not largely responsible for the expressions of 'Mercian separatism' which we see from the later tenth century onwards. The court of the five boroughs probably played an analogous role in 'Danish' areas. Many factors affected the stance taken by the nobles of Midland England in the tenth and eleventh centuries.

The alliances and connections among the nobility themselves were the stuff of local politics, but now all too often lost behind a host of unconnected references and unfamiliar names. But occasionally a line can be followed across the webs of family and other relationships. Archbishop Oswald was one of the most prominent ecclesiastics of the second half of the tenth century, Bishop of Worcester and Archbishop of York. His family came from the western edges of the Fenlands, and all his links remained there. His uncle was Oda, Archbishop of Canterbury, and the son of pagan Danish parents;[20] it was largely through him that Oswald was advanced. When Oswald was made Archbishop of York, he succeeded another relative, Archbishop Oskytel, also from the Fenlands,[21] who had a kinsman Thurcytel, abbot of Bedford and founder of Crowland.[22] Oswald himself was the founder of Ramsey abbey and the story of this family of spiritual nepotists is rounded off by Oswald's nephew and namesake who was a prominent monk at Ramsey in the reign of Edward the Confessor.[23] Archbishop Oda's brother and Oswald's kinsman was a landowner at Burwell as late as the 970s/980s.[24] Oswald founded Ramsey jointly with ealdorman Æthelwine, and both he and the abbey profited from Æthelwine's lands, kinsmen and clients in the Fenlands.[25] Oswald was also related to the wife of a local landholder, Athelstan son of Mann.[26] This Athelstan was a benefactor of Ely and especially Ramsey abbeys, and himself connected to Ælfhelm Polga whose extensive lands stretched from East Anglia into Bedfordshire and Huntingdonshire, who had a band of followers who rode with him and possessed his own longship.[27] To follow Oswald's family and links is incidentally to understand some of the reasons for the success of the tenth-century monasteries, which drew their patronage along these same lines of clientage and kinship. It is also to understand what the loyalty of a man like Oswald entailed, how much he brought with him, if not of automatic allegiance certainly of connection and influence.

Oswald's family were of Danish descent, but their loyalty to the southern king was unquestioned. Both Oskytel and Oswald were entrusted with the sensitive archbishopric of York, so often a centre of Northumbrian resistance.[28] They are a warning against a simple-minded view of ethnic politics in the later tenth century. The passion of the immigrant and convert could combine as here into a fervid allegiance. Moreover, it is clear how deeply this Danish family had entrenched itself in a couple of generations within the structure of local society. And at point after point in this web of connections royal activity was felt. Oda, Oscytel and Oswald were all royal appointments; Ramsey received the king's protection, like other abbeys; Æthelwine was the king's ealdorman and his family the recipients of royal patronage; Ælfhelm was a king's thegn or noble, sent his heriot (death duty) to the king and received in return protection of his will and bequests. If the endless alliances and ramifications which held local society together are apparent in Oswald's family, so too is the extent of royal involvement in that society by the late tenth century.

To understand local politics the rivalries and tensions as well as the kinship and clientage must be explored. In 975 Æthelwine and Oswald stood together; ranged against them was Ælfhere, ealdorman of the rest of Mercia. Their division was over the succession to the throne and Ælfhere attacked monasteries under the patronage of Æthelwine and Oswald.[29] The origins of the bitterness between them goes back to rivalry for power at the court of Edgar, and perhaps to the extension of Æthelwine's control in the Midlands at Ælfhere's expense.[30] Æthelwine and Oswald could be presented as closely associated with a monastic movement emanating from the southern court; here was an opportunity for separatist feelings. But they were far from being the major factor in the crisis of 975 in which the power struggles of great families played a major role.

About A.D.1004 a prominent noble, Wulfric Spott, founded the abbey of Burton-on-Trent. His family can be traced back to the 920s and 930s.[31] It had played a key role in the consolidation of southern control over the north Midlands and benefited from it. With royal blessing it acquired lands in Derbyshire and Nottinghamshire, even as far north as Lancashire. In 993 its loyalty was rewarded when Ælfhelm was appointed ealdorman at York; a few years later his brother Wulfric founded Burton. Royal grants, office and monastic patronage are the pattern of so many tenth-century families. But in 1006 Ælfhelm was murdered and his sons blinded at the king's command,[32] a fruit of the strains and suspicions of Æthelred's reign and the problems of ruling the North.[33] The events were a turning point in the family history. In 1015–16 members of this family were supporting the king's eldest son Edmund in his bid to gain the throne; the Danish invader Cnut had identified their importance and married Ælfgifu, daughter of the murdered Ælfhelm. In 1035 Ælfgifu and her relatives, now including perhaps Earl Leofric of Mercia, were still deeply involved in dynastic politics, supporting Ælfgifu's son Harold Harefoot.

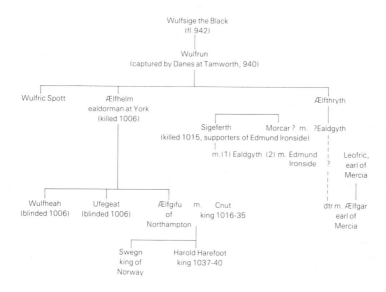

Figure 49. The family of Wulfric Spott.

This family was essential to anyone who wished to control the north Midlands in the tenth and eleventh centuries, partly as a result of deliberate royal policy, chiefly because of their extensive hereditary lands. Its alienation was fatal, as Æthelred found to his cost. But its rebellions and actions occurred within what had become an established pattern of separatist and dynastic politics. Only when Edmund appealed as a royal pretender to the sympathies of Mercians and Northumbrians did they rise, nor did they act again until the succession dispute of 1035. Acceptable, or more cynically, potentially success-ful political action had its parameters in the eleventh century. Rebellion as Mercians, or as a disgruntled family, was not legitimate, and unlikely to attract support; since men will support what they can argue is legitimate those conditions are inseparable. Only a southern prince with a claim to the throne could galvanize Mercian separatism or noble rebellion. To this extent unity was winning by the eleventh century and the East Midlands, like the rest of Mercia, becoming part of the kingdom of England.

The Monastic Revival

When the Vikings began their settlement of the East Midlands in the 870s they were pagan; 60 years later the son of Viking parents from the Fenlands was Archbishop of Canterbury and his nephew went on to be one of the leaders of the English movement for monastic reform and revival. The effects of the Vikings on the ecclesiastical history of England are often presented as disruption and destruction, but that is an exaggerated view. It was not simply their attacks which created the need for renewal and change in tenth-century monastic life; that was part of a wider European revival. When that revival occurred it found an enthusiastic response especially around the Fens where the new abbeys built up extensive estates. Their economic importance has already been charted, but, as at the conversion period, they were to play a role not only in the transformation of economic life but also in politics.

The religious life and organization of eastern England survived the earliest phases of Viking attack which were probably not aimed directly at this region. On the evidence of relic cults,[34] artistic output and occasional documentary proof, places like Breedon, Bakewell, Repton, Peterborough, Bardney and Derby had thriving, mostly monastic, communities as late as the 860s. Peterborough, for example, was still a functioning community managing its extensive lands in 852 when Abbot Ceolred made an agreement concerning Sempringham, Sleaford and other Lincolnshire properties.[35] Peterborough tradition has it that the abbey was totally destroyed in an attack by the great army in 870,[36] and there is nothing improbable in that date. The destruction of this venerable and important religious centre in 870 appears to have been complete. There is no record of the abbey for another century or so, and when bishop Æthelwold refounded it in the 960s only ruins were still standing.[37]

The fate of Peterborough appears to have been exceptional. Other religious centres were still functioning in the early tenth century and later, in spite of Viking attack. There was still a church at Breedon when Bishop Æthelwold held it in the 960s;[38] the sculptural output from the Bakewell centre (see fig. 50), and thus possibly the religious community which supported it, continued in the tenth century, and a community is recorded there in 949;[39] there was a 'little monastery' of St Mary at Huntingdon[40] and Castor near Peterborough still preserved its relics – and perhaps also its cult and religious life – in the 970s.[41] The evidence is fragmentary but evidence of any kind is fragmentary for this date. There is no reason to suppose that the destruction meted out at Peterborough was general. Peterborough was a large, wealthy and prestigious abbey; its wealth was the type of magnet which drew Vikings, its prestige may have made it a particular target for a Viking army clearly bent on demoralization and conquest. In Yorkshire the Vikings, once settled, were rapidly converted and co-existed happily with Christian institutions; there is no reason to think the situation was substantially different in eastern England. Destruction did occur, and especially the dispersal of monastic libraries like that at Breedon. Learning and its fragile products are an easy prey. But forms of organized religious life did survive the Viking settlements.

The situation did differ, however, from that of the early eighth century. There were some obvious changes. About the year 909 Edward the Elder

Figure 50. Sculptural fragments, many of the tenth and eleventh centuries, from Bakewell.

reorganized the English dioceses. At that date he controlled no part of the Danelaw and his new site for the bishopric of eastern Mercia was at Dorchester-on-Thames, where it remained until moved to Lincoln after the Norman Conquest. The bishopric of Lindsey may have continued in existence throughout the tenth century. But if the bulk of smaller monasteries survived in some form they were no longer the centres of learning or religious enthusiasm they had been in the period of conversion. That very assimilation to social structures which had been a key to their rapid success ushered in their demise. The control of lay families did not destroy them but it dulled the original ideals and often proved a threat to their property. There is little sign of a flush of new foundations or of significant new patronage by the ninth century. Viking attacks fell on a church structure resilient in its links with the local nobility but far from vigorous.

The tenth century was to change all this. A movement for monastic reform and revival was gaining momentum throughout Europe. It was aimed at the revitalization of monasticism so that it could fulfil its religious functions of prayer and of mediation with the divine, functions which mattered to benefactors and to society. The movement emphasized the celibacy of monks, as a way of perfection to enhance their acceptability as mediators with God and their efficiency as soldiers of Christ, but incidentally as a way of preventing the loss of monastic lands to the families of monks. The protection of the monastery's landed endowment was at the forefront of reformers' aims. Without guarantees that that endowment would be kept intact the functioning of the monastery as a community of prayer ceaselessly importuning God for its benefactors could not be fulfilled. Loss of property in the centuries since conversion had proved a major drain on the vigour of monasticism. The tenth-century reformers, like Bishop Æthelwold of Winchester and Archbishop Oswald, tackled the problem head on, seeking patronage for their new abbeys, lay protection but not interference, and the extension of abbey lands. These were seen as keys to the primary religious aims of the movement in the revival of an organized and continuous life of prayer and supplication. It is thanks to these bishops and the support they successfully attracted, especially from the king, but also from lay patrons, that the revival took off.

Its geographical spread reflected the sources of that patronage. It started as a court movement and always remained closely associated with the king; but southern kings had little land in the East Midlands. Here the patrons were the reformers themselves and members of the local nobility. Bishop Æthelwold secured grants from the king of decayed monastic sites often now in royal hands, like Ely, Barrow-on-Humber and Breedon.[42] He bought the island of Thorney, once the abode of hermits, for 40 mancuses of gold,[43] and originally had plans to refound Oundle.[44] Oswald persuaded ealdorman Æthelwine to commit to him his own small foundation of Ramsey[45] and Oswald's kinsman Abbot Thurcytel founded Crowland with his own patrimony.[46] These monk-bishops, with the knowledge of royal backing, were the driving force behind the first stage of the revival, and purchased land, persuaded patrons and occasionally manipulated the local courts to build up the original endowments. The monasteries they created produced a second and third generation of monastic bishops who continued the flow of patronage and protection. Eadnoth, one of the early monks at Ramsey, later became bishop of Dorchester-on-Thames and not only endowed Ramsey but created two new houses at St Ives and Chatteris, the latter one of the few nunneries of the revival.[47] In the mid-eleventh century two Peterborough monks, Æthelric and Æthelwine, became successive bishops of Durham, and the Durham monks later complained of their despoliation of their northern diocese to Peterborough's advantage.[48]

The revival could not have succeeded without lay support. Ealdorman Æthelwine of East Anglia provided the initial endowment of Ramsey.[49] Æthelwold's foundations of Peterborough and Crowland benefited from the gifts of two Lincolnshire thegns, Fræna and Frithegist, who gave lands in Lincolnshire and Northamptonshire.[50] The major foundations outside the Fenland concentration were all dependent on the initiative and support of lay nobles. Burton-on-Trent was the foundation of Wulfric Spott, using his

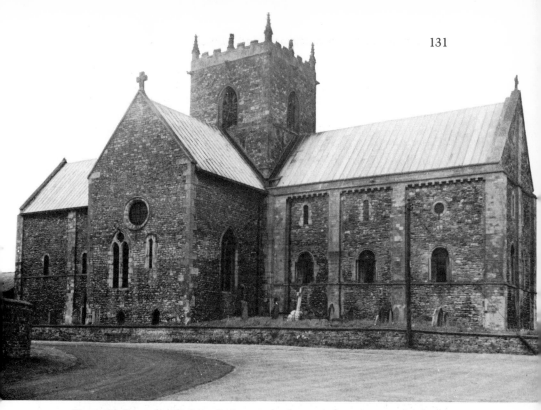

Figure 51. Stow church, Lincolnshire. Only the crossing and transepts contain original late Saxon work (reproduced by permission from H.M. and J. Taylor, *Anglo-Saxon Architecture*, vol. II, Cambridge University Press, 1965).

extensive lands,[51] and at a slightly later date in the eleventh century the family of the earls of Mercia became major patrons, founding Coventry and Stow (fig. 51)[52] and acting as patrons of Peterborough and Crowland.[53] This lay involvement is at first sight odd, since the apparent intention of the reformers was to loosen lay control in order to safeguard monastic land and the religious life. For the reformers noble patronage was essential and their plans could not have matured without it. But what motivated Æthelwine, or Wulfric, or the host of lesser lay patrons who followed in their footsteps?

The religious motive is primary. Æthelwine granted land at Stokely 'for the soul of his wife';[54] his wife gave Ramsey Sawtry together with her body, for her soul and as the price of her burial;[55] Wulfric founded Burton 'to the glory of God and the honour of my lord and for my soul'. Many of the grants which came to these monasteries were to secure burial and the prayers of the monks after death. To ask why tenth-century men and women patronized the monastic revival is an anachronistic question. In a Christian society where men cared for the future of their eternal souls and believed that the prayers of monks could assist in that salvation, patronage of the church was normal. What determines the level of lay patronage is then less the ebb and flow of lay piety than that of movements of religious reform and renewal. In the Anglo-Saxon period there were two such movements, at the conversion and in the tenth century, both of which attracted massive lay patronage.

But the incidence of lay piety is not the sole explanation of the geography of the reform, which did not sweep through the entire local nobility. The activities of Oswald and Æthelwold, and their local links, are one factor. Connection with these and with the royal court where the movement was centred are another. Wulfric and Æthelwine were both great men at the southern court; there they would have learnt of the new movement, conceived an enthusiasm for it, come into contact with the infectious energy of the reformers. There too they may have formed a desire to emulate the king in his foundations, perhaps to demonstrate their loyalty by furthering the movement he had sponsored. What the king was to the court and the great nobility a man like Æthelwine was in the Fenlands. If Æthelwine desired to adopt the lifestyle of the king and draw closer to him through sponsoring the same religious movement, similar motives moved his own local followers and clients. Finally it was the great nobles of the tenth century, men like Wulfric and Æthelwine, who had profited from the political opportunities offered by the enlarged kingdom of England, who had the wealth to endow the new monasteries. As a result the reform put down strong roots, but in particular areas. Through most of the East Midlands, where lay patronage was not forthcoming, the links with the southern court were more tenuous, its impact was marginal.

The strength of these motives can be gauged by the success of the reform. Nonetheless the effect of that reform was bound to be drastic in a society based on landholding. Many of the family functions of the monasteries remained, and proved another strand in the web of motives for patronage. The monks prayed for the souls of parents and spouses. The family of Eadnoth of Ramsey still endowed monasteries and a nunnery where their children could be provided for as monks and nuns.[56] But the more novel idea that land granted to the monastery was permanently diverted from hereditary family control proved more difficult to stomach. When the movement's royal protector, King Edgar, died in 975 and left a period of struggle and uncertainty over the throne, many acted to recover lands lavished on the abbeys by their relatives or acquired by zealous reformers in dubious ways. Peterborough, Oundle and Kettering were all seized by a certain Leofsige and remained uncultivated for two years;[57] Burwell was successfully reclaimed from Ramsey 'on the sole grounds of hereditary succession'.[58] Æthelwine himself repossessed land at Gedney and Tydd St Mary which Thorney had acquired.[59] The monasteries were engrossers of land in a society where livelihood and power were based on land; the desire to break hereditary control cut across strong feelings of family rights, which were, paradoxically, also motives for religious endowment. Æthelwine was a great friend of monks, but especially at what he saw as his family foundation of Ramsey; the interests of his kin led him to attack the property of other houses.

Attacks on the monasteries in the late tenth and early eleventh centuries do not so much indicate hostility to monasticism or the church, as they emphasize how little the reform had changed lay attitudes to the church, how deeply new views of church property cut into those attitudes. In the end the pattern reasserted itself wherever possible. Relatives of original founders like Oswald were still important in the mid-eleventh-century houses. Later patrons, from the king downwards, exhibited more tension and complexity in their relations with the abbeys. Edward the Confessor laid hands on Peterborough lands at Fiskerton, Fletton and Burghley, and had to be paid for their recovery.[60] The patronage of the house of Leofric of Mercia looks less disinterested than that of Æthelwine or Wulfric; Leofric's nephew and namesake became the pluralist abbot of all the abbeys in the family's control, Burton, Coventry, Crowland, Thorney and Peterborough.[61] A fine line separated the patronage and protection which Oswald sought from Æthelwine from the total control which Leofric established. That distinction may have been maintained in the enthusiastic commitment of the first generation, though even here family concerns remained; it had been lost by the mid-eleventh century. The parallel with the period of conversion is apparent.

But differences, some crucial to the fate of local monasticism, were there. The eventual pattern of the reform was the dominance of a few large houses, but the original intention was the revival of numerous monasteries, more like the situation of the eighth and ninth centuries. Æthelwold re-founded Ely, Peterborough and Thorney, but he may originally have hoped to revive Breedon, Oundle and Barrow, all in his hands. Other small houses, like St Ives and Chatteris, failed to grow. The accidents of initial endowment were crucial, as were successes in attracting further patronage. Survival and growth depended on the dynamism of a succession of abbots. The massive landed endowments of the conversion era were not forthcoming, and what the abbeys received were often scattered lands requiring constant defence and careful management. The new forms of land tenure and the land market, which the monasteries played their part in creating, produced a world of litigation. Added onto this was the growing burden of taxation, from the tributes to pay the Danes onwards. The monasteries of the tenth-century revival were born into a different world from that of the late seventh century and it took the sharp eye of a monastic imperialist to navigate it successfully.

Such were the abbots of Peterborough or Ramsey who founded the fortunes of these abbeys. From the beginning, a capacity to drive a hard bargain was a necessary adjunct of sanctity. Bishop Æthelwold got Water Newton cheap for Thorney, but when his royal protector died he had to raise the price from £20 to £33 and throw in land at Irchester, Titchmarsh and Water Newton into the bargain.[62] Bishop Ætheric acquired *Athelintone* for Ramsey by getting its Danish owner drunk and then tricking him into selling the land, on the mistaken assumption that the bishop had no money with him.[63] The other and more acceptable face of the coin was the careful, day-to-day estate management practised by the abbeys. Their endowments were substantial, but not so that they did not require constant attention, a driving force, as we have seen, in the economic growth of the region (see above, pp. 35–7).

Politics was one of the mixed motives in the foundation of the abbeys, and the greatest of them went on to play their own role in political life. Ramsey and Peterborough provided a succession of archbishops of York and bishops of Durham in the late tenth and eleventh centuries. Peterborough especially was the monastic home of archbishops Ealdulf and Ælfric of York and bishops Æthelric and Æthelwine of Durham.[64] That fact is testimony to the importance of Peterborough as a centre of religious training, but also a political move to draw the North more firmly into southern control. Ealdulf's appointment in 992/3 matched the appointment of Wulfric Spott's brother Ælfhelm to the ealdormanry. In both cases the loyalties of these men were judged to lie in the

Midlands and to the king. For churchmen like Ealdulf these attachments were focussed on the monasteries where they had been monks, monasteries often with strong royal sympathies. The new loyalties they created made the abbeys solvents of those older ties which formed separatist feeling.

In 1052 Leofric, nephew of the Earl of Mercia, became abbot of Peterborough. The saintly and simple Abbot Arnwig stood down to allow his appointment, which was in part political; the king was wooing his family.[65] Peterborough remembered him as a great abbot. They had lost lands in raising money for tribute[66] and in other ways, and it was Leofric who so restored the abbey's fortunes that the town became known as the 'Golden Borough'. He recovered property, made substantial personal gifts and undertook a new building programme. Leofric is the archetype both of a successful eleventh-century abbot and also of the renewed noble control of monasticism. His family connections hindered as well as helped Peterborough. Their rivalries with the queen's family incurred her enmity and led to her actions in depriving the abbey of gifts.[67] His final action was to embroil Peterborough in the events of the Norman Conquest. He died after an illness contracted at the Battle of Hastings. His successor failed to realize that William would be the eventual victor, and Peterborough lost much land in the aftermath of his miscalculation. All this combined with the natural geography of the area to make the Fens one of the last centres of resistance to the Conqueror, with the ex-Peterborough monk Æthelwine of Durham a companion to Hereward the Wake.

9 Boundaries and Divisions

The major political boundaries of the East Midlands were established during the seventh-century process of kingdom growth and again during the period of Viking invasion and southern conquest. Some of them follow basic geographical divisions but most have been altered or defined by political struggles and a few are lines on a map drawn almost entirely by the hand of politics. All of them result from competition for the control of land, more precisely of the tribute of land. As early as the *Tribal Hidage*, areas are assessed in units of 12, following the Mercian duodecimal monetary system (240 pennies=£1).[1] From the seventh century and before administration and especially taxation defined boundaries.

The northern boundary of Mercia was established during seventh-century wars with Northumbria but defined by geography. It followed the Humber and its tributary the Idle into the foothills of the Pennines; the boundary of Nottinghamshire, Lincolnshire and Yorkshire still follows the old course of the rivers Idle and Don.[2] The Humber and the marshlands which extended around it divided the peoples on its northern and southern banks. In the early eighth century a Northumbrian writer like Bede spoke of his area as Northumbrian, and of that to the south as *Suðanhymbra*, a term which went out of use in the eighth century to be replaced by *Mierce*, Mercians, or 'people of the border', again the Humber.[3] The successes of the seventh-century Northumbrians in establishing control south of the Humber rule out total geographical determinism, but the short-lived and ultimately unsuccessful nature of that control illustrate the problems of communication which the Humber posed. The battles of the seventh century were fought at Hatfield, on the Idle and on the Trent on that narrow strip of land which gave easy access north and south.

To the west the northern boundary of Mercia ran from the Humber to Whitwell Gate and Dore, that is towards the modern boundary of Derbyshire and Yorkshire[4] and on through the Peak. Bakewell was close to this northern boundary.[5] Roman and earlier earthworks here suggest that the Mercian boundary in this intractable country followed earlier frontiers between the British tribes of the Coritani and Brigantes.[6] The borders of the kingdom of Lindsey were similarly drawn by geography. The sea, the Humber estuary, the marshes and wastes of Trent and Witham made it a literal island – *Lindesege*, or Lindes island.[7] The natural barrier of the Fens, originally stretching up into south Lincolnshire, helped set the bounds of Lindsey as it separated Mercia and the East Angles (see fig. 52).

Geography helped set broad limits, but these were all political boundaries, fought over and defended as such. Edward the Elder fortified Bakewell in the early tenth century, seventh-century kings died in battle around the Trent and Humber, and if we hear little of such struggle around the Fens it may be more because of the accidental lack of sources than a sign of a peaceful frontier. The boundary of the Danelaw and the Five Boroughs, drawn in the late ninth and tenth centuries, is more obviously political.

A boundary between Danish and English was first explicitly defined in 886 in

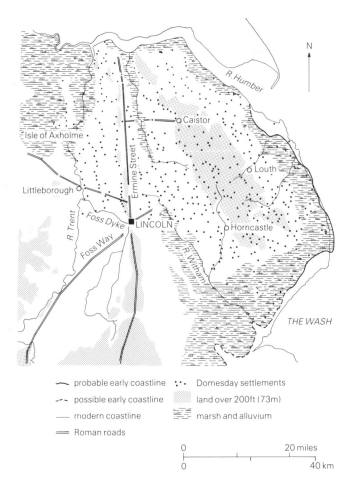

Figure 52. The kingdom of Lindsey (after D. Hill, *An Atlas of Anglo-Saxon England*, 1977).

a treaty between King Alfred of Wessex and the Viking king Guthrum;[8] it ran along the rivers Lea and Ouse north from London to Bedford and from there along Watling Street for an unspecified distance. Alfred's treaty has long been seen as defining the Danelaw and Danish England, as setting a significant boundary to Viking settlement. But the line it established was transient. It had almost certainly collapsed by the 890s, when the Danes built a fortress on the river Lea, and by the early tenth century Hertford, Bedford and Buckingham were all back in Danish control. As late as 912–14 Danish rule stretched beyond this theoretical boundary.

It was Alfred's children, Edward the Elder and Æthelflæd Lady of the Mercians, and his grandchildren, Athelstan and Edmund, who drew the significant boundaries of Danish England. At some date between 886 and 913 Æthelflæd and her husband Æthelred lord of the Mercians established Watling

Street as the boundary of English and Danish Mercia, in the course of unchronicled local struggles and negotiation. That boundary cuts across ninth-century Mercia along the useful dividing line of the Roman road: as long as such roads provided the easiest movement for armies neither side would have wished to cede it to the other. But the line was not arbitrary; it was drawn with a sensitivity to Mercian feeling (see fig. 53). It follows Watling Street between what is now Leicestershire (Danish) and Warwickshire (English), but at Mancetter the Danelaw boundary, as marked by the southern bounds of Leicestershire and Derbyshire, turns north. Watling Street runs on to the south of Tamworth and Lichfield, the political and ecclesiastical heart of the old Mercian kingdom. The rulers of English Mercia were clearly determined to retain control of this Mercian heartland; Tamworth and Lichfield remain in the tip of English Mercia, in Staffordshire. They were now frontier towns, a vulnerable position which probably explains why Stafford and not the older and more important centre of Tamworth became the new shire town.

The struggles of the first half of the tenth century effectively defined the Danelaw frontier and it was at this date that the boroughs on which both sides based their tactics were fortified. These boroughs, around which the Midland shires were formed, were clearly strategic, sited to command important routes along which armies might march, as Northampton does on Watling Street or Lincoln on Ermine Street; to control the river crossings where such roads were

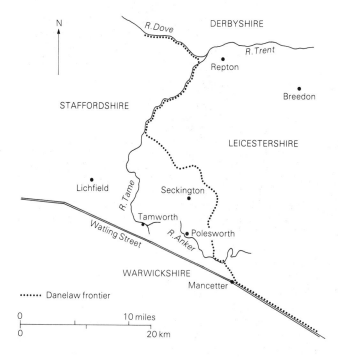

Figure 53. Shire boundaries and the Danelaw frontier around Tamworth.

most vulnerable, as at Nottingham and Stamford. At Derby, Nottingham, Stamford and Lincoln the towns stand at the south of the area defended, sited against attack from a southerly direction.[9] The frontier fought over was not Alfred's, which would take the Danelaw as far south as Bedford; that 'greater Danelaw' is as much a product of twelfth-century legal antiquarianism as of ninth- and tenth-century political realities. The line of the Danelaw was along Watling Street and the Welland, a definition which makes far better sense in terms of what we have seen of other evidence for Viking influence.

Such lines and boundaries take on meaning and force in their use and recognition and in the struggles over their definition. As long as they marked the edges of hostility they might be fortified. A series of small earthworks in Bedfordshire between the river Lea and Bedford, especially along the rivers Ouse and Ivel, may be the forts of the late ninth-century Danelaw frontier.[10] Battles fought on or near such frontiers show them to be a perceived reality and served to confirm that perception; again in the mid-tenth century it is Watling Street and the Welland that appear significant. In 937 Athelstan king of the English won a great victory at *Brunanburh* against a coalition led by Vikings associated with York and Dublin. *Brunanburh* is variously located in the Don valley, a northern tributary of the Humber,[11] or close to Watling Street in the forest of Bromswold in Northamptonshire;[12] in either case close to a line of old hostilities. A resurgence of Viking activity made the Danelaw boundary once more a battle ground between 939 and the early 940s. Olaf marched south from York and whereas he found succour to the north of Watling Street and the Welland, he attacked the English frontier towns of Northampton and Tamworth to the south. When he and King Edmund made peace they confirmed Watling Street as a boundary.[13]

Boundaries were neutral ground where kings could meet, neither far from his own territory, neither expressing subordination to the other or running the dangers inherent in a long journey into the other's kingdom. In 702 the kings of Mercia and Northumbria met to settle a dispute at Austerfield, just north of the river Idle.[14] In 829 Egbert came to Dore, and about 920 Edward the Elder came to Bakewell, in each case to meet with the rulers of northern Britain.[15] In 926 King Athelstan met Sihtric, king of the Northumbrians, at Tamworth and gave him his sister in marriage.[16] These boundaries had a reality beyond the actions of kings, sometimes separating different political attitudes and reactions. In the early 940s Leicester north of the Danelaw boundary appears to have offered no resistance to the Viking adventurer Olaf, whilst Tamworth, just south of that boundary, put up fierce opposition.[17] In 1065 the men of Lincolnshire, Nottinghamshire and Derbyshire joined a Northern rebellion against Tostig, an earl appointed from the south. They marched south, crossed the Northamptonshire border and then 'occupied' Northampton, a shire in Tostig's control; from here they sent their messages to the king.[18] Even if we allow for strong national or ethnic feelings, which seem unlikely, what determines the frontiers of such loyalties?

Lines defined through hostilities became the peacetime boundaries of administration, ceasing to be simply lines on a map fought over by kings. They determined where and to whom you paid tribute, in which court your cases were heard and thus what links of patronage and alliance you sought. Administrative boundaries played an important role in defining communities, turning groups on either side of an imaginary line in different directions, towards different lords and centres. By the late tenth century the Five Boroughs existed as an administrative unit with a court of their own.[19] They are a grouping of the five towns of Nottingham, Leicester, Stamford, Lincoln and Derby, together with their attached lands, and as an administrative unit it is unlikely that their origin is to be traced to the original period of Viking settlement. In the early tenth century, for example, Lincoln's links were north, towards York rather than south to the north-east Midlands. The Five Boroughs may represent a spontaneous alliance in the mid-tenth century against the threat of the York Vikings,[20] since they offered little resistance to Olaf this seems unlikely. More probably they are a defensive grouping organized by the southern kings to hold the area against threat from the north, either drawn together by Edmund after his recapture of the area in the early 940s, or even by Athelstan, whose policies in Mercia are obscure but important. Whatever its origin, the setting up of a local court to bind these towns together created new loyalties. In the working of that court friendships and alliances would be formed which made local thegns act, even rebel, together.[21] It was, as we have seen, such developments which infused political and administrative units with separatist feeling.

Major political and geographical boundaries became those of the shires, whose areas must also reflect estate patterns. Administrative development in the late Saxon period underlined the importance of the shire and its court and ensured that it became the significant local community for the nobility. The shires of the East Midlands were drawn up during the tenth and eleventh centuries by the kings of southern England. They were organized around the boroughs from which they take their names, Leicestershire, Derbyshire, Nottinghamshire and so on, and their origins lie in a military organization for the upkeep of urban defences. A shire was that area which *hyraď to* ('belonged to', 'was attached to') a central borough; as early as 917 and 918 towns like Stamford and Northampton had such areas associated with them,[22] the nucleus perhaps of a shire.

The boundaries of these shires utilized important physical features, like the Trent between Nottinghamshire and Lincolnshire, or old boundaries recently given new force, like Watling Street and the Danelaw boundary in the south of Leicestershire and Derbyshire. But these features may themselves represent in some cases older estate bounds, and shire boundaries must reflect in some part those of the estates and lands which maintained the central fortifications. Thus the suggestion that the Midland shires of the tenth century may in some cases follow Roman boundaries is not implausible. On the boundaries of Leicestershire lie Mancetter, High Cross, Caves Inn, Medbourne and Willoughby-on-the-Wolds, all strategic sites, probably old markets, positioned in Roman times where Roman roads crossed old estate boundaries (see fig. 54).[23] Since some continuity of estate boundaries through from Roman times now appears likely and with tenth-century shires made up of groups of estates such coincidence of bounds is probable. But it should not be exaggerated. Such coincidence will be neatest where, as in south Leicestershire, a major Roman road – Watling Street – would have proved a permanent feature of the agricultural and estate landscape, or in Rutland, where a very old estate pattern had been fossilized. Estate patterns had changed since Roman times, and other

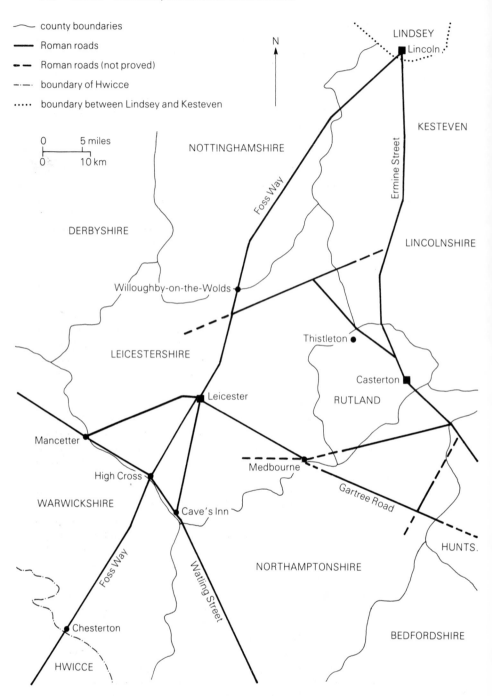

Figure 54. The relationship of select Roman settlements to the Roman road system and the later administrative boundaries (after C. Phythian-Adams, 'Rutland reconsidered', in *Mercian Studies*, ed. A. Dornier, 1977).

political factors affected shire boundaries. But such coincidences are a timely reminder that frontiers are defined not merely by the hostile actions of kings but by the detailed disposition of local landownership.

The shires of the East Midlands were not the creation of a single administrative decision, though all owe their existence to the increasing importance of the shire in the administration of tenth- and early eleventh-century England. Northamptonshire, Bedfordshire, Huntingdonshire certainly, and Derbyshire, Leicestershire and Nottinghamshire probably evolved during the tenth century, the three former in its first half.[24] But Lincolnshire, and the Five Boroughs in general, pose insoluble difficulties of dating. Lincolnshire, like Nottinghamshire, was first mentioned in 1016,[25] but Lindsey was also still an important unit. Lindsey was not only a nostalgic term of local description at this date, something which it remained until the twelfth century,[26] but an administrative area with its own ealdorman, Godwine.[27] By the time of Domesday, Lincolnshire and Lindsey were used interchangeably to describe the whole of Lincolnshire in the survey. Lincolnshire is also anomalous in being, together with Yorkshire to the north, one of the largest pre-Conquest English shires. Within it were two important towns, Lincoln and Stamford, both part of the Five Boroughs. Stamford is the only one of the Five Boroughs which did not become a shire centre, and together with Winchcombe in the West Midlands is the only non-shire town to receive a full survey in Domesday.[28] If Lincolnshire stands out for its great size, Rutland on its southern borders was out of line in the eleventh century as the smallest of the English shires. The administrative development of this area differed from that of the rest of England, though the situation there was probably less straightforward than appears, but the inadequacy of the evidence is a barrier to the solution of the problem.

Lincolnshire probably did not finally emerge in its modern boundaries before the eleventh century, some have suggested not before the end of that century.[29] Lindsey was used to describe the northern part of Lincolnshire in the eleventh century, and sometimes to describe the whole. The name of the old kingdom persisted as a geographical description and was frequently used when referring to the actions of local men, in rebellion and so on.[30] But it was given new force by the creation of an ealdormanry here, perhaps c.A.D.1000 as part of the defence of vulnerable areas like the Humber from Viking attack.[31] Stamford almost certainly once had its own shire, as did Winchcombe in the West Midlands,[32] which was later added to Lindsey to form the enlarged Lincolnshire. The original bounds of 'Stamfordshire' would have been marked to the south by the Welland, which was the limit of the territory of the Northampton army in the early tenth century.[33] The reasons for this anomalous development can only be conjectured. The north-east Midlands in the late tenth century had a court in the Five Boroughs which fulfilled many of the functions of shire courts elsewhere,[34] perhaps leaving the local shires less clear-cut, more fluid. The clear geographical boundaries of Lindsey, and its long history as a separate under-kingdom and bishopric, made it an obvious unit to retain.

The failure of 'Stamfordshire' is crucial to the development of Lincolnshire. As with 'Winchcombeshire' in the West Midlands, Stamford is in an area dominated in the tenth century by ecclesiastical estates and interests. The abbeys may have played a part in redefining local boundaries in the late tenth century, by which date their estates were a significant part of the local landscape. 'Stamfordshire' would also have contained part of what became Rutland. Rutland is a clear entity in Domesday Book, but it is not surveyed separately but included under Lincolnshire and Northamptonshire.[35] What gave Rutland its separate existence and held it apart from both these shires was the fact that it formed the dower land of Mercian queens.[36] Stamford once had land allocated to it for the upkeep of its borough defences; all early tenth-century military towns were so organized. But that area so grouped around Stamford failed to develop into a shire by the eleventh century. The need was less pressing, since the court of the Five Boroughs fulfilled many of the administrative and legal functions which were creating the tenth-century shires. Powerful vested interests of the queen, and later of the abbeys of the Fenlands, complicated the local situation. Rutland thus remained a separate small shire, and Kesteven and Holland, once part of 'Stamfordshire', were added to Lindsey to form Lincolnshire. The development of Lincolnshire illustrates the interaction of tenth-century administration, of older units and kingdoms and their boundaries, of ecclesiastical changes and of estate patterns in the formation of the shires of England.

The shire was the court for the local nobility; its activity helped give them a sense of community. Within the shire villages were grouped together into hundreds or wapentakes, which had their own courts where land transactions took place, cases of theft or violence were heard, some local policing functions organized. The hierarchy was more one of suitors than of function; it was the people who attended them rather than the cases they could hear which distinguished them. These groups of villages are called wapentakes in the Danelaw, that is in Leicestershire, Nottinghamshire, Derbyshire and Lincolnshire, and hundreds in the rest of the region; the Welland and the Watling Street are again the crucial division. Wapentakes were in existence by the late tenth century,[37] and may have been the creation of Viking rulers, possibly the York Vikings who alone controlled much of this area in the early tenth century. But the existence of hundreds not wapentakes in the East Riding of Yorkshire makes this unlikely, and suggests rather that they are the fruit of a reorganization imposed by the southern English kings. The wapentakes differ only in name from the hundreds of English Mercia, a difference in nomenclature arising from the different social structure of the north-east Midlands (see below, pp. 156–61).

If the boundaries of shires are often old, those of the hundreds and wapentakes appear to cut across old divisions, at least as they are represented by the sokes. In Lincolnshire some wapentakes divide the sokes.[38] There is little correspondence between ancient royal centres and wapentakes or hundreds.[39] The sokes had centred on such royal manors, where dues or tribute were paid.[40] Only a handful of wapentakes and hundreds are grouped around an ancient manor like the earliest estates: Newark (Nottinghamshire), Flitt and Luton (Bedfordshire), Wirksworth and Scardale (Derbyshire) are among the few examples. Only in Northamptonshire is the pattern preserved. The new units do not ignore older features. Their meeting places occupy established sites or reflect, as might be expected, lines of communication. Sparkenhoe wapentake in Leicestershire had its meeting place at Shericles farm (shire oak farm) on the Roman road from Leicester to Mancetter,[41] Wixamtree hundred in Bedfordshire met at Deadman's Oak, Willington, where many tracks and pathways met.[42] But the boundaries of these units show little correspondence with older patterns.

Many of their names are Scandinavian. Toseland hundred in Huntingdonshire met at Toli's grove,[43] Framland wapentake in Leicestershire at Fræna's grove overlooking the Wreake valley.[44] Gartree, a wapentake name in Leicestershire and Lincolnshire, may graphically preserve the picture of these courts. It is the 'spear-tree', from the Old Norse *geirr*, spear, the tree or post where the spears were brandished or hung at the wapentake meeting.[45] The Scandinavian names mirror the overall pattern of Scandinavian linguistic influence. In Lincolnshire half the wapentake names are Scandinavian, in Leicestershire far fewer.[46] Their names are no sign of their origin; it was English kings not Viking lords who redrew their bounds.

The redrawing of the boundaries of wapentakes and hundreds was contemporary with fundamental changes in the divisions and ownership of the land already discussed. This conjunction goes some way to explaining the novelty of their bounds. They are the neat grouping of villages around a central meeting place. Their boundaries, like those of the units of tenth-century estates, are those of individual settlements, of the villages and their fields. By the eleventh century the village appears as the most important unit in the sources. On page after page Domesday lists primarily villages, hamlets, individual settlements. But Domesday is a sharp reminder that the village has come into focus in the written sources because it has shifted in emphasis for the landlord. The changes in land ownership had made individual settlements, not large sokes, the units of most estates. Those settlements, the boundaries of their arable fields, their woods and pasture, had always been the most significant ones for the peasant who drew subsistence from them. The larger units of kingdom, shire, wapentake, soke were not irrelevant to the peasantry. Wapentake, soke, estate centre especially, determined where dues were paid, services performed, tribute taken, cases heard. But it was the boundary of the local landscape, known as we have seen in its intimate detail, which always figured most prominently in peasant life.

Part Three

PEOPLE IN THE LANDSCAPE

10   Social Structure

The nature and quality of a person's life in Anglo-Saxon England was not simply a question of the fertility of the soil, the nature of agriculture, the amount of royal tribute, although all these and other questions affected it. Many more fundamental factors determined the impact of some of these: the divisions between rich and poor, free and unfree; the ties of kin and clientage, the groups on which one could rely for protection or advancement. For the peasant, the nature of the bond with his lord was crucial; for the noble, his own lord and patron was an essential aid; for rich and poor, free and unfree, family and kin were ties which could not be ignored. Even more basic, determining day-to-day existence, participation in court or village life, were the most fundamental divisions between adult and child, man and woman.

Men, Women and Children

The world of political and economic life already outlined was a world apparently dominated by adult males. The sources, produced almost exclusively by and for such men, bring them into prominence. But as the more neutral cemetery evidence shows, the ratio of the sexes was then roughly as now, so that a history of East Midlands society which ignored women and children would exclude at least three-quarters of the population. Their submergence in the sources is so great that the task of recovering their lives poses constant problems.

The cemetery evidence, unlike written material, does not obscure women and children. Cemeteries are an 'extended social statement' from the past;[1] the job of the archaeologist and historian is to decipher that statement. The dead are arranged in cemeteries, grouped, buried in various ways, often with grave goods. All this can tell us of the social position of the dead in life, and of that of their surviving relatives. But burial and death are such significant events that they may distort the picture of normal lifestyle. The objects buried, for example, with a seventh-century woman may not simply be those she used in life, but may rather indicate the wealth of her relatives, what was considered appropriate to her station, what could be spared to be placed in the earth and lost and, most significantly, what was believed about the afterlife. Burial may represent not actual social status or relationships, but idealized ones; not us as we are, but as we would like to see ourselves. Cemetery evidence will be used throughout this chapter to recover a lost society, but it is subject to all the pitfalls of archaeological material. Grave-goods may tell us less of wealth than of belief.[2] If we look to death and its rituals to hold a mirror up for us to a lost world, we must remember that the rituals especially have left little trace in the soil.[3] In the Anglo-Saxon poem *Beowulf* the burning of the body of a prince was accompanied by dirges, the elaborate construction of a pyre hung round with weapons, and a crowd of mourners.[4] How little of this ceremony could have been recovered from a decorated urn and a handful of ashes?

Where grave-goods are found, their distribution between sexes and ages is significant in a society where the possession of certain objects marks status, rank and participation in social life.[5] In the sixth- and seventh-century cemeteries military equipment, shields and spears, helmets and swords, mark out male and especially adult male graves. At Puddlehill, Bedfordshire, a tall man was buried with his spear and shield;[6] at Bowers Low in Derbyshire a rich male grave of the seventh century was equipped with shield, iron spear and an 86cm sword with ornamented sheath.[7] The spear was the standard equipment of the adult male of these early centuries.[8] The prevailing lay culture was militaristic, as the poetry and annals show, but the widespread possession of weapons, especially in the early centuries, does not so much suggest a violent society as one in which military objects were used as indicators of status in life. Possession of spear, shield and so on showed a man to be adult, capable of taking a full part in social life, a part which might, and once had often, included war. As late as the tenth century the possession of weapons was the mark and proof of freedom, of the right to take part in the local courts.[9] Such symbols were formally handed over at the age of majority. In the tenth-century Blickling Homily on St Martin, the hero attained manhood at the age of 15 and took worldly weapons.[10] Possession of them marks the sixth- and seventh-century men buried in the Anglo-Saxon cemeteries as free, and adult.

There is no object or objects regularly associated with adult women which could have held any similar significance. There was apparently no comparable female transition to a full role in the community. Indeed the graves of women and children often show similarities in grave goods.[11] In terms of the community and the formal part they could play in it women and children were minors, under the control of their men. Instead women's grave goods vary enormously, often being the richest in the early cemeteries.[12] From the fifth to the seventh centuries women were buried with an assortment of knives, beads, brooches, rings, spoons, crystal balls and so on. At Totternhoe, Bedfordshire, one woman had with her in death a bone comb, leather purse, workbox with wool and thread, linen-bound knife, chatelaine, and beads and pendants of amber, paste, amethyst, glass, teeth and bone.[13] At Cow Low in Derbyshire a female body was buried with gold pins set with garnets, a wooden box, green glass vessel, ivory comb, needles, iron instruments and necklace. The female grave from Glen Parva (fig. 55) is far from unique. At least until the seventh century, when rich male burials become more important, it is in female graves that the most ostentatious wealth is found. Not all women's graves are rich, however; the majority contain much poorer equipment. But as in so many societies, the families of early Anglo-Saxon England indicated their wealth and status most openly on their womenfolk, decking them out even – perhaps especially – in death.

The division of labour between the sexes cannot be assessed from cemetery finds, though objects associated with textiles and their working are regularly found with women. Study of the bones from these cemeteries showed both men and women engaged in heavy manual labour (see above, pp. 23–4) though some distinctions of occupation are likely.

Restrictions on women, especially as landholders, may have been relaxed by the influence of the Christian church, so that it is unfortunate that most of our evidence dates from long after the effects of Christianity. Monasticism in the

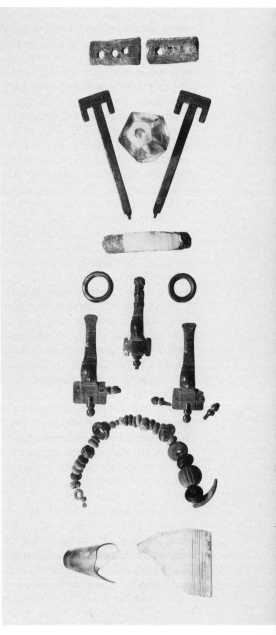

Figure 55. A female inhumation from Glen Parva. The grave-goods comprise a
fragmentary glass beaker, necklace, three brooches, bronze and ivory rings, a
facetted and perforated crystal, bronze girdle hangers and the bone plates of a
knife handle. The disposition of the brooches makes it clear that the body
was buried fully clothed (reproduced by permission of Leicestershire
Museums, Art Galleries and Records Service).

post-conversion period opened new opportunities for women. Nunneries, often double monasteries served by a community of priests, played a large part in the early period. Wulfhere's sisters, Cyneburga and Cyneswith, built a nunnery at Castor near Peterborough.[14] Repton was originally a double monastery under an abbess; Guthlac received the tonsure there under abbess Ælfthryth.[15] Near Bardney in the late seventh century was a religious house presided over by abbess Æthelhild, sister of the future bishop of Lindsey. It was a complex structure with enclosures, a separate men's dwelling, servants and priests.[16] Many others may have gone unrecorded, like Queniborough, Leicestershire, Cwene's *burh*, where *burh* probably indicated a monastic enclosure.[17] Monasticism here provided an opportunity for noble women to exercise power and influence, but it was itself moulded in that fashion by society's needs. The double monastery provided a niche for the daughters, widows and divorced wives of kings and nobles at a time when such women were not negligible.

The tenth-century reform found little place for them, not because they were now insignificant but because the religious currents of the day were limiting openings for women. Bishop Ætheric of Dorchester is said to have deliberately discouraged Cnut from founding a nunnery at Ramsey 'since it is clear what proximity of the two sexes brings both in profit and loss'.[18] Some families still tried to provide through the church for their female members. Eadnoth, a benefactor of Ramsey, founded a nunnery at Chatteris for his sister Ælfwyn to rule as abbess,[19] but in the climate of the tenth-century revival it did not flourish. The trend of church reform was now imposing its own pattern, and women were relegated to the status of benefactress.

That pattern was imposed on a society where women were important landowners. Æthelwold bought the site of Thorney abbey from a woman, Æthelflæd, for forty mancuses of gold;[20] Æthelflæd and Wulfgifu, wives of ealdorman Æthelwine, both made gifts to their husband's foundation at Ramsey.[21] Women, like men, have left their names to the places they owned in the ninth, tenth and eleventh centuries. Chellington, Bedfordshire, is Ceolwynn's *tun*; Darlton, Nottinghamshire, is Deorlufu's *ton*; Gunthorpe, Nottinghamshire, was once held by a woman with a Viking name, Gunnhildr's *thorpe*.[22]

Some women held their lands as heiresses in their own right and could transfer property rights in it. Æthelflæd, wife of Æthelwine, successfully claimed land at Sawtry as her paternal inheritance.[23] Such heiresses were married precisely to gain legitimate possession of the lands they controlled. Cnut's followers who settled in the Fenlands married local women to acquire lands there.[24] The practice was widespread after the Norman Conquest, when new Norman lords legitimized their conquest by marrying Anglo-Saxon women.[25] Geoffrey le Wirce, who held lands in Leicestershire, Nottinghamshire and Northamptonshire by 1086, had married an English wife Ælfgifu.[26] This use of women and marriage to legitimate the rights of conquerors is impossible unless women already possess rights over property which make them legal heiresses.

But it is as widows that women's rights to land are most important, in control of the dower land granted them at marriage. It is as widows that women occur most frequently in Domesday, from humble widows like Wulfwaru in

Northamptonshire with a single hide of land at Preston[27] to women like Godgifu/Godiva, widow of Earl Leofric, who held lands after the Norman Conquest in Leicestershire, in Nottinghamshire (including the great manor of Newark), and who is among a handful of landowners in Nottinghamshire and Derbyshire who had extensive rights of jurisdiction.[28] It is often as widows that we see them acting independently in the courts and defending their rights. Athelstan son of Mann gave his wife substantial dower land; she secured this and much of the rest of his land when she contested his will in her own favour.[29] It is fear of such action on the part of widows, as well as indication of the joint control of some property in marriage, that lies behind the joint gifts which church records are often careful to specify. Leofric and his wife Leoflæd jointly founded St Neots;[30] Ærnketel and Wulfrun together granted land to Ramsey.[31]

The capacity of women to hold and dispose of land is the essential background to the wider role some of them played. Whatever the truth of her ride through Coventry, the Lady Godgifu was certainly a monastic patroness with her husband, and in her own right at Stow in Lincolnshire.[32] Wulfric Spott's mother, Wulfrun, founded the religious house at Wolverhampton which bears her name; when the Viking Olaf attacked Tamworth c.940 she was important enough to be captured by him, and the event merited a reference in the laconic pages of the *Anglo-Saxon Chronicle*.[33] Wulfric's niece, Ælfgifu of Northampton, became the first wife of King Cnut, was regent of Norway for her eldest son, and in 1035–6 tried to place her son Harold Harefoot on the English throne.[34]

But as pawns in marriage politics, albeit with a future as regent or widow, women's significance is a function of their families and menfolk. During their husband's or father's lifetime land was often held for them by a male relative, hence the joint grants. Athelstan Mann's son left his daughter land bequeathed to her by her godmother; land passing from woman to woman but during his lifetime controlled by a man. Women's property rights in late Anglo-Saxon England were extensive, especially in relation to later developments, but they must be kept in perspective. In Northamptonshire only one out of 60 and more tenants-in-chief was a woman in 1086, and out of a host of landholders in 1066 only eight were women.

What landed rights they had were greater in eastern England than elsewhere. In the Nottinghamshire Domesday widows appear entitled to half a husband's land,[35] a provision which applied throughout the Danelaw, and which contrasted with the widow's third in southern England.[36] This may or may not be a 'Danish' peculiarity. If the impression is correct that the ninth to eleventh centuries saw advances in women's property rights this may have resulted from the increased use of testamentary disposition of land; the processes which were breaking up hereditary control and so opening landholding to a wider group of heirs, the growing land-market which widens the possibility of acquiring land, may all have played a part. But we are moving far into the realms of supposition.

Those realms include most of the early history of women. We see them as landholders, because in this capacity they entered the world-view of churchmen and the records of court and administration. The handful of dairymaids and female domestic slaves in late eleventh century Leicestershire, Northamptonshire and Nottinghamshire[37] are a poor indication of the activities of the rest of the female population. But if women are elusive, children are almost impossible to trace. That most of them died early, that those who survived passed into adulthood at a young age, has already been seen. In the early centuries there is little in the grave goods to distinguish children from adults. A child was buried according to the wealth of his/her parents, and the objects, at least, do not suggest that here was a society which recognized children as a distinct group, rather than as proto-adults. Yet at Raunds the children were apparently buried separately close to the south and east sides of the earliest church.[38] Perhaps Christian views altered the treatment of children; the evidence is too slim to say. Occasionally some human tragedy is frozen in the cemetery record. At Loveden Hill one grave contained a very old man, with advanced osteoarthritis, a lame dog and a small child; the child was buried in the man's arms and the dog at his feet, a group, perhaps, of the old and weak left at home and overtaken by some sudden disaster.[39] Such finds bridge the centuries with a sudden sense of empathy and contact, but they do little to help us understand the structure of this lost world.

Rich and Poor

Our sources pictured a landscape peopled by adult males, especially ecclesiastics and kings; its inhabitants were also predominantly rich. The poor, like women and children, are an elusive group. East Midlands society was unequal as far back as our sources take us; from the cemeteries of the fifth century to Domesday Book the distinctions between rich and poor are sharp.

The earliest cemeteries of the fifth and sixth centuries suggest a general level of relative poverty contrasted with a few wealthy groups. The picture is based on the paucity and poverty of grave-goods which is the norm at places like South Elkington or Leighton Buzzard. In the latter, many bodies were buried without grave-goods, or with a mere handful of beads, and only one grave showed pretensions, surrounded by a ditch and containing a spearhead, knife, ironwork and pottery.[40] The interpretation of these cemeteries is fraught with problems, since the absence of grave-goods may indicate varied beliefs, elaborate pre-burial rituals and so on, and graves with few goods are difficult to date. But the contrasts stand out between the majority, buried with knife, beads, perhaps a spearhead, and a wealthy minority. At Loveden Hill one cremation urn had been enclosed in a cist with two combs, a sword and a drinking horn,[41] another was accompanied by two metal vessels, a cloth-covered urn, bucket, drinking glass and sword.[42] They are typical of rich sixth-century male graves; status is indicated not by a quantity of objects but by a small number of status symbols, especially military equipment like the sword, whose meaning was fully understood by contemporaries.[43] The contrast with early women's graves, rich in quantity and quality of goods, has already been drawn.

By the seventh century social divisions in the grave-goods are starker, wealthy graves now distinguished by rich furnishings, numbers of prestige objects and elaborate barrows or cists constructed around them. Female rich graves are still well equipped, but it is now their male counterparts which

Figure 56. Silver-gilt round brooch with cloisonné garnets set on gold foil and the gold and garnet pendant cross from White Low (reproduced by permission of Sheffield City Museums).

stand out. At Loveden Hill the richest graves are usually the latest, one with a hanging bowl, sword and large bronze-bound decorated bucket.[44] The seventh-century woman buried at White Lowe, Derbyshire, had a gold cross and brooch (fig. 56), silver collar and glass vessels;[45] her neighbour in Galley Lowe could afford to be buried with a whetstone and 13 gold pendants, 11 set with garnets. Gold is never again found in the quantity in which it occurs in these seventh-century graves. Fine swords are buried in increasing quantity, as at Horncastle, Kirton-in-Lindsey, Colsterworth and Bowers Low. The Benty Grange warrior burial is one of the most important seventh-century finds. Its occupant was

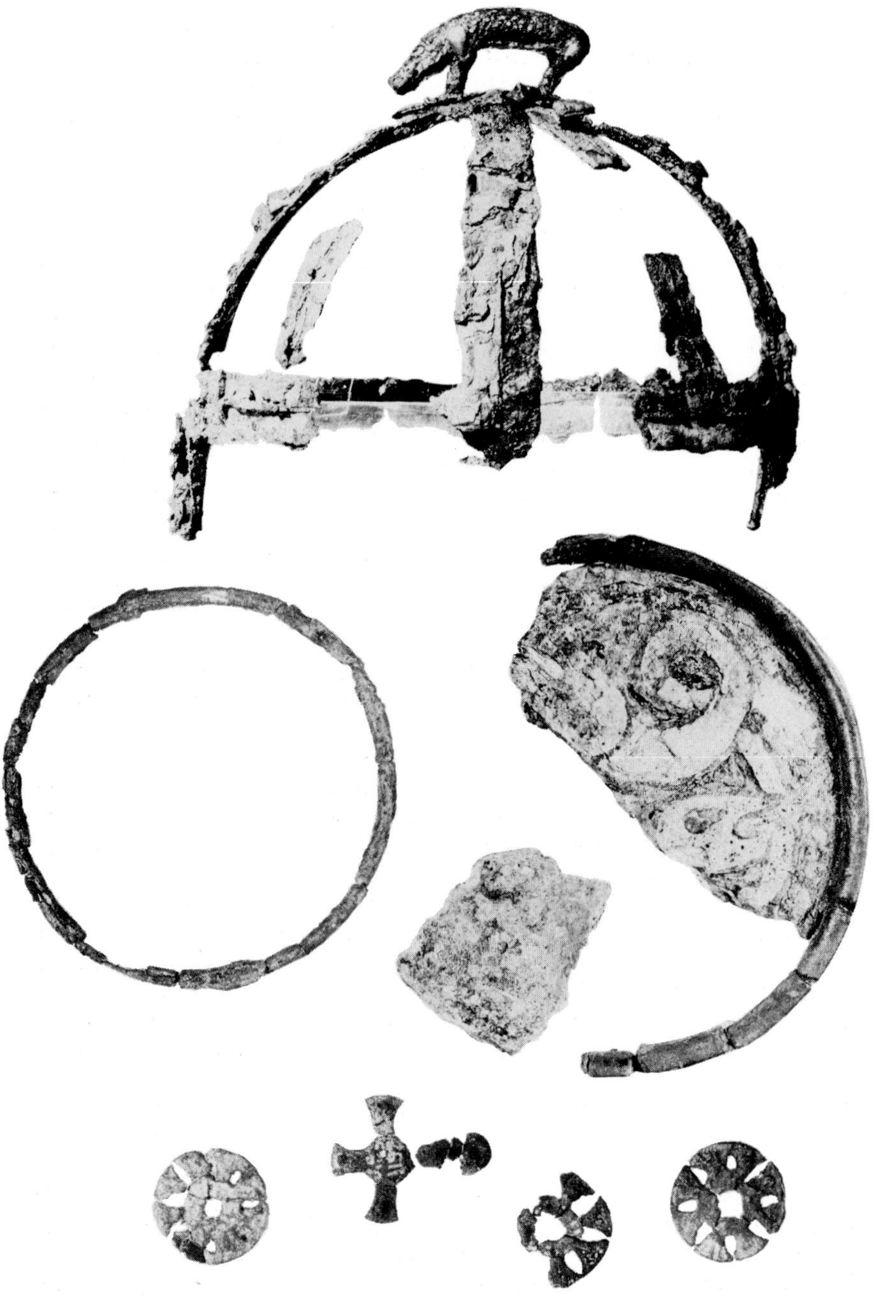

Figure 57. Iron framework of a helmet, part of an enamelled escutcheon and the silver border, cross- and wheel-shaped decorative pieces from a silver cup, all from Benty Grange (reproduced by permission of Sheffield City Museums).

buried with a silver-ornamented leather cup, two enamelled bronze discs, fine wire and braiding attached to what was once a silk garment, a woollen cloak and a helmet. The iron ribs of that helmet were once covered with horn plates, fastened with silver rivets and surmounted on its crown by a boar of bronze and silver gilt with eyes of garnet. On the nasal guard a silver cross indicated his Christian affiliation (see fig. 57).[46] Benty Grange is outstanding, but outstanding within a trend, as the Stoke Golding barrow in Leicestershire showed.[47]

The seventh century was, as we saw earlier, the age of the accumulation of and struggle for political power. The written sources described it in terms of the rise of dynasties and the battle for territory and loot. The graves tell of its social ramifications, of the increasing wealth and power of small groups of successful nobles and princes, and of their control over the acquisition and distribution of scarce and valuable objects. The finds in these graves are prestige objects, which marked out their owners in life, which were accumulated and redistributed in the halls of kings. Many are military, but not utilitarian, celebrating in bronze, silver and garnet the warrior prowess which brought power to their owners. These rare, sometimes imported goods and weapons which the nobility sought and kings gave away were the objects of war and looting. In the cemetery evidence the social changes which accompanied the kingdom-building and the rise of dynasties can be glimpsed, the unrivalled wealth of princes and nobles acquired in access to tribute, plunder and control of exchange.

The wealth of the few in the early Anglo-Saxon cemeteries contrasts with the low material standards of the many, both in these cemeteries and in settlement sites. Few of these have been excavated, but where they have, as at Maxey, little suggested ostentation or luxury. The pottery was local and roughly made by hand, consisting largely of cooking pots. There were simple bone objects, pins, combs and thread-pickers, and a very small proportion of the more valuable metalwork, only 25 iron objects, mainly knives, nails and pins, and a handful of copper alloy pieces.[48] Even allowing for the disappearance of wooden material, which played a large part in Anglo-Saxon life, this eighth- to ninth-century settlement shows nothing of the wealth of seventh-century graves. To compare the deliberate ostentation of death, the social statements of burial, with the chance finds of a settlement excavation, is not to compare like with like. Death and its accompanying rituals had religious and social significance which called for displays of wealth and status, and the inhabitants of Maxey would have stretched their resources to meet the demands of these events. The standards of everyday life, expressed in utilitarian artefacts and pottery, were probably more comparable across the whole social spectrum.

But the goods in the seventh-century graves told of the ability of their owners to take the surplus of others, through tribute and war. Status was demonstrated by the possession of rare objects, swords, drinking horns, gold brooches, glass cups, the product of the goldsmith, blacksmith, imports from the Rhineland. These changed hands between lord and follower. Lords were ring-givers, literally breakers-up or distributors of treasure, and weapon providers, attracting and retaining clients through the obligations created by such gifts. Access to these rare goods was all-important, whether to the stores of them in rival courts via plunder, or to the remnants of trade which still brought some of them from Europe. The basis of wealth was still land, and the labour and tribute of those who lived on it, which freed the lord and his followers for war. Possession of families, their land and labour, expressed in the unit known as the 'hide', or 'land of one family',[49] was the essence of social standing. When Frithuric founded Breedon-on-the-Hill he transferred to the monastery 31 hides; when Wulfhere founded Barrow-in-Lindsey he gave the 'land of fifty families'.[50] The inequality in the distribution of possessions marks an inequality in the distribution of power already deeply marked by c.A.D.700, founded already on concentrations of land.

At the end of the Anglo-Saxon period, in the tenth and eleventh centuries, those inequalities were still marked, even more securely based on land, though by now fuller sources show the wide variations which existed within the noble group. Archbishop Wulfstan of York, whose diocese stretched into Nottinghamshire, produced legal statements of the divisions within free society. In Mercia the *ceorl*, or free peasant, was worth 200 shillings; that is, that was the price paid in compensation if he were murdered. The thegn or noble was worth six times more at 1,200 shillings.[51] The distinction between freeman and noble was one which Wulfstan felt the need to define and redefine. Nobility went with land: the possession of military equipment, even a helmet, a coat of mail, a gold-plated sword, would not suffice to make a *ceorl* a thegn.[52] Wulfstan is indulging his rhetoric, since such valuable objects are unlikely to have been possessed by those without sufficient land. He is making a point about the minimum requirements for noble status, and land and its trappings are essential: 'If a *ceorl* prospered so that he possessed fully five hides of land of his own, a church and a kitchen, a bellhouse, castle gate, a seat and special office in the king's hall, then was he henceforth entitled to the rights of a thegn.'[53] The rights of a thegn included a privileged position in law courts, especially a high value on his oath which helped him clear himself and others in the court; it determined the level of compensation due to him if he was injured. To know who was and was not a thegn/noble was no mere question of social snobbery or idle social comment: 'And the thegn who prospered so that he served the king and rode in his household band . . . if he himself had a thegn who served him, possessing five hides of land . . . who attended his lord in the king's hall, and had thrice gone on his errand to the king, then he [i.e. the follower] was afterwards allowed to represent his lord with his preliminary oath, and legally obtain his [right to pursue a] charge . . .'[54]

The legal implications of status were one of the things which interested Wulfstan as potential sources of problem and friction in the court. Land was the simplest way of making status distinctions. Wulfstan was also a Christian social theorist, concerned like so many others in the early Middle Ages that society should mirror in its neat and orderly pattern the perfection of heaven.[55] These concerns might be considered sufficient in themselves to lead Wulfstan to comment on them. Those for whom Christian society, the working of the law or royal rights mattered had to make such definitions. The introduction to the Nottinghamshire Domesday states that the thegn who held six manors was distinguished from those with less, that those with full rights of jurisdiction (to hold courts for their tenants) were distinguished from those without.[56] It was a simple question of ensuring that the death duties (heriots) of the richest lords should go directly to the king. But Wulfstan speaks of an ideal past when these distinctions had applied clearly. His nostalgia may be that of the moralist in all times, for whom the golden age has always just passed away; it may also be that the northern and north Midlands society with which he was especially concerned posed particular problems c.A.D.1000 to the neat categories of his theory.

Society here, as it is revealed in Domesday, in the documents of the revived abbeys, in the place names, was much more highly stratified than his simplified distinctions suggest. The house of Leofric, with its lands throughout the Midlands, Wulfric Spott bequeathing land at some 70–80 named places,[57] enjoyed a level of landed wealth with which the legal theorists were not concerned. As Wulfric's will shows, it was wealth in land, but one which had generated cash; Wulfric left well over 200 gold coins to various beneficiaries. And it was still the wealth of an aristocracy which was a military elite. Wulfric left to the king, his lord, two silver-hilted swords, four horses, two saddled and two unsaddled, and the weapons due with them, the return of the gift of weapons from lord to man which still created the bonds of this noble society. Land and cash were the basis of noble wealth by the tenth century. The story was told in the twelfth century of a certain Ealdulf, a Fenland noble, who accidentally suffocated his own child in bed in a drunken stupor. He made amends by joining the community at Peterborough with gifts of land and money, adding the flamboyant aristocratic gesture of a spearful of silver bracelets and ornaments.[58] Ealdulf went on to become abbot of Peterborough and Archbishop of York.

An infinite gradation of middling nobility flesh out the Nottinghamshire Domesday scribe's men with six manors or more, or Wulfstan's prosperous thegns: Ælfric son of Mergeat in Leicestershire who held nine manors there in 1066,[59] Ælfstan of Boscome who had held seven manors in Bedfordshire.[60] They had their own 'men'. Godwin, Godmaer and Ælfgifu held land of Ælfstan and he had freemen in his allegiance.

With these lesser thegns and petty nobles, who held their land not of the king but of other lords, we enter that grey area which probably worried those like Wulfstan. They abound throughout the region, partly because Domesday has here bothered to record undertenants. At Carlton-in-Lindrick in Nottinghamshire, 2 carucates (far less than five hides) was shared among six men.[61] But these individuals were claiming the status of thegn/noble and each had a hall. At Eaton ten thegns each with his hall, held six and a half bovates between them.[62] The East Midlands was a region where freemen with little land still claimed noble status and privilege in the tenth and eleventh century. The local court and administrative unit here, as in Yorkshire, is instructively called a wapentake, a place where weapons were brought or brandished. The freemen who attended that court proved their right to be there by bringing their weapons, the symbol of their status as it had been of their sixth-century ancestors. Wulfstan's statements that land not weapons brought nobility applied particularly to such a society. The freemen of the East Midlands claimed their right to plead in the courts, but increasingly in tenth-century England only nobles enjoyed that freedom. To understand fully Wulfstan's problems in defining noble and non-noble by c.A.D.1000 we must first define free and unfree, a definition important at the lower end of society, but not identical to that of prosperous and poor.

Free and Unfree

The Domesday scribes divided the society of the East Midlands into six groups: thegns, freemen, sokemen, villeins, bordars and slaves (see fig. 58). The thegns we have already met; the others are less familiar. Robert de Tosny held Harby and Battesford in Leicestershire

> Harby . . . before 1066, 14 ploughs. In lordship four ploughs and eight slaves, and 28 sokemen and 7 villeins and 3 bordars have 13 ploughs.
> Bottesford . . . before 1066, 25 ploughs. In lordship 5 ploughs and 6 slaves; and 12 villeins and 60 sokemen and 5 smallholders have 15 ploughs . . .[63]

The slaves pose few problems. They belonged entirely to the lord and were numbered with his ploughs and chattels. At Thorney the slaves who tended the swine and worked in the dairy were objects of sale and purchase.[64] The rest of the inhabitants of a village in the control of a lord are, for one purpose, lumped together. The lord does not own them, as he does ploughs and slaves; nor does he pay their church or royal dues for them. Domesday lists them precisely because they owe royal dues, but it tells us little or nothing of the economic or social standing of villeins, bordars and sokemen, what made them separate groups.

The first distinction which mattered to them and to the social historian was economic. The villein was the more prosperous peasant farmer, the bordar a smallholder. On the lands of Burton abbey or on the Peterborough estates of the early twelfth century 2 bovates or 1 virgate (roughly speaking 30 acres) was a typical villein holding; bordars averaged between 5 and 8 acres.[65] These are ecclesiastical estates which may have imposed pressure for uniformity on peasant holdings, but they are our only evidence. The days when a hide (120 acres) was the land of a family had gone, though they may already have been past by the seventh century. The land of families had been divided, perhaps under pressure of gradual population growth, perhaps because of changes from the extended family holding joint property to the individual household of parents and children holding their own. A villein's 30-acre holding was adequate in subsistence terms. Out of its produce he provided for himself and his family and supplied the demands of the lord. Rather later in the Middle Ages, 15 acres was a bare subsistence holding in these circumstances.[66] The smallholders, who made up almost a fifth of the population, could not have achieved subsistence on their holdings, and must either have worked for a lord,

	Villeins	Bordars	Slaves	Sokemen	Freemen	Others
Beds.	1,854	1,147	480	107	—	3
Derbys.	1,858	738	20	128	—	92 (47 priests, 42 rentpayers)
Hunts.	1,935	482	—	20	—	63 (48 priests)
Leics.	2,630	1,371	402	1,903	6	111 (43 priests, 42 Frenchmen)
Lincs.	7,029	3,379	—	10,882	—	172 (122 priests)
Northants.	3,874	1,982	737	971	3	96 (68 priests)
Notts.	2,634	1,180	24	1,704	—	45
Rutland	730	114	—	8	—	7 (7 priests)

Figure 58. Domesday social classifications.

for other, prosperous peasants or eked out a living in other ways on the precarious margins of society. Some of these bordars were perhaps literally marginal, settled on the edges of the village, on newly-cleared land.[67]

Sokemen do not fit easily into divisions of society along purely economic lines. The size of their holdings varied enormously; what distinguished them was the extent of their service to the lord, what could be demanded of them. Such questions had obvious economic repercussions; what was owed to the lord determined what was left to the peasant. In the early twelfth century the abbot of Peterborough made a survey of his estates in which the dues and services of his peasant tenants were specified. At Collingham (Nottingham-shire) there were 20 villeins, each one of whom did one day's work each week for the lord and three extra works at harvest time. In addition the villeins brought 60 cartloads of wood to the lord's court, dug and carted 20 loads of turf or thatch, harrowed through the winter and paid £4 rent between them. The 50 sokemen on the manor worked for six days each year at the deer hedge, did three days' work in harvest, ploughed with their own ploughs four times in Lent, were responsible for ploughing, harrowing and reaping 48 acres and paid between them £12 per annum to the lord. Conditions varied. At Kettering, where there were no sokemen, the villeins worked three days each week on the lord's land.[68] Peterborough is an ecclesiastical estate, with heavy food require-ments met especially from the 'home' manors like Kettering, and the work-loads here may not be typical of all Domesday villeins. The sokemen too became more burdened with services in the late eleventh and twelfth cen-turies, so that the extent of their agricultural labour for the lord at Peter-borough may not be typical of all Domesday sokemen. But some things are clear. Villeins were much more heavily burdened with service than sokemen, and the lord's demands could make deep inroads into their time and labour. Sokemen did some services, but less frequently and often less onerous.

In this hierarchy of freedom and service which characterized tenth- and eleventh-century society sokemen were freer than villeins. In name and in services they recall the inhabitants of the *sokes*, the great estates like Gran-tham, Mansfield or Bolingbroke in Domesday, remnants of older estate patterns (see above, pp. 30–2). Soke means jurisdiction, control; it describes the lands, and inhabitants of lands attached to and paying their dues to the central hall of the lord. Sokemen were originally the inhabitants of such outlying lands, and sometimes still were in the eleventh century. In Not-tinghamshire Bothamsall had outlying sokeland at Elkesley; the population of Elkesley was six sokemen.[69] In the great estates of early England, especially where arable farms were not established, tenants still paid annual dues, a proportion of their crop, worked occasionally at the repair of the lord's house, the provision of his hunting and so on. As far back as we go in western Europe such enforced service and dues to overlords are found.[70] The vestiges of this system are apparent at Collingham, where the sokemen repaired the deer-hedge; they provided the renders in food which ninth-century Peterborough had expected from Sempringham. It was the rights to these dues and labour which were transferred in the early land grants, which always supported the noble and royal lifestyle.

Such rights were the basis on which heavier services could be built when such services were required. In general that requirement grew as the profits of plunder and war which had maintained the noble and churchmen of the seventh century dried up. In particular it grew with the development of the new estates of the ninth to eleventh centuries, often consisting of smaller fragments of the earlier estates, even in the case of tenth-century abbeys lesser landholdings than in the settlement era. These smaller estates were farmed more intensively, whether by a lay landlord who had time to devote to his one or two villages, or by efficient ecclesiastical estate managers. They characterized especially the lowland arable areas where smaller agricultural units were viable. And arable farming especially made heavy demands for labour. These were the circumstances which laid ever more onerous burdens on peasant families and gradually transformed many of them into a group distinguished by their heavier services, the villeins.

The distribution of sokemen and villeins illustrates this (above, fig. 58). In Huntingdonshire with a high proportion of ecclesiastical land, the bulk of the population were villeins, with an insignificant proportion of sokemen. In Lincolnshire, Nottinghamshire and Leicestershire, where church land is less significant, sokemen are a significant proportion of the population. Derbyshire is anomalous, but we have already seen reasons for thinking that here Domesday has omitted to include sokemen (see above, pp. 20–1). It is in Lincolnshire that the freer sokemen form the largest proportion of the population, over 50 per cent of all those recorded in Domesday. Seventy-one per cent of the population of the compact soke of Bolingbroke are sokemen, and they form 60 per cent of the population in the North Riding of Lindsey.[71] This free peasantry of Lincolnshire, and of parts of the Danelaw shires of Nottinghamshire and Leicestershire, are in part a remnant of an older situation, of the looser ties which bound peasant and lord before the heavy demands of tenth-century landlords. Many of the older estates were still in the process of fragmentation here, at Caistor, Horncastle, Greetham and so on. The local pastoral economy encouraged the survival of a free peasantry; landlords had less need for labour and exerted less pressure for increased service. But we must also recognize that Domesday is a social simplifier, lumping together groups who appear broadly similar, even though their origins may be diverse.

Lincolnshire not only has many sokemen but few smallholders. Many Lincolnshire sokemen may be smallholders, settled on newly-cleared land. Such peasants, like the older inhabitants of sokes, were loosely tied to a lord and his court, easy to define as sokemen. Later in the Middle Ages new land clearance and settlement, especially when it was not tightly controlled by ecclesiastical landlords, produced concentrations of free peasants. When local market and similar opportunities existed, this freedom was enhanced, since the smallholder can then supplement his income, is under less pressure to succumb to manorial lordship. In Lincolnshire and Huntingdonshire we see the two faces of tenth- and eleventh-century economic growth in its impact on rural society. In Huntingdonshire, monastic landlords who stimulated and benefited from that growth, anxious and able to enhance their control over the local peasantry; in Lincolnshire clearance, settlement, a land market beyond such control, producing a free peasantry. That free peasantry which is such a feature of areas of the East Midlands by the late eleventh century was both a survival and a new phenomenon.

Freedom is not an absolute. It is freedom *from* certain demands, exactions, from onerous labour services especially. It is also freedom *to* do other things, to sell land, to go with one's service to a new lord, to attend the local court of wapentake or hundred and have one's cases heard there. Villeins were in the process of losing these freedoms to do, sokemen still possessed most of them in the late eleventh century. Some of them had been defined and become important only during the later Saxon period. Freedom to sell land or go to a new lord only become questions of freedom when a land market has developed or the breaking up of older estates is creating many new lordships. Freedom to plead in court takes on new significance when land changes exacerbate litigation, and becomes more important when these courts are formalized and regularized as they were in the tenth century. Services were old, but these new questions sharpened the issue of freedom, made the need to prove and define it more pressing. Here is where the social pattern of the East Midlands and the concerns of Archbishop Wulfstan meet. The free peasantry here possessed, in large numbers, freedoms increasingly the prerogative of nobles. They proved those freedoms in court in the age-old way, with the brandishing of the weapons that symbolized them. Those concerned with the drawing of lines through society and with the definition of rights and duties found them especially anomalous, more so since weapons were still the symbols of status to a military aristocracy. Wulfstan tried to make land the criterion, but the changes resulting from legal and economic development had overtaken him. The free peasantry of the northern Danelaw remained significant long after the eleventh century,[72] in spite of increasing pressure from manorial lords and royal courts.

Social realities are rarely neat schema. A range of differences and distinctions cut through society, not all coinciding; differences of wealth and poverty, of amounts of labour service, of rights in the courts. Largely as a result of developments in the late Saxon period a parcel of such distinctions was coalescing, a combination of heavier labour services, restrictions on access to more formalized courts, restraints on the buying and selling of land on the new land market. This set of distinctions increasingly marked a line between sokemen and freemen on the one hand and villeins and bordars on the other – a line, however, which still awaited the activity of later royal lawyers to harden it into the clarity of freedom and serfdom.

Kin and Clientage

Freedom and unfreedom, wealth and poverty divided society, but some groupings were essential to all. Both peasant and noble were part of kin-groups to which they looked for aid, protection and the means of material wellbeing, whilst both peasant and noble increasingly felt the need for a lord or patron to whom they could turn for aid and who could extend their share of the good things of life.

No-one could stand alone in Anglo-Saxon England; there was a constant need for the help of family, lord, village community, little room for individualism. Legal cases reveal most clearly the ties and support which operated in all spheres of life. In the late tenth century the abbey of Ely bought land at Bluntisham, Huntingdonshire.[73] The land was purchased from a man,

Wulfnoth, and the price paid included not only the land, but men, stock and grain. The transaction was jeopardized by a claim on the part of the sons of Boge of Hemmingford that the land was theirs by hereditary right and Wulfnoth could not sell it. The case was judged in the shire court of Hunting-donshire, and there, under ealdorman Brihtnoth, the wise and old pronounced on the claims of Boge's sons. Wulfnoth and Boge's heirs were called to court, and Wulfnoth arrived accompanied by a host of men from six hundreds. It was with the help of these men, numbering according to the Book of Ely more than a thousand, that the case was finally decided in Wulfnoth's favour. The preliminary judgment was given to him, and he then called on the thousand men to swear to the justice of his case. The judgment turned on the knowledge of local men but its final resolution depended on Wulfnoth's ability to summon friends and supporters to swear an oath on his behalf. There was no hope in such a society for the friendless.

Protection, aid in court, help in seeking vengeance or compensation, land and the means of sustenance, all these had originally been provided by the family group, the oldest unit of social life. So fundamental and ubiquitous was that group that all obligations and dues were once laid upon it. We have seen before that the basic unit of dues and tribute was the hide, the land originally of a family, not of an individual. It was the family which provided for the elaborate and expensive burials in the sixth- and seventh-century cemeteries; the investment of so much effort in the dead itself argues a strong family sense. Throughout the period and at every social level which the sources allow us to explore the family is important. Kingdoms were family possessions in which all male members felt they had a right to share; monasteries were founded and controlled by family groups. Hereditary claim through the family remained the strongest claim to land in the late tenth century. The sons of Boge of Hemmingford lost Bluntisham because they could not prove their right, not because the court disregarded hereditary claims. Such claims overrode even judicial forfeiture. A lawful wife and heirs were still entitled to half his land, even if it were forfeit to king or lord for offences, so the Nottinghamshire Domesday claimed.[74] Family links provided land and advancement. We might call Archbishop Oswald's ecclesiastical dynasty in the late tenth century nepotists; the concept would have had little meaning when all men expected to share in the good fortune of members of their kin, even if that fortune were ecclesiastical office. Family provided for you in life and saw to the needs of your soul in death, for the wealthiest, in the family monastery itself.

So powerful and fundamental was kinship in this society that it acted as a type or model for other, newer bonds. When Wilfrid in the seventh century was building up his ecclesiastical empire he had himself made the heir of abbots and abbesses.[75] The claim was to be through kinship and the new kinship of the church. In the early eleventh century a priest, asked to give up the ties of family for the church, was to acquire a new group of colleagues, his fellow priests, who should compensate for the loss of the old by performing their functions for him, helping his case in the law courts and so on.[76] In both cases, however, a new group or bond was being offered to rival or replace that of natural family. Here it was the church, the new kin in Christ. By the eleventh century groups other than priests were banding together for mutual aid. In Cambridge a guild of townsmen had been formed, bound together by oaths and communal feasts, and taking on the functions of vengeance, aid in bringing men to court, the provision of proper Christian burial for its members.[77] For the townsmen, arguably uprooted from older structures, as for churchmen, ideally also divorced from ties of the flesh, new bonds perforce replaced the old. But more universally, and throughout the Anglo-Saxon period, the bond of lordship grew in importance for all social strata.

Lordship and kinship grew out of the same needs for aid and protection and were, in the ideal, mutually beneficial to lord and client, to all family members and warm in their expression. The two occasionally met and reinforced each other in ways which show how both derived their strength from tapping emotional bonding. It was common practice in the sixth, seventh and eighth centuries for the sons of nobles to be fostered at a royal or other court. There a young man entered a new family, formed a close tie with this surrogate kin and took his substitute parent as his lord. Young monks entering monasteries at a similar early age formed the same close bond with their spiritual father and lord, like that which bound Guthlac to the abbess of Repton under whom he had been tonsured.[78] Here and in the constant companionship of hunting and fighting and drinking together the ties of lordship were forged. Before he turned to the life of a hermit Guthlac had gathered together a group of young nobles and they had lived together on the proceeds of their looting.[79] As late as the tenth century a young man could still expect to spend a portion of his youth in the company of others at the court of a lord. The Blickling homilist shows St Martin taking worldly weapons at the age of 15 and then joining the company of the king's thegns; he spent the next three years of his knighthood (*cnihthad*) with them, and distinguished himself in their company.[80] Perhaps it was to such young men 'who rode with him' that Ælfhelm Polga made bequests in his will.[81]

By the tenth century and before, lordship was a social bond important beyond the ranks of the nobility and certainly not confined to groups of young warriors, even though as an ideal it was constantly reforged in that environment. Late in the tenth century, possibly in 997, Æthelred II issued a law code specifically to apply to the Danish areas of England; this third code of Æthelred is full, like its southern counterparts, of lords and lordship.[82] It is assumed that every man will have a lord who will bring him to justice, and help to clear him. The local nobility controlled the law courts; they had to be encouraged to bring their men to justice even if they could not be prevented from aiding their clients in court. Justice was secured through patronage. Whether a man was allowed to make money compensation or was sent to the ordeal might depend on whether his lord, and two other thegns, were willing to clear him with their oath;[83] the importance of establishing thegnly status is underlined. The more powerful a lord, the more he could sway a court. Ramsey abbey successfully defended a claim to land at Stapleford against Ælfnoth with the personal intervention of ealdorman Æthelwine, patron and protector of the abbey and chairman of the court. When Æthelwine died, Ælfnoth seized the land;[84] the removal of a powerful protector left institutions and individuals vulnerable, as all the abbeys found when their most powerful lord, King Edgar, died in 975.

The power which presidency of courts brought made an ealdorman like Æthelwine a desirable lord. Possession of royal office brought him more followers locally and adds another dimension to the acquisition of such office.

At the highest levels of the nobility, for the family of Wulfric Spott in the late tenth century, or of Leofric and Godgifu in the eleventh, it was the king's lordship alone which offered the extra benefits they sought in land and office. The will of Wulfric or of Ælfhelm Polga[85] was addressed to 'his dear lord' the king. It was through his bonds with these men, as we have seen, that the king ruled the East Midlands.

Everyone by the tenth century felt the need of a lord. Wulfric asked King Æthelred to be lord of his monastery; Archbishop Wulfstan assumed that a noble thegn would have others who followed him, rode in his service, attended him in the king's hall; residences like Goltho or Sulgrave were built to be a focus for the hospitality which bound them together; the poorest peasant could hope for nothing in the courts without one. Lordship had grown up to provide mutual aid, treasure rewarding service and the tie strengthened by shared danger and conviviality. 'The receiving of treasure . . . the place of feasting . . . the joys of the hall . . . the companions of warriors' was how the Anglo-Saxon poet remembered the ideal,[86] the lord a 'gold-friend', a 'treasure-giver' who sat on the 'gift throne'. The idea of protection lay behind the dues and services proffered by the peasantry to their lords, though here what might once have been seen as mutual benefits soon became one-sided. But in the upper ranks of society the ideal and reality behind the cold legal statements remained strong through to the end of the Anglo-Saxon period.

Lordship is everywhere in the legal and narrative sources of the late Anglo-Saxon period, and its prominence might argue that family was eclipsed. Certainly lordship had the advantage over kinship that it allowed choice; a lord could be chosen for his strengths whereas a family could not. But lordship may also require greater legal stress precisely because it is more artificial, whereas no man could avoid the ties of kin. Kinship remained the way that most people acquired the basic things of life: land or subsistence, a husband or wife were still given or arranged by the family group. Its ties remained powerful even after marriage, and it was kin who normally paid a man's fines or compensations in court even if it was lord who spoke for him.[87] It was to the aggrieved family that the wergeld or man-price of a murdered man was paid over as late as the eleventh century, paid by the murderer and his kin, in stages beginning with the head price at the graveside.[88] The kin-group here, as it applied at most social levels, was not a very wide one: father's and mother's immediate relatives and their children rather than a wider clan appear the operative kin.[89] At higher social levels ties of kin apparently encompassed a broader group; we have already seen the vague claims of kin which linked men like Ælfhelm Polga, Athelstan son of Mann, Archbishop Oswald (see above, pp. 125–6). This is not inconsistent. The kin as the group clearly defined to aid in the payment of a murder-compensation was a minimum group within which obligations were binding. The notion of kin encompassed a wider number of people, and one claimed kin if it were profitable and acceptable. To claim kinship with Archbishop Oswald was to hope for a share in the benefits he derived from close contact with the king; Oswald or Æthelwine accepted such claims insofar as they extended their influence in local society. If we see the broadest kin-group operating at the highest social levels it is no surprise. The greatly increased wealth of a section of the nobility after the unification of England may have reinforced kinship ties in late Saxon England. They were still too powerful for church reformers easily to break the link between family and monastery.

Conditions of Life

For Wulfstan, theorizing about thegns and their status, adequate land was the *sine qua non*, but he listed with it the necessary trappings. A thegn should possess the buildings in which to fulfil his station, a bellhouse, a fortification, a church and kitchen. The halls which the ten thegns at Eaton held are unlikely to have aspired to this degree of elaboration, but the tenth- and eleventh-century noble residences excavated at Sulgrave in Northamptonshire[90] and Goltho, Lincolnshire,[91] are closer to what Wulfstan had in mind. At Sulgrave the 25m-long hall was divided into five bays, with a cobbled porch at one end and a central hearth. The service end, from which the meal was brought, was screened off, whilst at the other end rose a two-storied, L-shaped chamber block which overhung the hall. A detached timber building near the porch was the kitchen, whilst a separate stone building was a tower or fortification, possibly tower and church combined. Nearby Earls Barton may be the tower-church originally attached to a thegnly residence,[92] and it is tempting to see the late eleventh-century Saxo-Norman towers of Lincolnshire in the same light (fig. 59). Sulgrave is the reality behind Wulfstan's theory and shows a late Saxon thegn in Northamptonshire living in a style hitherto associated only with twelfth-century or later manorial lords. At Goltho a series of halls, dated

Figure 59. The eleventh-century towers of Earls Barton and Glentworth churches.

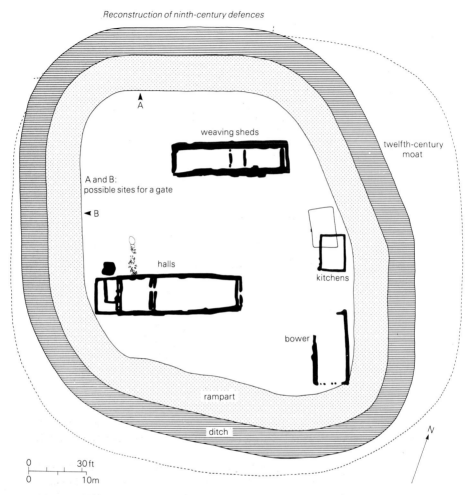

Reconstruction of ninth-century defences

weaving sheds

twelfth-century moat

A and B:
possible sites for a gate

halls

kitchens

bower

rampart

ditch

0   30 ft

0   10m

Figure 60. The ninth- and tenth-century buildings and defences at Goltho (reproduced by permission of Guy Beresford).

from the ninth century onwards, were built. Again the lord's hall is the central feature, with a raised dais for dining at the east end. With a kitchen block and other chambers it surrounds a courtyard, the whole complex surrounded during the tenth century with a timber palisade (see fig. 60). The 18 m hall with a court around it which the abbot of Peterborough undertook to build for the abbot of Ramsey at Whittlesey Mere must have been similar.[93]

The hall was the centre of the noble life-style. Ealdorman Æthelwine had one at Upwood; he retained it even after granting the land to Ramsey so that he might continue to enjoy the excellent local hunting, fowling and hawking.[94] The hall and kitchen imply a household and the entertainment of followers. A Danish follower of Cnut who settled near Ramsey in the eleventh century entertained king and bishop in his hall.[95] His household included a steward to oversee the entertainment; that of the lady Ælfhild had a chaplain to whom

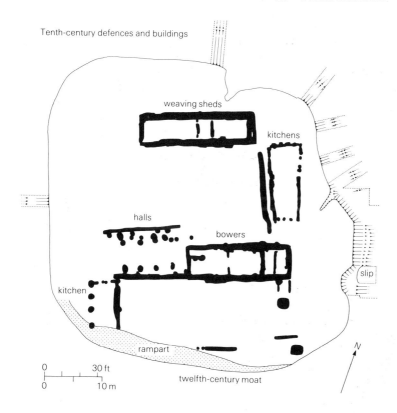

Tenth-century defences and buildings

weaving sheds

kitchens

halls

bowers

kitchen

slip

rampart

0   30 ft

0   10 m

twelfth-century moat

N

she left land at Clapton, Northamptonshire.[96] The households, the entertain-ment, the buildings confirm a separate lifestyle, a local dominance and for many nobles already a permanent residence.

The thegnly halls of late Saxon England were built of wood; in spite of the availability of good stone, the buildings of eastern England were largely of wood. As at Sulgrave, the church/fortification stood out as the only stone building, and many earlier churches, apart from the grandest like Brixworth, may have been wooden. At Raunds the first small church there probably had a wooden chancel attached to its stone nave.[97]

Villages and peasant dwellings have been little excavated. The Continental villages of the migration period contained large three-aisled halls or long-houses with ancillary buildings. Few of these have been found in the early English settlements, rather sunken-floored huts, like those at Salmonby, Lincolnshire,[98] predominate, their floors often covered in accumulated rub-bish. From these squalid structures a view could emerge of the early Anglo-Saxon settlers as poor squatters, but it would be a picture both premature and inaccurate. Middle Saxon settlements like Maxey had larger houses, and in any case the reviled sunken-floored buildings could be large and impressive. That at Upton, Northamptonshire, measured some $9 \times 5\frac{1}{2}$m, and was apparently a specialized weaving house; when the building was burnt down loom weights threaded on sticks fell from a rack or cupboard against the end wall.[99] Many

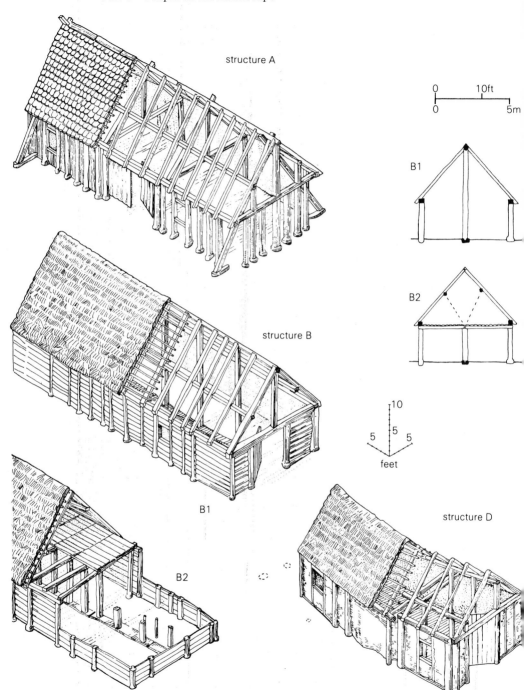

structure A

B1

B2

structure B

B1

B2

structure D

0   10ft

0   5m

10

5   5

5   5

feet

Figure 61. Tentative reconstruction of three houses at Maxey, Northants. (reproduced by permission of P. V. Addyman from his 'A Dark-Age Settlement at Maxey, Northants.', *Medieval Archaeology*, VIII, 1964).

sunken-floored pits were rubbish pits, or kitchens or storerooms, their accumulations of rubbish indicating not so much squalid habits of their former inmates, but the infill after the site was abandoned. The larger wooden houses appear now only as post-holes, small features easily lost in earlier and inadequate excavation or difficult soil conditions.

Carefully excavated late Saxon settlements like St Neots, Huntingdonshire, have given a clearer picture of the houses and construction techniques of the Anglo-Saxons.[100] Several large timber houses were found, one 'boat-shaped' and measuring $11\frac{1}{2} \times 6$m; the shape is dictated more by questions of stability in the wind than by the hankerings of a seafaring nation.[101] Most of the buildings at St Neots had walls set into horizontal wooden foundation beams, with superstructures of timber or wattle and daub which have left no remains. Not even nails were found, the joints apparently being all carpentered and secured with wooden pegs. At Maxey some of the large rectangular houses were of post-hole construction, that is the supports for the wall were not set into a horizontal beam but directly into the ground, into specially dug holes. Others were of palisade construction, closely-set timbers, or of panels of wattle and daub set in trenches (see fig. 61). At both St Neots and Maxey there were numerous small sunken-floored pits, separate from the living accommodation, some obviously firepits with hearths, some with proper entrances and lined with wicker, perhaps used as storage cellars. In neither case were there longhouses of the Continental type where all activity, even the stabling of animals, went on under the same roof. There were separate buildings for specialized functions. No trace was found of nails, stone, tiles or slate: these were houses of wood or wattle and daub, roofed with shingles, turf or thatch.

Knowledge of urban dwellings is growing rapidly with the careful excavation of sites such as Flaxengate in Lincoln.[102] Construction techniques were similar to those in rural areas. Overlapping or abutting horizontal boards or planks were attached to posts set directly into the ground. The houses were single storey with a centrally placed hearth, though there is some evidence for internal partitioning and a cross passage joining opposite doors. The floors were of beaten earth, clay or grassy material such as straw or brushwood, though the disappearance of planks over the centuries may give a false picture. The life expectancy of such buildings, subject especially to the rotting of posts and fire, was very low; in some cases as little as five years, with most probably unstable within 15 to 20 years. Fire was a common hazard. Almost all the buildings constructed on the Flaxengate site before c.1040 show signs of fire destruction, in some cases possibly even a deliberate prelude to rebuilding.

The domestic economy was based on wood, and its disappearance in most soil conditions means that the archaeological picture of lifestyle is very incomplete. Cooking pots are the most regular find, followed by bowls. The output of the pottery industry of a place like Stamford confirms this; cooking vessels, with and without lids, large bowls and spouted pitchers formed the bulk of production (see fig. 62). Tableware was largely wooden, with pottery used for cooking. The large cooking pots were designed for slow cooking, placed in the ashes to simmer,[103] with skillets for higher-temperature use. Plates and other flatware were little produced, and the predominance of bowls in the pottery tableware may indicate that porridges and stews were the predominant cooked diet. Even drinking vessels were mostly wood or leather.

Figure 62. Large bowl in Lincoln fine-shelled ware and large container in Lincoln sandyware (reproduced by permission of the Trust for Lincolnshire Archaeology).

The few pottery ones made were often goblet-shaped in imitation of the high-value metalware used only by the wealthy. Pottery copies of expensive metal objects occur from very early. In the seventh century a bronze cauldron was buried in a rich grave to the south of Louth at Stenigot; pottery copies of these valuable objects have been found at Harston (Leicestershire) and elsewhere.[104] The ubiquitous wood was even used for chalices. Archbishop Wulfstan, as always attempting to regulate conduct, tried to outlaw them in his rules for the priests of his diocese; they posed obvious problems of purification.[105]

Metalwork played a small but important part in lifestyle. Craftsman-produced objects fashioned from it, especially weapons, were the objects of status and prestige throughout the Anglo-Saxon period. It was sparingly used by the poor. At Maxey only 25 iron objects were found, and it was only in a larger and more prosperous settlement like St Neots that any quantity of ironwork was in use. Knives, pins, nails, more rarely weapons, were the only metal objects likely to be found in most households; the importance of the weapons brandished at the wapentake should not be underestimated. Metal was used especially for tools, of agriculture or of woodwork, gradually coming into use for the iron plough share, fashioned into axes, adzes, chisels and planes.

The cemeteries of the fifth and sixth centuries thus reveal a community with a comfortable as well as a wealthy segment. The richer graves have complete sets of expensive weaponry, which we have come to associate with the nobility, but many graves contained metal objects. At Loveden Hill iron knives, bronze brooches, bronze tweezers and iron shears are relatively common and spears are widespread. Even Elkington, generally considered a poor cemetery, yielded ironwork as well as beads.[106] Death called for display, and more than a tiny minority of these earliest settlers could afford it.

The home production of textiles was a regular female task. Loom weights, usually of pottery or unbaked clay, are a common find; the loom was standard household equipment. It may have been a horizontal or a beam-tensioned loom; either would have involved the weighting of the warp threads in this way. Loom weights become rarer in late Saxon contexts. None were found at Flaxengate, although this may merely indicate that spinning not weaving was carried out on the site.[107] Their absence may indicate the gradual spread of the two-beam vertical loom or the treadle-operated one, neither of which required the weighting of warp threads. However, as St Neots and other sites have shown, the older types of loom continued in use to the end of the period even if a new technology was coming into use alongside them. Wool was the most common material, woven in plain weave or twill. Wool-braid was tablet-woven, and a rare example of it was found in the cemetery at Fonaby, near Caistor.[108] Linen and silk were known, though imported silk marked out the princely, like the Benty Grange warrior. Linen, though prestigious, was more widely used. At Totternhoe, Bedfordshire, a seventh-century woman was buried wearing linen slippers.[109] Graves in the same cemetery contained two workboxes with wool fibre, thread and a small roll of material. The role of even the most prosperous women in the domestic provision for their families was emphasized in death.

The dress of the early inhabitants of the East Midlands can be reconstructed only tentatively, and mainly from cemeteries. The dead were buried clothed, and it is especially from the graves of the wealthy that some idea of clothing and adornments is gained. Garment fastenings, such as those manufactured in Lincoln at Flaxengate in the tenth century, seem unknown before the Viking arrival. Before this garments were secured by a variety of pins, brooches and ribbons, for both sexes. The jewellery found in so many early graves is an elaboration of basic, utilitarian necessities. Single brooches fastened cloaks at the shoulder, whilst pairs of brooches, with beads slung between them, could secure a cloak across the breast. Clasps or brooches gathered the sleeve at the wrist. At Kempston, Bedfordshire, a seventh-century woman had small circular brooches fastening her sleeves, a string of beads, several silver rings on her fingers and a small gold and garnet ornament,[110] a concern for ostentation as well as utility. Wealthy women of the pagan period were often buried with the chatelaine which hung from their girdles, including tweezers and cosmetic brushes,[111] and with the bone combs with which they dressed their hair. Wealthy men of the fifth and sixth century carried less ornamentation, though those who could afford it were buried with a buckled sword- or knife-belt hanging from the right shoulder with sword or knife in its leather-ornamented sheath.

It is only occasionally that the graves show a lighter, less utilitarian side of life. One skeleton at Tugby, Leicestershire, had been buried with bone dice and 46 discs, for playing a game similar perhaps to draughts;[112] one of the cremations at Cold Eaton was accompanied by 28 bone playing-pieces.[113] They are a welcome antidote to a sober picture, an eccentric comment on some individual's view of the afterlife, if not of this.

11 Religion and Belief

> The wine halls crumble; the rulers lie low, bereft of joy; the mighty
> warriors have all fallen in their pride by the wall . . . Everything is full
> of hardship in the kingdom of earth; the decree of fate changes the world
> under the heavens. Here possessions are transient, here friends are
> transient, here man is transient, here woman is transient. So spoke the
> wise man in his heart . . . Well is it for him who seeks mercy, comfort
> from the Father in heaven, where for us all security stands.[1]

The cultivation of the land, the demands of tribute, the need for lordship,
these took up the lives of the Anglo-Saxons and shaped their activities and
concerns. But other beliefs and ideas, like those expressed in the Anglo-Saxon
poem, *The Wanderer*, grew out of and affected those lives, and must be
understood if we would see them as a whole. The poet expresses a fatalism
characteristic of much early Germanic literature, but his world-view is one
already affected by Christianity. The conversion to Christian belief was a
major and apparent change and we must decide how far it altered religious
ideas, how far it was itself assimilated by a different culture.

Beliefs

The only statements of belief which the pre-Christian inhabitants of the East
Midlands have left are their cemeteries. It is a very partial statement, not only
because of the limitations of archaeology and the loss of so much, but because
it speaks primarily of beliefs about the dead and the afterlife. The dead have
been objects of fear, veneration and cult in many societies, including that of
early Anglo-Saxon England. They are a liminal group; that is, they are seen to
stand on the margin of two worlds, on the threshold which links the afterlife
and the here and now. As former members of human society they are bound to
it and its concerns, and can be called on in need or propitiated in fear. As the
dead they have passed beyond this world and are able to draw awesome power
from the next. In early England the dead were often buried on the outskirts of
settlements or on high places remote from habitation. Hall Hill cemetery near
West Keal, Lincolnshire, stands on a spur overlooking the Fens to the south of
the Wolds; Loveden Hill has a similarly prominent position. Such sites take up
least good arable land and place the dead at a healthy distance from the living.
Early cremation rituals, and even grave-goods, may mark a ritual purification,
a destruction of a man and his goods and any power he might retain through
them over the living.[2] At the same time the dead and their ambiguous power
were turned to the protection of the community. They were buried on its
boundaries of which they became protectors. Burial mounds marked part of
the tenth-century bounds of Water Newton, Huntingdonshire,[3] and the early
burials in the Roman road at Aldwincle, Northamptonshire, were in a road
acting as a land boundary.[4] Such boundary burials are common.[5] In their

barrows and cemeteries the dead defined and protected the boundaries of their old communities.

The early cemeteries with their grave-goods argue already for a belief in the afterlife. The goods buried were, as we have seen, those most closely associated with the person, or rather with his or her status, the objects most regularly worn to denote position in this life and so to indicate it in the next. The occasional finds of food in graves indicate most clearly a belief in some existence beyond the grave. At Sandy, Bedfordshire, about three quarters of charred wheat was found near the cremations, whilst at Totternhoe two jars packed to stand upright in the grave of a young man may once have held liquids.[6] At Borrowash, Derbyshire, the burnt bones of ox and sheep accompanied the burials.[7] The jars and pots often found in graves probably once contained food or drink. How much of this is provision for afterlife, how much propitiation of the dead, how much destruction of their hold on life and how much social statement about their surviving families, are questions that the grave goods alone cannot answer.

Beyond their concern for the dead the pre-Christian beliefs of the Anglo-Saxons are little known. The position of some of their sacred sites is still represented in a handful of pagan place-names; they are far from a complete picture, but the record of the last places where such practices lingered.[8] The Old English words *weoh*, *hearg* and *wig*, all meaning a heathen sanctuary, survive in place names like Wyham and Wyvill (Lincolnshire), Wysall (Nottinghamshire), Wyfordby (Leicestershire) and Harrowden (Northamptonshire). We need not assume any elaborate ecclesiastical structure similar to the Christian church. Wulfstan in the early eleventh century spoke of the survival of sacred stones, trees and wells,[9] and for the bulk of the population rituals associated with such sites in springtime, at harvest, at death may have been most important. A more organized concern with the gods and their worship, like the Christian religion later, may have characterized kings and nobles. Wensley in Derbyshire was Woden's grove, but Woden was especially the god of a military elite. The kings of the Mercians traced their descent from him,[10] an annexation to their blood-line which marked their successful grasp on power.

Christianity was to be, in the words of St Paul, the putting on of a new man. In practice conversion was a process of mutual assimilation in which Christianity changed as much as existing ideas. Nowhere is this more apparent than in attitudes to the dead. Christianity took them over, brought them literally to the centre of the community, having neutralized their capacity for evil and transformed selected ones into saints. In the Christian community at Raunds the dead were not buried on the fringes of the community but at the side of the church, in the centre of the community.[11] The existing Christian emphasis on the holy dead and on the power of their relics must have smoothed the transition from old belief to new religion, with these Christian ideas brought to prominence in the process.

The church took over the ritual stages essential to safe transition from this world to the next and to the security of those left behind. How central this function was is shown in the church dues, first defined in the tenth century but incorporating older ideas. It was the possession of a graveyard, that is the ability to provide for the rituals of the dead, which gave a church rights to tithes and dues.[12] A 'soulscot' or mortuary payment was one of the dues specified.[13] Grave goods had been replaced by a gift to the Christian church. By the tenth century and probably before the wealthiest provided generously to secure burial in the church itself, purchasing the special efficacy of the holiest places, close to the relics of the saints. Æthelflæd, one of the wives of ealdorman Æthelwine, gave land at Sawtry to Ramsey as the price of her burial there,[14] and Ærnketel secured the same benefit for himself and his wife with land, 15 pounds of gold, and the chattels he had on the day of his death.[15] Control of the rituals of burial were the incidental origin of much of the church's wealth.

Those personal trappings designed to announce status in the afterlife had no function in a religion which preached theoretical equality beyond the grave. But the relatives of the Christian dead continued to make such statements, perhaps for the consumption of the living, in funerary monuments. The many carved crosses, like those at Bradbourne, Eyam, Rothley (fig. 63), Bakewell, Stapleford, were mostly not preaching crosses but funerary monuments. So too were the hogback tombstones of the tenth century, like that at Hickling, Nottinghamshire (fig. 63), based on stone or wooden reliquaries and sarcophagi, 'houses of the dead'.[16] In the tenth and eleventh centuries a burgeoning lay piety and the cash to express it produced a great investment in death. Decorated gravestones, like that at St Mark's Lincoln,[17] the numerous

Figure 63. Hickling hogback tombstone (*left*, seen from above) and the Rothley Cross.

examples in south Nottinghamshire and Bedfordshire[18] and those mass-produced at Barnack,[19] bear witness to the continued concern with the proper burial of the dead.

The pagan veneration of the dead and their power merged readily into the Christian cult of the holy dead expressed in relics. Relics were central to Christian worship. Lists of the resting places of the saints existed by the ninth century, not so much to guide pilgrims as to celebrate the massing of power they represented,[20] the spiritual riches of a kingdom. Possession of relics was eagerly sought by religious houses, and in the competitive world of the tenth- and eleventh-century Fenlands some dubious practice arose from the fervour. The relics of St Felix had been brought from Dunwich to Soham by monks fleeing from Viking attack. Both Ramsey and Ely were anxious to acquire them. The Ramsey monks set out by boat in quest of them, overcame local resistance to the loss and carried them off singing psalms. When noise of the translation, not apparently a silent affair, reached Ely, the monks from there sailed out in an even larger company to recover them. In a thick fenland fog, which the Ramsey monks chose to interpret as a miraculous intervention, the two boatloads of monks passed without seeing each other.[21] The holy rivalry of these two abbeys had seen other instances of body-snatching. In 1016 the Ramsey monks were en route back from the battle of Ashingdon carrying the body of their dead abbot. They rested the night at Ely. There the body was stolen whilst the Ramsey monks slept deep in a drunken stupor induced by the saintly Ælfgar, retired bishop of Elmham and monk of Ely.[22]

Relics moved constantly. Patrons endowed their favourite houses with them. Ealdorman Æthelwine brought the bodies of Ethelbert and Ethelred to Ramsey;[23] Cnut transferred Wigstan from Repton to Evesham.[24] Retiring ecclesiastics brought them as gifts when they sought the security of a monastery for their final years. When Ælfweard bishop of London retired to Ramsey in 1044 he brought the jaw bone of St Egwin and the blood-stained cowl which had covered the head of the martyred Ælfheah.[25] The monastic engrossers of the late tenth century sucked in relics as they did land. Peter-borough got the bodies of Saints Cyneburga and Cyneswith from nearby Castor, and of the virgin Tibba from Ryhall,[26] and added them to a collection which later boasted the arm and ribs of St Oswald, two teeth of the martyr-king Edward, the arm of St Swithin and the hair of St Ethelwold.[27] The latest examples of the lists of Saints Resting Places, like that of the twelfth-century Peterborough monk Hugh Candidus, celebrated the monasteries as the power-houses of the Christian community.

The Christian cult of relics has always proved a stumbling block to the rational or cynical modern mind. They are easily dismissed as the beliefs of the poor and ignorant, cynically manipulated to their own profit by greedy monks. They are certainly a part of a system of belief now alien to us and difficult to understand, but they were central to the Christian experience of their day, to that of learned monks and bishops, of noble families and kings. So much which has survived from early England is concerned with this cult. Saints' Lives like that of Wigstan produced at Repton,[28] resting place lists, records of acquisitions and translations are a significant proportion of the fragmentary written sources. Churches were built, rebuilt and remodelled to incorporate the needs and demands of those who wished to see and touch the holy relics. At Repton the church was extended over the free-standing royal tomb to bring it into the church building and stairs were provided at either side of the nave to give access to the shrine.[29] Wing in Buckinghamshire was remodelled in the tenth century to provide passages to its relic crypt.[30] Some of the finest Anglo-Saxon sculpture was once part of stone reliquaries, like the rows of dancing figures at Breedon, the fragment of a similar frieze at Castor (above, fig. 40), and the Wirksworth slab (fig. 64). The latter, slightly coped in shape, was originally the

Figure 64. The Wirksworth slab.

top of such a shrine. Its iconography presents the death of the Virgin, the descent into Hell, Ascension and apocalyptic representation of the Lamb on the Cross as a prelude to the mission of the Church. It is eloquent of the central place of death, judgment and resurrection in the beliefs of the Anglo-Saxon church. In stone and in parchment the priorities of the Anglo-Saxons are frozen. It is not simply an accident of survival which brings them to the fore; their survival results from the effort originally invested in them.

The saints and their relics took over the defensive and familial functions of the pagan dead, protecting their followers and watching over their families. The cult of relics draws its strength from belief in the power of the dead and their continued interest in the world they have left. The physical remains of the holy, objects which had touched them or been used by them, partook of the power and virtue of the Saints, a power rendered benign by their sanctity and by Christian ritual, now enhanced in the world beyond death and tapped through these objects by those on earth. The saints were intercessors and patrons,[31] partial in their favours to followers and devotees like any lord. Saints and their relics offered immediate aid, and like the prayers of monks, a communal route to salvation. Salvation through the merits and aid of others was an idea which arose readily from the society of Anglo-Saxon England. In a world where every man looked to others for aid, to his family, patron or village community for protection and the means of existence, the idea of salvation as an individual quest was foreign. The holy dead were spiritual lords and family, in physical contact with particular places and people through their relics. The

Anglo-Saxon no more expected to stand alone in death and judgment than he did in his earthly life.

The saints of the early English church were readily recognizable to their devotees. They were heroes who grappled with the forces of evil in personal combat with demons and spirits. St Guthlac was born a noble warrior and lived a life of battle and tribute before his conversion. That turning-point took him into a new realm of heroic endeavour as a hermit in the wastes of the Fenlands at Crowland. There his battles were with the flesh, and with demons, on one occasion an entire army of them. As a spiritual hero he won the respect of a warrior age. As a holy man he received frequent visits, including those of the exiled Æthelbald, future king of Mercia. His prestige aroused the emnity of his servant, who once planned to kill him 'in order that he might take Guthlac's place and enjoy the respect of kings and princes'.[32] Guthlac was a Christian hero for a warrior culture. He is in the tradition of heroic Christian ascetics whose subdual of the flesh was a metaphorical death which put them in contact with the powers of the afterworld.[33] Like the hero Beowulf his battles are literal ones, epic deeds against monsters of the dark.

Seventh-century Christianity was not a pacifist creed. The helmet of the Benty Grange warlord carried a Latin cross on the noseguard. Lay ideals and ecclesiastical culture interacted deeply in a society where the clergy were drawn from the ranks of nobles reared in warlike traditions. In 747 the synod of *Clofesho* had to forbid the recitation of the Christian liturgy as if it were a tragic secular poem.[34] Tatwine, monk of Breedon-on-the-Hill and Archbishop of Canterbury, was a product of the synthesis. His learning was that of an eighth-century Christian world still struggling to keep alive the culture of Rome. His major work was a manual of instruction in Latin grammar. It was Latin grammar in the service of Christian education, like that which Guthlac underwent for two years, learning to read the scriptures, mastering the canticles, hymns, psalms and customs of the church. But Tatwine also composed 40 riddles, a typically Anglo-Saxon, oral form, where the worlds of Mediterranean Christianity and eighth-century Mercia meet. A down-to-earth wit and earthy humour appear in the riddle for squinting eyes 'which look at different things'[35] or for a table 'whose habit is to satisfy men with varied dishes' but which is often 'eagerly plundered by robbers, who tear off my dress, leaving behind my naked body'.[36] But it is Tatwine's riddles on the arrow, sword, sheath, quiver and whetstone which take us straight into the world of the hero-saint Guthlac, of the early cemeteries and the culture of the lord's hall. The fusion of Christianity and military ideals was still vigorous in the tenth and eleventh centuries, where sculptures like the Bakewell cross shaft depict warriors and the abbot and monks of Ramsey fought together at the battle of Ashingdon.[37]

> I wish to preserve the things that are mine and give them willingly to whoever pleases me and is obedient to my authority. If indeed Christ is prince of all things, shall he not have the portion which religious men gave him for the redemption of their souls . . . by [the monks'] prayers we can be snatched from our enemies.[38]

For a thegn like Ælfwold, brother of ealdorman Æthelwine, the spiritual hierarchy of Christ and his monastic followers paralleled the worldly one he

Figure 65. Christ in Majesty, Barnack.

understood. Emphasis was on Christ the King, the triumphant judge, the majestic prince as in the eleventh-century Barnack Christ in Majesty (fig. 65). The apocalypse and the day of judgment portrayed at Wirksworth, or in the angels of the apocalypse at Bakewell or Eyam, strike the theme of power which was the face Christ turned to the Anglo-Saxons. Gifts to the patron saints of churches laid these saints under the obligation of reciprocal response just as the gift of lord to man. Wealth displayed status for churches as for individuals. A great bishop or abbot like Leofric of Peterborough embellished his church with candlesticks, a great table, feretories, vestments and a cross for the altar. Poverty was a dubious virtue. To the family of flesh and blood the church added spiritual relatives, powerful dynastic saints like Guthlac or Wigstan for royal families. Additional kin were created even in this world when rebirth at the baptismal font brought a new set of parents. Wulfric Spott, for example, was linked to the family of Morcar, one of the most powerful men in the north Midlands, as the godfather of Morcar's daughter,[39] a welcome alliance sealed in the water of baptism.

Tatwine's riddles are part of an oral culture, of dramatic gesture and ritual performance. When King Æthelred of Mercia granted land to Saxulf they joined hands, took a turf from the land and placed it on a gospel book before a multitude of men.[40] Wulfnoth and his thousand followers proved their title to land, just as others cleared themselves, with an oath sworn orally in court.

These rituals set apart the action from everyday life, called on the witness of unseen powers, and their efficacy lay in perfection of performance, correctness of detail. An oath in court was void if incorrectly worded; God was placated with rituals performed with concern for minutiae. Tatwine and his fellow monks used Roman ritual books, and Roman Christianity triumphed in England because the apostolic tradition offered a guarantee of correct observance. A church like Brixworth seems to have been designed for a three-dimensional presentation of the liturgy, with architectural possibilities for the use of music, for the voices of angels ringing out from a height (as we know was the case at Essen in Germany); the liturgical sequence for a great feast like the Ascension could be given a dramatic splendour in such surroundings.[41] The tenth-century monasteries had as a major aim the performance of the cycle of Christian ritual, and benefactors endowed them to ensure that aim. Christianity elaborated rituals and provided a new and sumptuous spectacle of religion; but ritual itself and the attitudes of mind which sustained it were already rooted in Anglo-Saxon culture.

The Christian church could never have succeeded in its mass conversion without a dialogue with existing social norms in which its own beliefs were modified or re-ranked in new priorities. But Christianity brought its own defined voice to that dialogue and its impact should not be minimized. Tatwine's riddles are part of Anglo-Saxon oral culture, but they are dwarfed in size by his grammatical work whose origins lay in the Mediterranean. Brixworth had its ambulatory for the clergy to process around the relics of the dead, but the church was a novel stone building, built on the plan of a Roman basilica with westworks perhaps set aside for the instruction of catechumens in the new faith. Guthlac fought demons but with the Christian weapons of prayer, a warrior but one cast in a new role symbolized in the transition from a life of loot and pillage via lengthy instruction to tonsure and initiation at Repton. Christian kings and their dynastic saints fulfilled old demands on kingship, guaranteeing the good fortune and protection of their people, but the holy monk kings like Æthelred of Mercia who retired to Bardney signal the entry of a new theme. The Christian church brought eastern England into contact with ideas and traditions born far away on the shores of the Mediterranean. Through its specialized clergy and education it became the guardian and teacher of these new ideas.

From the first the monasteries were centres of education. Tatwine got his learning at Breedon, Guthlac at Repton. Tatwine's grammar was a functional, educational work for instructing monks in Latin. The revival of the monasteries in the late tenth century brought a revival of learning in its wake, with an influence on the church beyond the abbey gates. Bishops were chosen from the ranks of the monks. Ælfweard bishop of London, Ætheric and Eadnoth bishops of Dorchester, were educated at Ramsey[42] and a series of archbishops of York and bishops of Durham were drawn from Peterborough. The monasteries were the major sources of learning for humbler ecclesiastics, like Morcar son of Leofsige, a deacon in Lindsey, whose father gave lands to Ramsey in exchange for his son's education.[43]

In 1018 Edmund, the new Bishop of Durham, asked the Peterborough monks to instruct him in the monastic rule. It was an education fashioned to the needs of monks that the abbeys provided. At Ramsey a life of the founder, St Oswald, was written by the monk Byrhtferth. Oswald's Continental contacts had brought to Ramsey a French monk, Abbo of Fleury, a noted contemporary scholar and historian.[44] Abbo composed a life of St Edmund the martyred king of East Anglia, and a grammar for the instruction of the children committed to the abbey. It was at Ramsey that the only two *computus* known from Anglo-Saxon England were produced, one of them again by Byrhtferth.[45] A computus is at first sight a work of mathematics, astronomy, history, medicine, theology, music and grammar, a broad compendium of knowledge. But it was knowledge organized and relevant to a central purpose typical of the concerns of the learned. The computus was an ecclesiastical calendar used to calculate the movable feasts of the church. It takes us back to the questions of ritual and correct observance essential to early religion.

The Bishop of Durham in 1018 asked for instruction in the monastic rule of life. That followed at Peterborough and the late tenth-century abbeys was the rule of St Benedict. Rules of life by which communities of monks and other clergy ordered their existence were known in England from the seventh century,[46] though the earliest were often diverse, eclectic and not always followed. The aim of the tenth-century revival was the strict imposition of the Benedictine rule and with it of a life of celibacy. The monastic rule epitomizes the extent to which Christianity demanded, even if it did not always achieve, a new life for its adherents. The result of the tenth-century changes was a new emphasis on the separate way of life of the clergy and a renewed demand for Christian moral standards to be enforced more widely. The church, especially a religious house with its patron saint, had always presented a new allegiance and focus of loyalty, but as long as the house was a family foundation, the saint a family patron, old loyalties readily coexisted. The tenth-century reformers tried to change this. They encouraged monks in particular, but the clergy in general, to see themselves as a separate group or order in society, with a new set of rules and allegiances.

In the early eleventh century a Northern writer, presumably in the York diocese, drew up a set of rules for the priests of the diocese, in which the clergy are encouraged to see themselves and act as a group, taking over the functions of lord and family: 'If anyone offer wrong to any priest, all his colleagues are to be zealous about obtaining the compensation, with the help of the bishop, and in every matter of law they are to be, just as it is written "as if one heart and one soul".'[47]

He did not demand celibacy of his parish priests; the religious houses did. Celibacy and the monastic rule combined to separate the monk from family and to mark his entry into a new community. The breaking of family ties was, as we have seen, only partially successful, but the new community often took a strong hold on the affections of its members, reared and educated there from a young age. Many bishops, former monks of Ramsey or Peterborough, retired there to die. These ideals were not new, but they triumphed in the tenth and eleventh centuries.

The current of reform reached out to lay society, emphasizing questions of sexuality and marriage which were moral issues with wide repercussions in a society based on land and family. *The Northumbrian Priests' Law*, which would have applied in Nottinghamshire and possibly Lindsey, typifies these attitudes. On lay morality it emphasizes four areas: heathen practices, the keeping of the Sabbath, the payment of church dues and sexual offences. Its first concern was the vigorous life of the church itself, essential to the final stages of missionary activity as to all other aims; hence its emphasis on church dues and their regular payment. The church was concerned with the definition and spread of the Christian life, for laymen but especially therefore for the clergy; its author was worried about pollution, about those sins which made the layman, but especially the priest, unclean, and in the latter case unfit for his ministry – most notably sexual offences. The laity must recognize and heed the separate, holy nature of the church; the sabbath and its activities were to be a day in every sense set apart.

The author's concerns led him into the sphere of marriage regulation. He forbade the taking of more than one wife, required the legal betrothal and wedding of a woman, forbade divorce and remarriage, and incest, including incestuous marriage with spiritual relations like godparents. Those who died in incestuous unions forfeited Christian burial.[48] Marriage was still essentially a lay affair and the church's involvement in it peripheral. Laymen at all social levels saw marriage as a question of family land and property, the getting of heirs, and divorce, remarriage after divorce or the marriage of cousins was still widely practised. It is doubtful whether the full legal processes of marriage which are here envisaged were fulfilled in most unions. Marriage was a regulated family affair, sexual mores personal except insofar as they involved the question of a woman's virginity and thus paternity. The Christian ideals the *Law* enunciated cut across and impeded these social functions of marriage. The efficacy of its author's demands is doubtful; only gradually and at certain social levels did the pattern he required come to be followed.

Here and elsewhere the tenth-century reformers and their successors were reiterating ideals already old with a renewed vigour. The movement for reform and regeneration of which they were a part emphasized the gap between the practice of lay society and the Christian ideal. The assimilation of Christian beliefs to lay practice had never been total and the tenth century sharpened a potential conflict always inherent. Christianity had added important new elements to Anglo-Saxon belief.

Church and People

The author of the *Northumbrian Priests' Law*, like Archbishop Wulfstan whose work he knew, grew out of the revival of learning and of church organization, especially of monasticism, which marked the tenth century. But in his concern with the parish clergy and certain aspects of lay morality he strikes a new emphasis. Tenth-century developments in land-holding and parish formation had brought the parish clergy into novel prominence, in few areas more so than in the East Midlands. The parish priest brought the Christian church into direct and regular contact with a wide social spectrum. Wulfstan stepped in to provide a way of life for this clergy, to make of them obviously worthy ministers of sacred rituals, to guide them in the demands they made of their lay flocks. His requirements were sometimes unrealistic, but they were called for by a new relationship between church and people which had come into being in the late Saxon period, and which calls into question the nature of religious provision before this and the extent of the earlier conversion.

In the seventh and eighth centuries church structures mirrored those of political power as the conversion progressed through an alliance of churchmen, kings and great nobles. Thus when the bishoprics were set up late in the seventh and early in the eighth century they followed the divisions of contemporary politics. Theodore, coming as he did from the Mediterranean, sought urban centres like Leicester and Lincoln, but Leicester was the episcopal seat for the diocese of the Middle Angles,[49] Lincoln for Lindsey.[50] Early monasteries like Barrow, Partney, Peterborough or Breedon were the foundations of royal or noble families on their own lands. It was from these monasteries especially that missionary activity and the provision for religious needs was organized. Frithuric gave Breedon to Peterborough in the late seventh century 'so that they should found a monastery at Breedon and appoint a priest of good repute to minister baptism and teaching to the people assigned to him'.[51]

Monasteries, or minsters – the word derives from *monasterium* – were churches from which a community of clergy served a large area. They were still recognizable in the eleventh century.[52] They might be chief minsters, founded on important royal or episcopal estates like Bakewell, Southwell or Stow, or other old minsters, perhaps like the community of seven priests who served the church of St Alkmund in Derby in the late eleventh century.[53] By the tenth century they were mother churches, the baptismal church for a wide area where church dues like tithe or payments for lighting (that is, dues of wax) or burial were made. The church at Aylesbury in Buckinghamshire had rights to church dues from eight hundreds;[54] St Wulfram's, Grantham, had the tithes and ecclesiastical customs from the wapentake of Wivebridge and from *Treos* hundred.[55] These tenth-century claims to dues mark the original areas which the minster churches had served.

The earliest church buildings which survive confirm a picture of religious activity concentrated on particular centres, though this evidence must be read with a realization that if local churches were built early they would have been small, wooden and likely to have disappeared. Brixworth and buildings like it were not parish churches. Divided into four cells, with its narthex, aisles and chapels, presbytery and absidal chancel, Brixworth was a late seventh-century minster, monastic or royal church. So too was eighth- and ninth-century Repton with its monastic community. The narthex at Brixworth may be a sign of its original function as a baptismal church for a wide area, set aside for the instruction of catechumens.

These minsters were the major centres of religious provision. Priests were sent out from here; the Council of *Clofesho* in 747 spoke of priests apparently under the jurisdiction of abbots or abbesses.[56] The laity came here for baptism, perhaps burial and to pay their dues. The earliest sunken mausoleum at the monastery/minster of Repton may have doubled service as a baptistery. The minster churches were the foundations of kings and nobles at the centres of their estates. They were supported by the religious dues of those estates just as tribute supported the lord, and in turn they supplied the religious needs of the people. But those estates were, as we have seen, large and the areas served by the minsters wide. The jurisdiction of Southwell minster in the tenth century

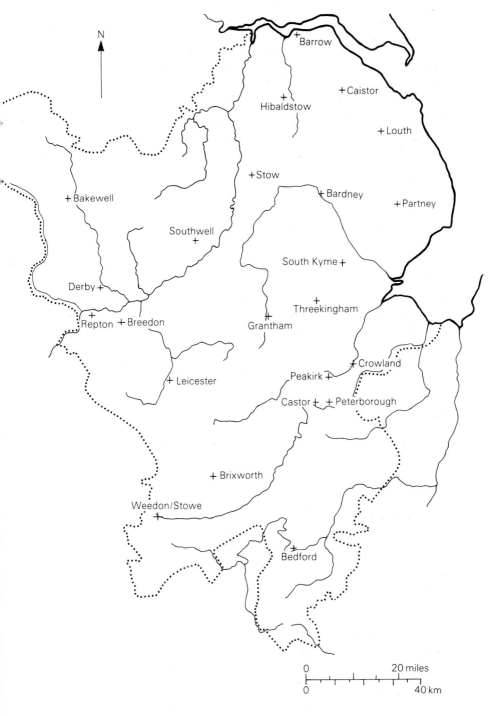

Figure 66. Known minsters in the East Midlands.

may be some indication. Southwell once served the settlements of Hal-
loughton, Gibsmere, Upton, Morton, Goverton, Bleasby, Kirklington, Normanton, Halam, Fiskerton and Farnsfield.[57] The geographical distribution of
the minsters themselves reflects political and other motives of their noble and
royal founders rather than a desire to provide equally and adequately for the
religious needs of the community. The provision of minsters shown in fig. 66 is
unlikely to be complete, but the map gives some indication of how thin and
irregular such a religious provision based on the minsters must have been.

When the minsters and their rights were recorded in the tenth and eleventh
centuries they were already losing their dominant position. The changes in
estate divisions between the ninth and eleventh centuries had been
accompanied by ecclesiastical change. The creation of rural parishes and
parish churches went hand in hand with the fragmentation of great estates;
one was a precondition of the other.[58] The parish church was the manorial
church with burial rights, the church set up by the lord to which burial and
other dues formerly paid to the minsters had been diverted. Not until a
village's ecclesiastical dues were free to go to its own priest could a priest and
church be supported, a parish system as we know it come into being. That
freedom was achieved when the village passed into individual ownership,
ceased to be an integral part of a large estate-structure. The rights of the old
minsters were guarded and defended. At first a thegn was permitted to give
only a third of his tithe to his own church, and then only if it had a graveyard;
the rest went to the old minster.[59] But the statement and defence of these rights
was necessary because they were being challenged; the definitions of minster
and parish churches found in the laws were called for in the same way as
Wulfstan's rules for the clergy. The tenth and eleventh centuries were a great
age of church building. Most of the surviving Anglo-Saxon church fabric dates
from this time, and this is not merely a sign that older buildings were decayed
or rebuilt. Where excavation has occurred, as at Raunds, there is no evidence
for a church before the first tiny tenth-century structure.[60] The building of
churches does not necessarily mean the formation of parishes; a two-tier
system of baptismal churches and lesser chapels without rights to tithe and so
on could easily coexist. But the combination of church building, changes in
land holding and concern over tithe payments suggest that the late Saxon
period in the East Midlands was a time of rapid parish formation.

Thegns built churches and supported priests on land often newly acquired or
recently freed for their ownership. One symbol of a nobleman's status
c.A.D.1000 was his possession of a church.[61] The new parish churches often
expressed the wealth and confidence of the nobility who founded them. They
were owned by their builders. The church at Ratcliffe-on-Soar was built by
Sewy who held the village in Domesday.[62] As property, they were inherited
and transferred. The priest Godric owned a church in Lincoln in the mid-
eleventh century, which he had inherited from his mother Garwine.[63] He tried
to give it to Peterborough when he became a monk there, but his fellow
citizens objected, not because churches could not change hands, but because
they claimed no-one could grant possessions outside the city. The church of St
Mary Huntingdon certainly did change hands several times in the mid-
eleventh century, until at the time of Domesday it was held as a pledge for
debt.[64] The building of a church increased a person's assets since tithes which

Figure 67. Surviving Anglo-Saxon
church fabric (including the
Saxo-Norman towers of Lincolnshire)
(after H.M. and J. Taylor,
Anglo-Saxon Architecture,
1965).

would have gone to the old minster were now retained. The proliferation of parish churches reflects not only the piety and wealth of the local nobility, but something of their canniness.

Changes in land ownership, especially in eastern England, were one factor in rapid parish development, but it was not only the nobility who founded parishes. The new monasteries built churches on their estates combining an undoubted zeal for conversion with that pressing desire to realize assets to the full. In Lincolnshire, Nottinghamshire and Derbyshire groups of freemen or thegns founded and held churches together.[65] Such churches, founded by a group within the village, are a reminder of the peculiar social structure of the area. Yet they must indicate the desire of communities to have a church and priest of their own. Religious enthusiasm and piety played a large part in parish growth.

Nowhere is this more obvious than in the towns, where parishes and churches proliferated. Here the number of churches blossomed far beyond the simple question of provision for religious need. By A.D.1100 and possibly by the time of Domesday, Lincoln had 35 parish churches, whilst in Domesday, which under-records churches, Derby had six.[66] Their proud founders occasionally recorded their benefaction, as in the dedication stone at St Mary le Wigford, Lincoln (fig. 68). Parish development in the towns is linked to their burgeoning wealth in the late Saxon period, and the remoteness of the East Midlands from episcopal control in the tenth century meant that there was little check on this enthusiasm. This growth in the number of parishes brought

Figure 68. Dedication stone of St Mary-le-Wigford, Lincoln, The inscription in Old English fills the top triangular portion of a Romano-British memorial stone. It reads in translation 'Eirtig had me built and endowed to the glory of Christ and St Mary' (reproduced by permission from R.C. Collingwood and R.P. Wright, *Roman Inscriptions in Britain*, Oxford University Press, 1965).

with it regular religious provision in towns and villages. The local priest became for the first time a normal feature of the community and arguably the real conversion of the bulk of the population began.

The priest was maintained on a portion of land (glebe) and a share, not necessarily the whole, of the ecclesiastical dues of his parishioners. The normal size of the glebe was probably little more than a peasant holding of 30 acres; when Domesday specifies a larger one, as the half hide (60 acres) at Buckworth, Huntingdonshire, or two hides (240 acres) at Bottlebridge, it may be precisely because these were exceptional.[67] Church dues were in theory extensive. Tithes of stock and produce, church scot, a load of grain in November and the first fruits at Martinmas, plough alms of a penny on every plough paid at Easter, light dues of a halfpennyworth of wax at Candlemas, Easter and All Saints, and the soulscot or mortuary payment were a formidable list.[68] All parish churches did not possess all these rights; Wulfstan was concerned that many of them went unpaid and not all those which were paid went to the priest rather than the lord. But the setting up of parishes may have had a similar effect to that of the new estates of the tenth century, namely the more determined exaction of dues. Parish development brought the priest and his sacraments into the heart of the local community; it also brought the man to whom dues were paid to live among them. The priest held a normal landholding in the village, yet enjoyed dues often onerous to provide. The tension inherent in the position of the parish clergy lay behind Wulfstan's attempts to define the separate status of the priest.

Tenth-century development had brought priest and people together at a time of lay religious enthusiasm and exposed each to the scrutiny of the other. Lay piety is most obvious in parochial growth and church-building itself, but it is evident in the crude religious sculpture produced in the East Midlands at this date: it is sculpture distinguished by quantity not quality. In the cross fragments of Gunwade, Moulton or Nassington in Northamptonshire, of Crowle in Lincolnshire (fig. 69), the round-shafted crosses of the Peak District or the decorated grave-slabs found throughout the region, it is the mass piety of lay patrons not the high artistic output of monastic centres like Breedon, Peterborough or Repton which we are seeing, and it is an expression of lay piety difficult to parallel on this scale from southern England.

The face-to-face intimacy of priest and congregation was epitomized in the church building itself. Many tenth-century churches were small. The first church at Raunds measured no more than 5.7 × 4.3m externally, with a tiny chancel.[69] The surviving church at Wittering is small in dimension and its huge chancel arch brought priest and people together (fig. 70). These were not buildings designed to separate off and guard the priest and his mysteries. The effects of such proximity are not necessarily simple. It fuelled religious enthusiasm and brought the reality of religion into daily existence; in so doing it may have offset heretical development.[70] Yet, especially when combined with the payment of church dues, it fostered that criticism of the clergy which elsewhere formed the basis of eleventh-century heresy.[71] It prompted reformers like Wulfstan to consider urgently the need to cleanse and organize the clergy.

The *Northumbrian Priests' Law* was aimed at a parish clergy still integrated into their local society. They are married, or have a permanent house-mate;

Figure 69. Crowle cross shaft.

the deacon of Lindsey whose son was educated at Ramsey was not exceptional.[72] They might be drunkards or tavern-minstrels,[73] need to be warned against carrying weapons in church or fighting.[74] Their command of the intricate rituals of the church was not always great; they were to be wary of performing the annual services in the wrong order, of misconducting the ordeal.[75] They were not to celebrate mass more than three times a day, nor in an unconsecrated building, without a consecrated altar, without wine, with a wooden chalice and so on.[76] They were to be ready to admonish their flock,[77] a difficult task for men who lived constantly among them. The aim of the author is to set the clergy above reproach, more fundamentally to separate them by style of life from their flock. The purity of the minister and the correctness of the rituals must be obvious to parishioners in daily contact with the blemishes in both, and are necessary to the effectiveness of the sacramental duties of the priest.

In the *Northumbrian Priests' Law*, in the synods referred to there and in the *Canons Enacted under King Edgar*,[78] the aim was to purify and underline the separate status of the clergy for a ministry now so publicly carried out. The attempts failed, at least in view of later complaints about the parish clergy. It is ironical that the religious enthusiasms which created and resulted from the parish structure of eastern England in the tenth and eleventh centuries, which fed on a new intimacy of priest and people, should have resulted in attempts to separate clearly the clerical order and its lifestyle from that of laymen.

Figure 70. Saxon chancel arch of Wittering church (reproduced by permission from H.M. and J. Taylor, *Anglo-Saxon Architecture*, vol.II, Cambridge University Press, 1965).

Epilogue

By the tenth and eleventh centuries the social and economic picture of the East Midlands is, largely thanks to a relative and novel abundance of documentation, becoming clear. It is a picture of economic growth, of urban and industrial development; of the curtailing of freedom for many yet equally of a large group of prosperous minor nobility; of parish formation and ecclesiastical provision alongside the rise of new monastic estates; of a region now part of the larger political unit of England, now dominated by great nobles and churchmen whose rise had been an offshoot of the unification of England.

By the tenth and eleventh centuries our picture is clear precisely because of improved documentation, and as the source material (or lack of it) determined so many of the questions which could and could not be asked about the entire period, there must be a suspicion that the social and economic structures we see in the late Saxon period are not new, but merely have the illusion of novelty because they are visible for the first time. Is the picture already old? Have significant changes occurred between the fifth and eleventh centuries?

Some aspects of the region's life had altered slowly if at all. Society remained deeply unequal throughout, and the elites of church and nobility were sustained in the eleventh century as in the sixth and seventh by the enforced diversion of peasant surpluses and labour. The contrast between a Leofric or Wulfric at the end of the Saxon period and a royal official like Blæcca or a prince like Frithuric at the beginning should not be overdrawn. The powers which each wielded over the lives of others was essentially similar and sustained on the same basis.

The kin-group and family remained throughout an important unit in the lives of all men and women, whether we are looking at the burial of the dead in a sixth-century cemetery or the motives for monastic foundation in the late tenth. The records show the wide family connections of the tenth- and eleventh-century nobility and churchmen. This is an inevitable function of the concerns and origin of our sources, and we should be wary of generalizing from it to the size and nature of the operative kin-group at all levels of society and through the whole period. 'Claiming kin' may be most actively pursued when and where there is most to gain; the kin-group may vary according to circumstances, as the persistence of the household unit even in extended kin-systems demonstrates. The late Saxon nobility are certainly atypical in the extent of their influence and power. Although it is safe to conclude that the family was the most significant community in the life of every man and woman it would be unwise to generalize about its composition from limited examples drawn from the upper levels of society.

Beyond these and similar continuities important changes did occur which are more than the illusions of fluctuating source material. The scanty written records of town growth and industry at the end of the period are backed by archaeological excavation and by the evidence of coinage, both confirming a rapid economic advance from the late ninth century onwards. This is a significant take-off, even though we should not ignore the importance of exchange in the earlier centuries. The relationship between town growth and the less well understood rural and agrarian economy is problematic. Towns called into being by the Viking invasions, by the needs of defence and by royal action provided markets which must have stimulated different attitudes to exchange and production in the countryside. Yet that town growth cannot itself be explained solely in terms of external factors. If some rural change was triggered by urban stimulus, developments in the countryside fed the urban phenomenon. Town and industrial growth, if not origins, can be explained only in relation to an expanding local market. New patterns of landholding, and especially the possibility of a land market opened up by invasion and by changes in landholding and inheritance, ramified through the agrarian economy. New types of estate were formed, demonstrably different from those of the sixth and seventh centuries, with novel needs and demands and in some cases with a capability and desire to produce for and sell on an expanding market. All this makes it likely that the picture of, for example, changing boundaries of freedom and serfdom, or the large group of lesser nobility which can be identified in the tenth and eleventh centuries are relatively new.

Older answers to the problem of change within this period, especially in the East Midlands, tended to be couched in racial or ethnic terms. The region was twice invaded, by Germanic, for want of a better word, Anglo-Saxon invaders in the fifth and sixth centuries, by Vikings in the ninth, tenth and eleventh. In both cases invaders remained as settlers, but the view that these settlements transformed the region is now highly suspect. The scale of both movements has been much disputed, and if no firm and final answer has emerged it is clear that neither can any longer be seen as sufficient in size, nature or motivation to alter radically patterns of settlement, agriculture or economy. At these levels, where we are concerned with the mechanisms of exploitation whether of people or of land, invasion and take-over may be expected to have a minimal impact – unless, that is, the invasion produces a total overwhelming of the native population which in neither instance appears to have been the case.

At other levels invaders may play a more important role. Their arrival inevitably creates new circumstances or alters old ones, and both they and the existing inhabitants react to these changes. Thus the coming of the Anglo-Saxons contributed to that situation of local conflict and petty war which marked the centuries of transition from Roman Britain, and consequently played a part in the emergence of a society dominated by princely warlords (whether British or Anglo-Saxon). Viking invasions led to fortification and spurred town growth and thus new royal demands. They contributed, if sometimes very indirectly, to the new administrative and political groupings of the late Saxon period, if only to the extent that some of these were organized against them. Viking rule was the spur and the legitimation for West Saxon kings to conquer and assimilate the East Midlands into the kingdom of England. Vikings were a factor accelerating existing changes in landholding patterns and the land market.

At the end of the period when the evidence is fuller we can begin to explore how these foreign groups were perceived. Byrhtferth, writing the *Life of Oswald* at the end of the tenth century, knew and thought it worth recording that Oswald's grandparents, his uncle Oda's parents, were pagan Danes – pagan and Danes, both attributes seemed significant in the ancestry of two future archbishops. In the eleventh century new Danish landlords stood out in the Fenlands. The sharp practice of land-hungry churchmen was not specifically directed against them, though that was how it was remembered at Ramsey almost a century later. Danish settlers certainly filled the unenviable position of 'comers-in' in all societies; legitimate objects of suspicion, with at least a temporarily high profile. But awareness of them was not constant; some of it was affected by the post-Norman Conquest perspective on the late Anglo-Saxon past and other evidence suggests a fairly rapid assimilation into local society.

It would be foolhardy to write the Germanic invaders and Danish settlers out of the history of the East Midlands, but dangerous to interpret that history along ethnic lines. If a Christian community under a British overlord maintained itself within the defences of fifth and sixth-century Lincoln it probably looked little different from the Anglo-Saxon overlords and communities elsewhere in Lincolnshire: all were faced with the unstable situation of invasion and local power struggles. Eventually the successful leaders of this political world came to identify themselves (and thus by association their followers) through ancestry and affiliation. Since most of these successful leaders saw themselves as pagan Germanic in origin that became the dominant picture of East Midlands history. But their political myth-making should not blind us to the possibilities of British survival. Tenth- and eleventh-century southern observers might speak of the Danelaw, but we must be aware that questions of separatism were more complex than racial divisions. Invasion and new lordship rather than Anglo-Saxon or Danish race were the crucial factors.

The coming of Christianity and its gradual extension are certainly as significant if not more so than the ethnic identities of invaders. Christianity not only contributed new beliefs, it created new loyalties and groupings; monasteries and to a much lesser extent dioceses played an important role in economic and political as much as in religious life. The growth of parishes with their demands for tithes and other payments affected the day-to-day life of the village community. The church acquired new estates and made new demands, first in the conversion period and then again in the tenth century, affecting landholding and inheritance at the upper levels of society and freedom and villeinage at the lower.

Between the fifth and the eleventh centuries the East Midlands were never a single coherent political unit. Their history was continually affected by broader political changes. They were involved first in the rise of the dynasty and kingdom of Mercia and the local wars of the sixth to eighth centuries over tribute and loot. By the tenth century they were incorporated in the kingdom of England ruled over by southern, West Saxon kings through powerful local officials and families. These political and administrative changes, like the ecclesiastical developments, belong at the centre not on the margins of the region's history. Kingdoms, ealdormanries and shires created communities which took on real meaning as they were expressed in their courts and meetings. The transformation of landholding, arguably so important in the agrarian economy, came about as much because of ecclesiastical need for land and royal need for followers as because of the arrival of new Viking landlords or of fresh economic demands. Even the lives of peasant farmers, arguably remote from the courts of kings, bishops and nobles, were touched by changing demands for tribute and by new estate patterns largely determined by changes in the structure of power. The search for turning points in history is in many ways a futile, even an illegitimate quest. But if we must mark them in the East Midlands it should not be by the arrival of Anglo-Saxons or Danes, but by the coming of Christianity, the rise of Mercia and the growth of the kingdom of England.

Abbreviations

Note Places of publication are given only for works published outside the United Kingdom. In abbreviating less frequently cited periodicals the commonly accepted usage of *Soc.* for *Society*, *J.* for *Journal*, *Trans.* for *Transactions* etc. has been followed. Other abbreviations are listed below.

Anglo-Saxon Cemeteries	Rahtz, P., Dickinson, T. and Watts, L. (eds.), *Anglo-Saxon Cemeteries, 1979*, The fourth Anglo-Saxon symposium at Oxford (BAR 82, 1980)
Arch.J.	*Archaeological Journal*
ASC	*Anglo-Saxon Chronicle*, ed. and trans. in *EHD*, I and II, references are by year of entry in this edition.
ASE	*Anglo-Saxon England*, ed. P. Clemoes
BAR	British Archaeological Reports (British Series unless otherwise indicated)
Bede, *Eccles.Hist.*	Bede, *Ecclesiastical History of the English People*, ed. and trans. B. Colgrave and R.A.B. Mynors (1969)
BL	British Library
BNumJ	*British Numismatic Journal*
CBA	Council for British Archaeology
Chron.Ram.	*Chronicon Abbatiae Rameseiensis*, ed. W.D. Macray (Rolls Series 83, 1886)
DB	Domesday Book
Dornier, *Mercian Studies*	*Mercian Studies*, ed. A. Dornier (1977)
Darby, *Domesday England*	H.C. Darby, *Domesday England* (1977)
EHD	*English Historical Documents*, I, ed. D. Whitelock (2nd edn, 1979), II, ed. D.C. Douglas and G. Greenaway (2nd edn, 1981)
EHR	*English Historical Review*
Fl.Wig.	Florence of Worcester, *Chronicon ex Chronicis*, ed. B. Thorpe (2 vols, 1848–9)
Hugh Candidus, *Chronicle*	*The Chronicle of Hugh Candidus, a monk of Peterborough*, ed. W.T. Mellows (1949)
Liber Eliensis	*Liber Eliensis*, ed. E.O. Blake (Camden 3rd ser. 92, 1962)
Meaney, *Gazetteer*	A. Meaney, *A Gazetteer of Early Anglo-Saxon Burial Sites* (1964)
Med. Arch.	*Medieval Archaeology*
Robertson	*Anglo-Saxon Charters*, ed. A.S. Robertson (1939)
S.	P.H. Sawyer, *Anglo-Saxon Charters, an annotated list and bibliography* (1968). All references to charters are cited by their number in this list.
Stenton, *Preparatory*	F.M. Stenton, *Preparatory to Anglo-Saxon England*, ed. D.M. Stenton (1970)
TRHS	*Transactions of the Royal Historical Society*

Notes

1 The Land

1. A.E.B. Owen, '*Hafdic*, a Lindsey name and its implications', *J. English Place-Name Soc.*, VII (1974–5), 45–56.
2. H.E. Hallam, *The New Lands of Elloe* (1954), 15, 17–18.
3. J.H. Tallis and V.R. Switsur, 'Studies on south Pennine peats, VI: a radio-carbon pollen diagram from Featherbed Moss, Derbyshire', *J. Ecology*, LXI (1973), 743–51.
4. S. 679 and J.E.B. Gover, A. Mawer and F.M. Stenton, *Place-Names of Nottinghamshire* (1940), 10.
5. *DB*, I, 230r.
6. K. Cameron, 'Anglo-Saxon and Danish period', in *Nottingham and its Region*, ed. K.C. Edwards (1966), 199.
7. C. Hart, 'Hereward the Wake', *Procs. Cambs. Antiquarian Soc.*, LXV (1974), 28–40 at p. 38.
8. H.E. Hallam, *Rural England 1066–1348* (1981), 96.
9. *DB*, I, 209r.
10. Hallam, *Rural England*, 94–103.
11. *ASC* 'A', 917.
12. M.W. Barley, 'Lincolnshire rivers in the Middle Ages', *The Architectural and Archaeological Society of the County of Lincoln. Reports and Papers* (1938), 21.
13. A. Rogers, 'The origins of Newark, the evidence of local boundaries', *Trans. Thoroton Soc.*, LXXVIII (1974), 16.
14. J. Steane, *The Northamptonshire Landscape. Northamptonshire and the Soke of Peterborough* (1974), 135.
15. Simeon of Durham, *Historia Regum*, 764, *EHD*, I, 267.
16. *DB*, I, 212r.
17. *Leis Willelme* 26, printed in F. Liebermann, *Die Gesetze der Angelsachsen* (Halle, 1903), I, 510; *Leges Edwardi Confessoris* 12, *ibid.*, 637–8.
18. *Leges Edwardi Confessoris* 12.9, *ibid.*, 639.
19. B. Eagles, *The Anglo-Saxon Settlement of Humberside* (BAR 68.1, 1979), 182.
20. A.E. Brown and A. Hannan, 'Watling Street and the Gartree Road, some work on two Roman roads in Northamptonshire', *Northants. Arch.*, XIII (1978), 91.
21. S. 556.
22. S. 566.
23. I.D. Margary, *Roman Roads in Britain* (1967), 238ff.
24. Steane, *op. cit.*, 62 and 64.
25. S. 977; A.E. Brown, T.R. Key and C. Orr, 'Some Anglo-Saxon estates and their boundaries in south west Northamptonshire', *Northants. Arch.*, XII (1977), 171.
26. N. Brooks, 'The development of military obligations in eighth- and ninth-century England', in *England before the Conquest*, ed. P. Clemoes and K. Hughes (1971), 69–84.
27. *DB*, I, 280r.
28. *DB*, I, 337r.
29. *ASC* 'A', 873, 874.
30. *ASC* 'C', 1013.
31. *ASC* 'A', 918 (*recte* 915), 921 (*recte* 918), 923 (*recte* 920).
32. J. Dyer, 'Earthworks of the Danelaw frontier', in *Archaeology and the Landscape*, ed. P.J. Fowler (1972), 222–36.
33. *DB*, I, 337r.
34. *Ibid.*, 280r.
35. *Ibid.*, 284v, 288r, 283r, 347r, 273r.
36. *Ibid.*, 375v, 376r, 343r.
37. T.A.M. Bishop, 'The Norman settlement of Yorkshire', in *Essays in Economic History*, ed. E.M. Carus-Wilson, II (1962), 10–11.
38. *DB*, I, 284r.
39. *Tatuini Opera Omnia*, Corpus Christianorum, Ser. Latina, 133 (1968), 172.
40. *Ibid.*, 173.
41. Felix, *Life of Guthlac*, ed. and trans. B. Colgrave (1956), ch. 24.
42. *Chron. Ram.*, 127–8.
43. Abbo of Fleury, *Vita Sancti Eadmundi*, Patrologiae Cursus Completus, ed. J.P. Migne, 139 (Paris, 1880), col. 509.
44. Beowulf, *Anglo-Saxon Poetry*, trans. R.K. Gordon (1926), 28–9.
45. S. 495, traced and discussed by

Brown, Key and Orr, *op. cit.*,
155–63.
46. S. 1014.
47. S. 922.
48. S. 768.
49. S. 977.

2   The Agrarian Economy

1. J. Hatcher, *Plague, Population and
the English Economy* (1977), 68 and
references. Cf. Darby, *Domesday
England*, 89.
2. J.F.R. Walmsley, 'The *censarii* of
Burton Abbey and the Domesday
population', *North Staffs. J. of Field
Studies*, VII (1968), 73–80.
3. J.C. Russell, *British Medieval
Population* (Albuquerque, 1948),
22–33, and cf. J. Krause, 'The
medieval household: large or small',
Economic History Rev., 2nd ser., IX
(1957), 420–32.
4. Based on Darby, *Domesday England*, 338–45.
5. D. Owen, 'Chapelries and rural
settlement; an examination of some
of the Kesteven evidence', in
*Medieval Settlement, Continuity
and Change*, ed. P.H. Sawyer (1976),
66–71.
6. M.W. Barley, 'The medieval period',
in *Nottingham and its Region*, ed.
K.C. Edwards (1966), 204–13.
7. H.E. Hallam, *Rural England 1066–
1348* (1981), 95.
8. R. Millward, 'Leicestershire from
1100–1400', in *Leicester and its
Region*, ed. N. Pye (1972), 236.
9. Hallam, *op. cit.*, 97.
10. A. Boddington and G. Cadman,
'Raunds – an interim report on
excavations 1977–80', *Anglo-Saxon
Studies in Archaeology and
History*, 2, ed. D. Brown, J.
Campbell and S. Chadwick Hawkes, BAR 92 (1981), 103–22.
11. *Ibid.*, 122.
12. See e.g. P.H. Sawyer, *From Roman
Britain to Norman England* (1978),
ch. III.
13. E.g. by Hatcher, *op. cit.*, 58–61.
14. M.E. Jones, 'Climate, nutrition and
disease: an hypothesis of Romano-
British population', in *The End of
Roman Britain*, ed. P.J. Casey (BAR
71, 1979), 231–51.
15. Boddington and Cadman, *op. cit.*,
110 fig. 1.8, 118–22.

16. L. Wilkinson, 'Problems of analysis
and interpretation of skeletal
remains', in *Anglo-Saxon
Cemeteries, 1979*, ed. P. Rahtz, T.
Dickinson and L. Watts (BAR 82,
1980), 221–31.
17. P. Addyman, K.R. Fennell and L.
Biek, 'A dark-age settlement at
Maxey, Northamptonshire', *Med.
Arch.*, VII (1964), 42, 59, 65.
18. Robertson, no. 7.
19. Wilkinson, *op. cit.*, 230.
20. Robertson, no. 39.
21. Darby, *Domesday England*, 361.
22. *DB*, I, 233r.
23. *Ibid.*, 213r.
24. *Ibid.*, 273r.
25. Addyman *et al.*, 'Maxey', 65 and 71.
26. Robertson, App. 2, no. 9.
27. *DB*, I, 215v.
28. J. Clutton-Brock, 'The animal
resources', in *Archaeology of Anglo-
Saxon England*, ed. D.M. Wilson
(1976), 378.
29. *DB*, I, 211v.
30. *Ibid.*, 215v.
31. *Ibid.*, 209r.
32. D. Owen, *Church and Society in
Medieval Lincolnshire* (1971); 67.
33. P.H. Sawyer, 'The wealth of England in the eleventh century',
TRHS, 5th ser., XV (1965), 162–3.
34. Clutton-Brock, *op. cit.*, 382.
35. *DB*, I, 205r.
36. *Ibid.*, 192rv, 196v.
37. *Ibid.*, 280r.
38. *Tatuini Opera Omnia*, Corpus
Christianorum, Ser. Latina, 133
(1968), 203.
39. Robertson, App. 2, no. 9.
40. *DB*, I, 280r.
41. S. Applebaum, 'Roman Britain', *The
Agrarian History of England and
Wales*, I.ii, ed. H.P.R. Finberg
(1972), 83–7.
42. P. Addyman, 'Late Saxon settlements in the St Neots area III: The
village and township of St Neots',
Procs. Cambs. Antiquarian Soc.,
LXIV (1972–3), 94.
43. P.J. Fowler, 'Agriculture and rural
settlement', in Wilson (ed.), *op. cit.*,
27.
44. Addyman *et al.*, 'Maxey', 20–1.
45. P. Everson, 'An excavated Anglo-
Saxon sunken-featured building and
settlement site at Salmonby,
Lincolnshire, 1972', *Lincs. History
and Archaeology*, VII (1973), 71.
46. Addyman, 'Late Saxon settlements,

II', 76.

47. M. Gelling, 'English place-names derived from the compound *wicham*', in *Place-name Evidence for the Anglo-Saxon Invasion and Scandinavian Settlements*, ed. K. Cameron (1977), 8–26.

48. G. Foard, 'Saxon settlement in Northamptonshire', *World Archaeology*, IX (1978), 358–74.

49. Cf. M. Bloch, 'The rise of dependent cultivation and seignorial institutions', *Cambridge Economic History of Europe*, I, ed. M.M. Postan (1971), 272–6, and M.I. Finley, *Ancient Slavery and Modern Ideology* (1983), 67–8, 77–8, 147.

50. See e.g. G.R.J. Jones, 'Early territorial organization in Gwynedd and Elmet', *Northern History*, X (1975), 3–27, and 'Multiple estates and early settlement', in Sawyer (ed.), *op. cit.*, 15–40.

51. BL, MS Harl. 3271, f. 6v, and see C. Hart, 'The Tribal Hidage', *Trans. Royal Historical Soc.*, 5th ser., XXI (1971), 133–57.

52. Bede, *Eccles. Hist.*, bk. 5, ch. 19.

53. B. Cox, 'The place-names of the earliest English records', *J. English Place-name Soc.*, VII (1976), 12–66.

54. *DB*, I, 209r.

55. *Ibid.*, 219r.

56. M.W. Bishop, 'Multiple estates in late Anglo-Saxon Nottinghamshire', *Trans. Thoroton Soc.*, LXXXV (1982 for 1981), 37–47.

57. The fullest and best description of these estates is still F.M. Stenton, 'Types of manorial structure in the northern Danelaw', *Oxford Studies in Social and Legal History*, II (1910), 3–96.

58. J. Campbell, *Bede's Reges and Principes* (Jarrow Lecture, 1979).

59. Bede, *Eccles. Hist.*, bk. 4, ch. 19.

60. S. 1805.

61. W.T. Potts, 'The pre-Danish estate of Peterborough Abbey', *Procs. Cambs. Antiquarian Soc.*, LXV (1974), 13–27.

62. C. Phythian-Adams, 'Rutland reconsidered', in Dornier, *Mercian Studies*, 63–84.

63. J. Campbell, 'The first century of Christianity in England', *Ampleforth J.*, LXXVI.1 (1971), 13–14.

64. R. Powell, 'The Lichfield St Chad Gospels', *The Library*, 5th ser., XX

(1965), 26.

65. T.M. Charles-Edwards, 'The distinction between land and moveable wealth in Anglo-Saxon England', in Sawyer, *op. cit.* (1976), 180–7.

66. J. Campbell, 'Bede's words for places', in *Names, Words and Graves: Early Medieval Settlement*, ed. P.H. Sawyer (1979), 47–8.

67. See, e.g., G. Fellows-Jensen, *Scandinavian Settlement Names in the East Midlands* (Copenhagen, 1978), 89, 372.

68. A.E. Brown, T.R. Key and C. Orr, 'Some Anglo-Saxon estates and their boundaries in south-west Northamptonshire', *Northants. Arch.*, XII (1977), 155–76.

69. S. 495.

70. S. 977.

71. Bishop, 'Multiple estates', 42–5.

72. D. Knowles, *The Monastic Order in England* (1966), 702–3.

73. *Chron. Ram.*, ch. 25.

74. S. 792.

75. S. Raban, *The Estates of Thorney and Crowland* (1977), 19–20.

76. Robertson, no. 39.

77. E. King, *Peterborough Abbey 1086–1310, A Study in the land market* (1973), 6–11.

78. R.V. Lennard, *Rural England 1086–1135* (1959), 357–8, 361–2 and 378–9.

79. J. Raftis, *The Estates of Ramsey Abbey* (Toronto, 1957), 7 and n.44.

80. *Anglo-Saxon Charters*, II: *Charters of Burton Abbey*, ed. P.H. Sawyer (1979), xxxviii–xlvii.

81. *Ibid.*, xliii.

82. C. Hart, 'Athelstan 'Half King' and his family', *ASE*, II (1973), 115–44.

83. *Chron. Ram.*, 130–43.

84. P.H. Sawyer, personal communication.

85. P.A. Stafford, 'The "farm of one night" and the organization of King Edward's estates in Domesday', *Economic History Rev.*, 2nd ser., XXIII (1980), 491–502.

86. *DB*, I, 273r.

87. *Ibid.*, 209r and v.

3   Towns, Trade and Industry

1. J. Campbell, 'Bede's words for places', in *Names, Words and Graves: Early Medieval Settlement*, ed. P.H. Sawyer (1979), 34–42.

2. On St Paul-in-the-Bail I am grateful for information on recent redating of the church and cemetery to the Trust for Lincolnshire Archaeology; full report to be published in the Archaeology of Lincoln series. On Blæcca the praefectus of Lincoln, Bede, *Eccles. Hist.*, II, 16.

3. D. Hill, 'Continuity from Roman to medieval: Britain', in *European Towns, their Archaeology and Early History*, ed. M.W. Barley (1977), 293–302.

4. M. Hebditch, 'A Saxo-Norman pottery kiln discovered in Southgate St, Leicester, 1964', *Trans. Leics. Arch. and Hist. Soc.*, XLIII (1967–8), 4–9.

5. C. Colyer and R.H. Jones, 'Flaxengate', *Lincs. History and Archaeology*, XII (1977), 75–6, and B.G. Coppack, 'The excavation of a Roman and medieval site at Flaxengate', *ibid.*, VII (1974), 74–5.

6. R.A. Hall, 'The pre-conquest *burgh* of Derby', *Derbys. Arch. J.*, XCIV (1976 for 1974), 16–23.

7. *DB*, I, 280r.

8. Meaney, *Gazetteer*, 159, and A. Ozanne, 'The Peak dwellers', *Med. Arch.*, VI–VII (1962–3), 28–9.

9. 'Barton-upon-Humber, Castledyke South', *Med. Arch.*, XXVII (1983), 184; J.R. Watkin, 'A Frankish bronze bowl from Barton-on-Humber', *Lincs. History and Archaeology*, XV (1980), 88–9.

10. *Liber Eliensis*, 19.

11. C. Arnold, 'Wealth and social structure: a matter of life and death', in *Anglo-Saxon Cemeteries*, 81–142.

12. R. Hodges, 'State formation and the role of trade in Middle Saxon England', in *Social Organization and Settlement*, ed. D. Green, C. Haselgrove and M. Spriggs (BAR International Ser., Suppl. 47. ii, 1978), 439–53.

13. J.P.C. Kent, 'From Roman Britain to Saxon England', in *Anglo-Saxon Coins*, ed. R.H.M. Dolley (1961), 7–8 and 20.

14. D.M. Metcalf, personal communication. For full discussion of *sceattas* see *Sceattas in England and on the Continent*, ed. D.M. Metcalf (BAR forthcoming).

15. D.M. Metcalf, 'Monetary affairs in Mercia in the time of Æthelbald', in Dornier, *Mercian Studies*, 91–4.

16. D. Perring, *Early Medieval Occupation at Flaxengate* (Archaeology of Lincoln, Report no. IX.1, 1981), 44.

17. A. Everitt, 'The primary towns of England', *Local Historian*, XI.5 (1975), 266–7.

18. *Ibid.*

19. S. Reynolds, *Introduction to the History of English Medieval Towns* (1977), 27–34.

20. S. Harvey, 'Royal revenue and Domesday terminology', *Economic History Rev.*, 2nd ser. (1967), 221–8.

21. C. Blunt, C.S.S. Lyon and I. Stewart, 'The coinage of southern England, 796–840', *BNumJ*, XXXII (1963), 1–74.

22. H.E. Pagan, 'Coinage in the age of Burgred', *BNumJ*, XXXIV (1965), 11–27, and C.S.S. Lyon, 'Presidential address: historical problems of the Anglo-Saxon coinage 2: the ninth century', *ibid*, XXXVII (1968), 230–4.

23. H.R. Mossop, *The Lincoln Mint* (1970), plate 1, nos. 1–6.

24. *Ibid.*, plate 1, nos. 7–11, and C.S.S. Lyon, 'Some problems in interpreting Anglo-Saxon coinage', *ASE*, V (1976), 191.

25. F.W. Kuhlicke, 'The Bedford Mint', *Bedfordshire Mag.*, XIII (1972), 168, and C. Blunt, 'The coinage of Athelstan, King of England 924–39', *BNumJ*, XLII (1974), 44–5.

26. *Ibid.*

27. *Ibid.*, 112.

28. M. Dolley, 'The Anglo-Danish and Anglo-Norse coinages of York', in *Viking Age York and the North*, ed. R.A. Hall (1978), 28.

29. D.M. Metcalf, 'Continuity and change in English monetary history c.973–1086, Part 2', *BNumJ*, LI (1981), 76–7.

30. *Ibid.*, 53.

31. *Ibid.*, 76–7, and Metcalf, personal communication. See M. Blackburn and D. Metcalf, 'Five finger exercises on the List hoard', in *Viking Age Coinage in the Northern Lands*, ed. M.A.S. Blackburn and D.M. Metcalf (BAR International ser. 122, 1981), 511 and *passim* for discussion of statistical problems in estimating mint output.

32. D.M. Metcalf, 'Geographical patterns of minting in medieval England', *Seaby's Coin and Medal Bull.* (1977), 354.

33. *Idem*, 'The ranking of boroughs, numismatic evidence from the

reign of Æthelred II', in *Ethelred the Unready*, ed. D. Hill, BAR 59 (1978), 210–12.

34. R.H.M. Dolley and D.M. Metcalf, 'The reform of the English coinage under Eadgar', in Dolley (ed.), *Anglo-Saxon Coins*, 136–68.

35. P. Stafford, 'Historical implications of the regional production of dies under Æthelred II', *BNumJ*, xlviii (1978), 40; M. Dolley, on Caistor, *BNumJ*, xxviii (1955–7), 88–92; on Torksey, *Numismatic Chron.*, xvi (1956), 293–5; on Louth, *BNumJ*, xxviii (1955–7), 499–504; 'A possible sixth Anglo-Saxon mint in Lincolnshire', *BNumJ*, xxix (1958–9), 51–4. F. Elmore Jones, 'A note on the mint at Horncastle', *BNumJ*, xxxvii (1968), 191–2.

36. D.M. Metcalf, 'Geographical patterns of minting', 354 and 391.

37. P. Stafford, 'Historical implications', 39 and n.31.

38. D.M. Metcalf, 'The ranking of boroughs', 170–3 and *passim*.

39. J.H. Williams, 'Northampton', *Current Arch.* no. 79 (1982), 253.

40. C. Mahany and D. Roffe, 'Stamford, the development of an Anglo-Scandinavian borough', *Anglo-Norman Studies*, v (1983), 197.

41. R.H. Wildgoose, 'Defences of the pre-conquest borough of Nottingham', *Trans. Thoroton Soc.*, lxv (1961), 19–26.

42. *DB*, I, 280r.

43. D. Hill, 'Late Saxon Bedford', *Beds. Arch. J.*, v (1970), 96–100.

44. J. Hassall and D. Baker, 'Bedford: aspects of town origins and development', *Beds. Arch. J.*, ix (1974), 79.

45. II Athelstan 12, 13 and 13.1.

46. R.A. Hall, 'The pre-conquest *burgh* of Derby', *Derbys. Arch. J.*, xciv (1976 for 1974), 19.

47. *ASC* Mercian Register 917.

48. Hall, *op. cit.*, 21.

49. Perring, *op. cit.*, 44.

50. *Ibid.*, 36 and 43.

51. L. Adams, 'Early Islamic pottery from Flaxengate, Lincoln', *Med. Arch.*, xxiii (1979), 218–9.

52. J. Williams, 'The early development of the town of Northampton', in Dornier, *Mercian Studies*, 149.

53. Mahany and Roffe, *op. cit.*, 197–219, and K. Kilmurry, *The Pottery Industry of Stamford*, Lincolnshire (BAR 84, 1980), 30.

54. *Ibid.*, 176–7 and 186–7.

55. Reynolds, *op. cit.* (1977), 37–42.

56. Perring, *op. cit.*, 41–2.

57. M. Blackburn, C. Colyer and M. Dolley, *Early Medieval Coins from Lincoln* (Archaeology of Lincoln, Report no. VI.1, 1983), 42.

58. P. Addyman and J.B. Whitwell, 'Some Middle-Saxon pottery types in Lincolnshire', *Antiquaries J.*, l (1970), 96–102.

59. P. Addyman, 'Late Saxon settlements in the St Neots area, II, Little Paxton', *Procs. Cambs. Antiquarian Soc.*, lxii (1969), 77; *idem*, 'Late Saxon settlements . . . III, The Village and Township of St Neots', *ibid.*, xliv (1972–3), 82.

60. Kilmurry, *op. cit.*, 134, 155–6.

61. *DB*, I, 338v, 345r, 351r and v, 354v, 355r, 356r.

62. Williams, *op. cit.*, 141–9.

63. E.M. Jope, 'The Saxon building-stone industry in southern and midland England', *Med. Arch.*, viii (1964), 91–118.

64. Kilmurry, *op. cit.*, 171.

65. *Ibid.*, 172.

66. *Geþyncđo* 6, *EHD*, I, 469.

67. Kilmurry, *op. cit.*, 172.

68. *DB*, I, 203r.

69. *Ibid.*

70. *Ibid.*, 280r.

71. *Ibid.*, 336r.

72. H.R. Loyn, 'Anglo-Saxon Stamford', in *The Making of Stamford*, ed. A. Rogers (1965), 25.

73. T.C. Lethbridge, 'The Anglo-Saxon settlement of Eastern England', in *Dark Age Britain*, ed. D.B. Harden (1956), 120–2.

74. J.G. Hurst, 'The pottery', in *Archaeology of Anglo-Saxon England*, ed. D.M. Wilson (1976), 299 and 307.

75. P.V. Addyman, K.R. Fennell and L. Biek, 'A dark-age settlement at Maxey, Northamptonshire', *Med. Arch.*, viii (1964), 69; Addyman, 'Late Saxon settlements in the St Neots area, III', 91ff.

76. *DB*, I, 344r, 360v, 219v, 210v, 214r.

77. Asser, *Life of King Alfred*, ed. W.H. Stevenson (1959), 87.

78. Williams, 'Northampton', *op. cit.* in n. 39, 345.

79. H.M. Taylor, *Anglo-Saxon Architecture*, III (1978), 742–3.

80. Jope, *op. cit.*

81. *Chron. Ram*, 165–6.

82. R. Cramp, 'Anglo-Saxon sculpture of the Reform period', *Tenth-century Studies*, ed. D. Parsons (1975), 184–6.
83. S. 1624.
84. *DB*, I, 272v.
85. *Ibid.*
86. Perring, (*op. cit.* in n. 16), 41–2; *The Vikings in England*, E. Roesdahl, J. Graham-Campbell, P. Connor and K. Pearson, ed. 101–3.
87. *Ibid.*
88. J.E. Mann, *Early Medieval Finds from Flaxengate*, Archaeology of Lincoln, XIV.1 (1982), 44–5.
89. *Op. cit.* in n.46.
90. *Op. cit.* in n.4.
91. Hurst, *op. cit.*, 301–3.
92. Kilmurry, *op. cit.*, 30ff.
93. Addyman, 'Late Saxon settlements in the St Neots area, III', 80.
94. Hurst, *op. cit.*, 323.
95. Kilmurry, *op. cit.*, 13–24.
96. L. Musset, 'Pour l'Étude des relations entre les colonies scandinaves d'Angleterre et de Normandie', *Melanges de Linguistique et de Philologie, in memoriam F. Mosse* (Paris, 1959), 330–9.
97. S. Lyon, 'Analysis of the material', in Mossop, *Lincoln Mint, op. cit.* in n.23, 13–15.

4 Sources and Problems

1. F.M. Stenton, 'The supremacy of the Mercian kings', *EHR*, xxxiii (1918), 433–52.
2. ASC 'E' 870, and Stenton, 'Medeshamstede and its colonies', *Preparatory*, 179–81.
3. *Anglo-Saxon Charters, II: Charters of Burton Abbey*, ed. P.H. Sawyer (1979).
4. *Chron. Ram.*; Hugh Candidus, *Chronicle*; *Liber Eliensis*.
5. *Life of Guthlac*, ed. and trans. B. Colgrave (1956).
6. *Chronicon Abbatiae de Evesham*, ed. W.D. Macray, Rolls Series, 29 (1863), 325–37, discussed by D. Rollason, *The Search for Saint Wigstan*, Vaughan Paper no. 27 (Univ. of Leicester, 1981).
7. P. Wormald, 'Bede, Beowulf and the conversion of the Anglo-Saxon aristocracy', in *Bede and Anglo-Saxon England*, ed. R.T. Farrell (BAR 46, 1978), 42–9.
8. Stenton, 'Lindsey and its kings', *Preparatory*, 127–30, and D. Dumville, 'Kingship, genealogies and regnal lists', in *Early Medieval Kingship*, ed. P.H. Sawyer and I. Wood (1977), 90.
9. M.T. Clanchy, *From Memory to Written Record* (1979), 12–17.
10. Stenton, 'Medeshamstede', *Preparatory*, 182.
11. *Liber Eliensis*, 98–9.
12. P.H. Sawyer, *From Roman Britain to Norman England* (1978), 136–42.
13. Meaney, *Gazetteer*, 40–1.
14. T. Bateman, *Vestiges of the Antiquities of Derbyshire* (1848), and *Ten Years Diggings in Celtic and Saxon Grave Hills* (1861).
15. 'Medieval Britain in 1972, pre-Conquest', *Med. Arch.*, xvii (1973), 146; C. Hills, 'The archaeology of Anglo-Saxon England in the pagan period, a review', *ASE*, viii (1979), 318.
16. See, e.g., D.H. Kennett, 'Seventh-century cemeteries in the Ouse valley', *Beds. Arch. J.*, viii (1974), 99–108, and A. Ozanne, 'The Peak dwellers', *Med. Arch.*, vi–vii (1962–3), 15–52.
17. T.C. Lethbridge, 'The Anglo-Saxon settlement of Eastern England', in *Dark Age Britain*, ed. D.B. Harden (1956), 119.
18. S.C. Hawkes and G.C. Dunning, 'Soldiers and settlers in Britain, fourth to fifth centuries', *Med. Arch.*, v (1961), 1–70.
19. Hills, *op. cit.*, 298–9.
20. J.N.L. Myres, *Anglo-Saxon Pottery and the Settlement of England* (1969).
21. Hills, *op. cit.*, 308–9.
22. J.K. Sørensen, 'Place-names and settlement history', in *Names, Words and Graves: Early Medieval Settlement*, ed. P.H. Sawyer (1977), 1–33.
23. B. Cox, 'The place-names of the earliest English records', *J. English Place-Name Soc.*, viii (1976), 12–66 and J. Campbell, 'Bede's words for places', in Sawyer (ed.), *Names, Words and Graves*, 34–51.
24. B. Cox, 'The significance of the distribution of English place-names in -hām in the Midlands and East Anglia', reprinted in *Place Name Evidence for the Anglo-Saxon Invasion and Scandinavian Settlements*, ed. K. Cameron (1977), 55–98.

25. Sørensen, *op. cit.* in n.22, 16.
26. See, e.g., K. Cameron, 'Scandinavian settlement in the territory of the Five Boroughs: the place-name evidence', in Cameron (ed.), *op. cit.*, 115–38.
27. G. Fellows-Jensen, *Scandinavian Settlement Names in the East Midlands* (Copenhagen, 1978).
28. Discussion in *ibid.*, 357–62.
29. Bede, *Eccles. Hist.*, 336 and 192.
30. *Ibid.*, 192.
31. ASC 'E', 963, printed in *Two of the Saxon Chronicles Parallel*, I, ed. J. Earle and C. Plummer (1952), 117.
32. Fellows-Jensen, *op. cit.*, 299–328, esp. 327–8.
33. *Ibid.*, 13–14.
34. M. Gelling, 'The charter bounds of Æscesbyrig and Ashbury', *Berks. Arch. J.*, LXIII (1967), 5–13, and *idem*, *Signposts to the Past* (1978), 181–3.
35. Cf. Sawyer, *Roman Britain to Norman England*, 156.
36. U. Weinreich, *Languages in Contact: findings and problems* (The Hague, 1963), *passim* and esp. 47–62; and P.H. Sawyer, *Age of the Vikings* (2nd edn, 1971), 169–71.
37. Gelling, *Signposts to the Past*, 236–40.
38. S. Harvey, 'Domesday Book and Anglo-Norman governance', *TRHS*, 5th ser., xxv (1975), 175, but cf. Clanchy, *op. cit.*
39. Fellows-Jensen, *op. cit.*, 291.
40. R.I. Page, 'How long did the Scandinavian language survive in England? The epigraphical evidence', in *England before the Conquest*, ed. P. Clemoes and K. Hughes (1971), 165–81.
41. M. Wakelin, *English Dialects, An introduction* (1977), 130–8.
42. See, e.g., G. Jones, 'Multiple estates and early settlement', in *Medieval Settlement, Continuity and Change*, ed. P.H. Sawyer (1976), 15–40; G.W.S. Barrow, *The Kingdom of the Scots: government, church and society from the eleventh to the fourteenth century* (1973), 7–68; Sawyer, *Roman Britain to Norman England*, ch. III.
43. A.K.G. Kristensen, 'Danelaw institutions and Danish society in the Viking Age: *sochemanni, liberi homines* and Königsfreie', *Medieval Scandinavia*, VIII (1975), 27–85, and

O. Fenger, 'The Danelaw and the Danish law', *Scandinavian Studies in Law*, XVI (1972), 85–96.

5 The End of Roman Britain

1. Bede, *Eccles. Hist.*, 48–50.
2. Cf. *ibid.*, 68, 186, 560.
3. Gildas, *The Ruin of Britain and other works*, ed. M. Winterbottom (1978), 26.
4. J. Whitwell, *The Coritani* (BAR 99, 1982), 153–5.
5. *Ibid.*, 155–7.
6. K.R. Fennell, 'Pagan Saxon Lincolnshire', *Arch. J.*, CXXXI (1974), 287.
7. C.F.C. Hawkes, *Arch. J.*, CIII (1946), 89–90.
8. B. Eagles, 'Anglo-Saxons in Lindsey and the East Riding of Yorkshire in the fifth century', in *Anglo-Saxon Cemeteries, 1979*, ed. P. Rahtz, T. Dickinson and L. Watts (BAR 82, 1980), 285–7.
9. Whitwell, *op. cit.*, 158.
10. See Eagles, *op. cit.*
11. D. Kennett, 'Seventh-century cemeteries in the Ouse Valley', *Beds. Arch. J.*, VIII (1974), 99 and esp. n.8.
12. Meaney, *Gazetteer*, 189.
13. C. Hills, 'The archaeology of Anglo-Saxon England in the pagan period, a review', *ASE*, VIII, 302–4.
14. W. Davies, 'Annals and the origin of Mercia', in Dornier, *Mercian Studies*, 19.
15. Meaney, *Gazetteer*, 201.
16. T.H.Mck. Clough, A. Dornier, R.A. Rutland, *Anglo-Saxon and Viking Leicestershire* (1975).
17. A. Ozanne, 'The Peak dwellers', *Med. Arch.*, VI–VII (1962–3), 15–52.
18. M. Faull, 'British survival in Anglo-Saxon Northumbria', in *Studies in Celtic Survival*, ed. L. Laing (BAR 37, 1977), 1–55, esp. 20.
19. Fennell, *op. cit.*, 285–6.
20. ASC 'A', 571.
21. P. Hunter Blair, 'The battle at Biedcanford in 571', *Beds. Mag.*, XIII (1971), 27–30.
22. Stenton, 'Lindsey and its kings', *Preparatory*, 129.
23. D. Dumville, 'Kingship, genealogies and regnal lists', in *Early Medieval Kingship*, ed. P.H. Sawyer and I. Wood (1977), 72–104, esp. 90.
24. I am grateful to the Trust for

Lincolnshire Archaeology for advance information on the redating of this church and cemetery; full report to appear in the Archaeology of Lincoln series.

25. Bede, *Eccles. Hist.*, 192.
26. *Ibid.*
27. K. Cameron, '*Eccles* in English place-names', in *Place-name Evidence for the Anglo-Saxon Invasion and Scandinavian Settlements*, ed. K. Cameron (1977), 1–7.
28. M. Gelling, 'English place-names derived from the compound *wīchām*', ibid., 8–26.
29. M. Gelling, *Signposts to the Past* (1978), 101.
30. J. Steane, *The Northamptonshire Landscape, Northamptonshire and the Soke of Peterborough* (1974), 33.
31. *Ibid.*, 77.
32. M. Todd, *The Coritani* (1973), 89, and Whitwell, *op. cit.*, 101 and 160.
33. D. Hall and P. Martin, 'Brixworth, Northamptonshire, an intensive Field Survey', *J.Brit.Archaeol.Ass.*, 132 (1979), 1–6.
34. G. Foard, 'Saxon settlement in Northamptonshire', *World Arch.*, IX (1978), 358–74.
35. T.M. Charles-Edwards, 'Kinship, status and the origins of the hide', *Past and Present*, LVI (1972), 3–33.
36. Hills, *op. cit.*, 317.
37. M. Faull, 'British survival in Anglo-Saxon Northumbria', in Laing (ed.), *op. cit.*, 5–7.
38. Hills, *op. cit.*, 318.
39. *Ibid.*, 318, and Fennell, *op. cit.*, 286.
40. L. Wilkinson, 'Problems of analysis and interpretation of skeletal remains', in *Anglo-Saxon Cemeteries*, 221–31.

6   Kings, Kingdoms and Churchmen

1. W. Davies and H. Vierck, 'The contexts of Tribal Hidage, social aggregates and settlement patterns', *Frühmittelalterliche Studien*, VIII (1974), 223–93.
2. Bede, *Eccles. Hist.*, 290.
3. BL MS Harley 3271, f. 6v., with full discussion in Davies and Vierck, *op. cit.*, and C. Hart, 'The Tribal Hidage', *TRHS*, 5th ser., XXI (1971), 133–57.
4. W. Davies, 'Annals and the origins of Mercia', in Dornier, *Mercian Studies*, 17–29.
5. Felix, *Life of Guthlac*, ed. and trans. B. Colgrave (1956), chs. 25, 27 and 40.
6. P. Hunter Blair, 'The Northumbrians and their southern frontier', *Archaeologia Aeliana*, 4th ser., XXVI (1948), 98–126.
7. Bede, *Eccles. Hist.*, 294.
8. S. Revill, 'King Edwin and the battle of Heathfield', *Trans. Thoroton Soc.*, LXXIX (1975), 40–9.
9. Bede, *Eccles. Hist.*, 290.
10. *The Blickling Homilies*, ed. R. Morris, Early English Text Society (repr. 1967), 89 and 95.
11. Eddius, *Life of Wilfrid*, ch. 20.
12. 'Barton-upon-Humber, Castledyke South', *Med. Arch.*, XXVII (1983), 184.
13. Bede, *Eccles. Hist.*, 190–2.
14. *Ibid.*, 336.
15. He appears in the charter S.1183, dated 772 x 787.
16. J. Campbell, *Bede's reges and principes*, Jarrow Lecture, 1979.
17. W. Davies, 'Middle Anglia and the Middle Angles', *Midland History*, II (1973), 18–20.
18. J. Campbell, 'Bede', in *Latin Historians*, ed. T.A. Dorey (1966), 181–2.
19. *Ibid.*
20. H. Mayr-Harting, *The Coming of Christianity to Anglo-Saxon England* (1972), 30–9.
21. Bede, *Eccles. Hist.*, 278.
22. *Ibid.*, 280.
23. D. Whitelock, 'The pre-Viking age church in East Anglia', *ASE*, I, 14.
24. Bede, *Eccles. Hist.*, 370.
25. *Ibid.*, 312.
26. *Ibid.*, 246.
27. *Ibid.*, 370.
28. H.M. Taylor, 'Corridor crypts on the continent and in England', *N. Staffs. J. of Field Studies*, IX (1968), 17–52.
29. H.M. Taylor and J. Taylor, *Anglo-Saxon Architecture*, I (1965), 108–14.
30. *Ibid.*, 384–6.
31. E. Gilbert, 'Brixworth and the English basilica', *Art Bull.*, XLVII (1965), 1–20, dating the building to the mid-eighth century.
32. R. Bailey, *The Early Christian Church in Leicester and its region* (Vaughan Paper, no. 25 Univ. of Leicester, 1980), 16–18.
33. Cf. W. Levison, *England and the*

Continent in the Eighth Century
(1946), 259–65.

34. J. Campbell, 'The first century of
Christianity in England', *Ampleforth J.*, LXXVI (1971), 13–14.

35. Bede, *Eccles. Hist.*, 246.

36. Felix, *Life of Guthlac*, ed. Colgrave,
ch. 20.

37. Eddius, *Life of Wilfrid*, ed. and
trans. B. Colgrave (1927), ch. 67.

38. Hugh Candidus, *Chronicle*, 50–1.

39. Bede, *Eccles. Hist.*, 246, 528.

40. Quoted in Stenton, 'Medeshamstede and its colonies', *Preparatory*,
182.

41. Bede, *Eccles. Hist.*, 336; Hugh Candidus, *Chronicle*, 7–10, and S.68.

42. Letter of Boniface to Æthelbald,
EHD, I, 820.

43. *ASC* 'A', 716.

44. *Ibid.*, 757.

45. D. Hill, *Atlas of Anglo-Saxon England* (1981), 83.

46. Letter of Alcuin to Osbert, *EHD*, I,
855.

47. R. Cramp, 'Schools of Mercian
sculpture', in Dornier, *Mercian
Studies*, 194–211.

48. *Ibid.*, figs. 57a, b, c; 59, 60a and p.
210 and 219.

49. R. Cramp, 'The Anglian tradition in
the ninth century', in *Anglo-Saxon
and Viking Age Sculpture and its
Context*, ed. J. Lang (BAR 49, 1978)
esp. her phase V, and 'Schools of
Mercian sculpture', 224.

50. D. Rollason, 'The cults of murdered
royal saints in Anglo-Saxon England', *ASE*, XI (1983), 3–5.

51. Simeon of Durham, *Historia
Regum*, 801, *EHD*, I, 276.

52. Roger of Wendover, *Flores
Historiarum*, 872, *EHD*, I, 282.

53. I am grateful to Professor Martin
Biddle for advance information on
the results of the Repton excavations. Much of what follows is
based on his findings.

54. See H.P.R. Finberg, *Early Charters
of the West Midlands* (1972), 218. I
am informed by Professor Biddle
that the burial is confirmed in a
reference in a Much Wenlock MS
pre-1104.

55. D. Rollason, *The Search for Saint
Wigstan* (Vaughan Paper no. 27,
Univ. of Leicester, 1981).

7 The Vikings and the Danelaw

1. *ASC* 'A', 874.

2. *Fl. Wig.*, I, 267.

3. *ASC* 'A', 841.

4. See, e.g., *ibid.*, 853.

5. I am grateful to Professor Martin
Biddle for information on his
excavations at Repton prior to
publication.

6. M.A. O'Donovan, 'An interim
revision of episcopal dates for the
province of Canterbury, 850–950, pt
I', *ASE*, I (1972), 27–8, 43–4; 'pt II',
ibid., II (1973), 95–6.

7. See their witness to S.878, 891, 899,
904 etc.

8. Treaty of Alfred and Guthrum, ch.
1, *EHD*, I, 416.

9. *ASC*, *Mercian Register*, 909, and D.
Rollason, 'List of saints' resting-places in Anglo-Saxon England', *ASE*,
VII (1978), 63 and 87, for their movement of relics there; *ASC*, *Mercian
Register*, 918, for Æthelflæd's burial
there, and Æthelweard, *Chronicle*,
ed. A. Campbell (1962), *s.a.* 910 for
her husband's burial there.

10. S.224 and P.H. Sawyer, 'The
charters of Burton Abbey and the
unification of England', *Northern
History*, x (1975), 28–39.

11. Æthelweard, *Chronicle*, ed.
Campbell, 51.

12. C. Phythian-Adams, 'Rutland
reconsidered', in Dornier, *Mercian
Studies*, 63–84, and esp. his 'The
emergence of Rutland and the making of the realm', *Rutland Record*, I
(1980), 5–12.

13. M. Dolley, *Viking Coins of the
Danelaw and of Dublin* (1965), 18.

14. *ASC* 'A', 914, 917 and *Liber Eliensis*, 98.

15. R. Hall, 'The pre-conquest *burgh* of
Derby', *Derbys. Arch. J.*, XCIV (1976
for 1974), 16–23.

16. *Liber Eliensis*, 98–9.

17. *ASC* 'A', 923, recte 920.

18. I. Stewart, 'The St Martin coins of
Lincoln', *BNumJ*, XXXVI (1967), 49–
54, and A. Smyth, *Scandinavian
York and Dublin*, II (New Jersey and
Dublin, 1979), 7.

19. F. Barlow, *The English Church,
1000–1066* (1963), 215.

20. *ASC* 'A', 'B', 'C', 'D', 942 and 'D',
943, and Smyth, *op. cit.*, II, 89–103.

21. *Ibid.*, 1–14.

22. Dolley, *op. cit.*, 25.

23. Simeon of Durham, *Historia Regum*, 939, *EHD*, I, 279.
24. *ASC* 'A', 'B', 'C', 'D', 942.
25. Many references are brought together and discussed by H.M. Chadwick, *Studies on Anglo-Saxon Institutions* (1905), 198–201.
26. III Æthelred c. 1.1.
27. Cf. F.M. Stenton, *Anglo-Saxon England* (3rd edn, 1971), 506–7.
28. See the figures compiled by G. Fellows-Jensen, *Scandinavian Settlement Names in the East Midlands* (Copenhagen, 1978), 232, table 3.
29. K. Cameron, 'The minor names and field names of the Holland division of Lincolnshire', in *The Vikings*, Proceedings of the symposium of the faculty of Arts of Uppsala, ed. T. Andersson and K.I. Sandred (Uppsala, 1978), 81–8.
30. K. Cameron, 'The Scandinavian settlement of eastern England: the place-name evidence', *Ortnamnsällskapets i Uppsala Årsskrift (1978)*, 7–17.
31. D. Wilson, 'The Scandinavians in England', in *The Archaeology of Anglo-Saxon England* (1976), 396–7.
32. D.M. Wilson, 'The Vikings' relationship with christianity in Northern England', *J. British Archaeol. Ass.*, xxx (1967), 37–46 and D. Whitelock, 'The conversion of the Eastern Danelaw', *Saga-book of the Viking Society for Northern Research*, xii (1941), 159–76.
33. E.g. P.H. Sawyer, *The Age of the Vikings* (2nd edn, 1971), 154–71.
34. P.H. Sawyer, *From Roman Britain to Norman England* (1978), 155–163.
35. Fellows-Jensen, *op. cit.*, 27.
36. Sawyer, *Roman Britain to Norman England*, 163, and Fellows-Jensen, *op. cit.*, 327–8.
37. Fellows-Jensen, *op. cit.*, 252.
38. *Ibid.*, 272–3.
39. *Ibid.*, *passim*.
40. *Ibid.*, 13–14.
41. M.F. Wakelin, *English Dialects. An Introduction* (1972), 137.
42. Sawyer, *Roman Britain to Norman England*, 162.
43. See above n.36.
44. D.M. Wilson, *The Viking Age in the Isle of Man* (Odense, 1974), 8–9.

8 The Last Century of Anglo-Saxon Rule

1. Life of Oswald, *EHD*, I, 913–4.
2. *ASC* 'C', 1013.
3. *Anglo-Saxon Charters, II: Charters of Burton Abbey*, ed. P.H. Sawyer (1979), xliii, and P. Stafford, 'The reign of Æthelred II, a study in the limitations on royal policy and action', in *Ethelred the Unready*, ed. D. Hill (BAR 59, 1978), 36.
4. *ASC* 'E', 1035.
5. *ASC* 'C' and 'B', 957.
6. *ASC* 'C', 1016.
7. D. Rollason, 'The cults of murdered royal saints in Anglo-Saxon England', *ASE*, xi (1983), 15–22.
8. *Ibid.*, 15 and 18.
9. M.A. O'Donovan, 'An interim revision of episcopal dates for the province of Canterbury, 850–950: part I', *ASE*, i (1972), 37–8.
10. On him and his family, A. Williams, 'Princeps Merciorum gentis: the family, career and connections of Ælfhere, ealdorman of Mercia, 956–83', *ASE*, x (1982), 143–72.
11. See C. Hart, 'Athelstan Half-King and his family', *ASE*, ii (1973), 115–44.
12. On Wulfric's family, Sawyer, *op. cit.* (1979), xxxviii-xliii.
13. *ASC* 'C', 1013.
14. Florence of Worcester, *Chronicon ex chronicis*, ed. B. Thorpe (1848–9), I, 993.
15. IV Edgar 2.1, *EHD*, I, 435.
16. P. Wormald, 'Æthelred the Lawmaker', in Hill (ed.), *op. cit.*, 61.
17. See, e.g., the St Brice day massacre of Danes, *ASC* 'C', 1002.
18. P. Stafford, 'The Laws of Cnut and the history of Anglo-Saxon royal promises', *ASE*, x (1982), 173–190.
19. Williams, *op. cit.*, 161–6.
20. *Vita Oswaldi*, *Historians of the Church of York and its Archbishops*, ed. J. Raine, I (1879), 401 and 404.
21. *Chron. Ram.*, 23–4.
22. *Liber Eliensis*, 105 and 96 n.5.
23. *Chron. Ram*, 112–14, 159–60.
24. *Ibid.*, 48–9.
25. *Ibid.*, 51, 52–5, 57, 79–80 etc.
26. *Ibid.*, 61.
27. *Anglo-Saxon Wills*, ed. D. Whitelock (1930), no. 13, and p. 134.
28. D. Whitelock, 'Dealings of the kings of England with Northumbria in the

tenth and eleventh centuries', in *The Anglo-Saxons, Studies . . . presented to B. Dickins*, ed. P. Clemoes (1959), 75–6.

29. Williams, *op. cit.*, 167–9.
30. *Ibid.*, 160–9.
31. See above, n.12.
32. *ASC* 'C', 1006.
33. Stafford, 'Æthelred II', 31–3.
34. D. Rollason, 'Lists of saints' resting-places in Anglo-Saxon England', *ASE*, VII (1978), 64–8, on the dating of the early portion of the *Secgan*.
35. Robertson, no. 7.
36. *Two of the Saxon Chronicles Parallel*, ed. J. Earle and C. Plummer, I (1892), 71.
37. Hugh Candidus, *Chronicle*, 27–8.
38. S.749.
39. S.548.
40. S.792.
41. Hugh Candidus, *Chronicle*, 50–1.
42. *Liber Eliensis*, 73–6; S.782; S.749.
43. S.792.
44. Hugh Candidus, *Chronicle*, 28.
45. *Chron. Ram.*, 35–8.
46. S. Raban, *The Estates of Thorney and Crowland* (1977), 8–9.
47. C. Hart, 'Eadnoth first abbot of Ramsey and the foundation of Chatteris and St. Ives', *Procs. Cambs. Antiquarian Soc.*, LVI–LVII (1964), 61–7.
48. Simeon of Durham, *Historia ecclesiae Dunhelmensis*, in *Opera Omnia*, ed. T. Arnold, I (Rolls Series, 1882–5), 87, 89, 91–2, 94.
49. *Chron. Ram.*, 52–5.
50. C. Hart, *Early Charters of Eastern England* (1966), nos. 345 and 346; Raban, *op. cit.*, 12.
51. S.1536 and Sawyer, *op. cit.*, xv-xxxiv.
52. S.1226, 1233 and 1478.
53. Hugh Candidus, *Chronicle*, 66; Raban, *op. cit.*, 12.
54. *Chron. Ram.*, 51.
55. *Ibid.*, 50.
56. On this family see Hart, 'Eadnoth of Ramsey'.
57. *Liber Eliensis*, 85.
58. *Chron. Ram.*, 51.
59. Raban, *op. cit.*, 16–17.
60. Hugh Candidus, *Chronicle*, 67.
61. *Ibid.*, 66–7.
62. Raban, *op. cit.*, 16.
63. *Chron. Ram.*, 135–6.
64. Hugh Candidus, *Chronicle*, 47, 72–4 and J. Cooper, *The Last Four Anglo-Saxon Archbishops of York*

(Borthwick Papers no. 38, 1970) and above n.48. Archbishop Cynsige more likely endowed it as his burial place than originated here.
65. *Two of the Saxon Chronicles Parallel*, ed. Earle and Plummer, I, 183.
66. Hugh Candidus, *Chronicle*, 65.
67. *Ibid.*, 72–3.

9 Boundaries and Divisions

1. C. Hart, 'The kingdom of Mercia', in Dornier, *Mercian Studies*, 46.
2. S. Revill, 'King Edwin and the battle of Heathfield', *Trans. Thoroton Soc.*, LXXIX (1976 for 1975), 48 and map 42, and cf. the county boundaries pre-1974.
3. P. Hunter Blair, 'The Northumbrians and their southern frontier', *Archaeologia Aeliana*, 4th ser., XXVI (1948), 105–13.
4. *ASC* 'A', 829 and 942.
5. *Ibid.*, 923, *recte* 920.
6. Hunter Blair, *op. cit.*, 121, and R. Millward and A. Robinson, *The Peak District* (1975), 118–20.
7. Stenton, 'Lindsey and its kings', *Preparatory*, 134.
8. Alfred and Guthrum, 1, *EHD*, I, 416, and R.H.C. Davis, 'Alfred and Guthrum's frontier', *EHR*, XCVII (1980), 803–10.
9. C. Mahany and D. Roffe, 'Stamford, the development of an Anglo-Scandinavian borough', *Anglo-Norman Studies*, V (1983), 214–15.
10. J. Dyer, 'Earthworks of the Danelaw frontier', in *Archaeology and the Landscape*, ed. P.J. Fowler (1972), 222–36.
11. M. Wood, 'Brunanburh revisited', *Saga Book of the Viking Society*, XX.3 (1980), 200–17.
12. A. Smyth, *Scandinavian York and Dublin*, II (New Jersey and Dublin, 1979), 51–5.
13. Simeon of Durham, *Historia Regum*, 939, *EHD*, I, 279.
14. Eddius, *Life of Wilfrid*, ed. and trans. B. Colgrave (1927), chs. 46–7.
15. *ASC* 'A', 929, and 923, *recte* 920.
16. *ASC*, 'D', 925, *recte* 926.
17. *Ibid.*, 943.
18. *Ibid.*, 1065.
19. III Æthelred 1.1, *EHD*, I, 439.
20. Mahany and Roffe, *op. cit.*, 214–16.
21. *ASC* 'C', 1013, 1015.
22. *ASC* 'A', 917; *Fl. Wig.* 918.

23. C. Phythian-Adams, 'Rutland reconsidered', in Dornier, *Mercian Studies*, 78.
24. See C. Hart, *The Hidation of Northamptonshire* (1970), 13–14, 45 and *passim*, and cf. C. Taylor, 'The origin of the Mercian shires', in *Gloucestershire Studies*, ed. H.P.R. Finberg (1957), 17–45, and H.M. Chadwick, *Studies on Anglo-Saxon Institutions* (1905), 202–4. For the shire courts of Northamptonshire and Huntingdonshire operating by the late tenth century and before see *Liber Eliensis*, 85 and 99.
25. *ASC* 'C', 1016.
26. See the making of the Lindsey survey in the early twelfth century.
27. *ASC* 'C', 1016 and cf. *ibid.*, 993.
28. On Stamford, H. Loyn, 'Anglo-Saxon Stamford', in *The Making of Stamford*, ed. A. Rogers (1965), 15–33.
29. C. Hart, 'Athelstan *Half-King* and his family', *ASE*, II (1973), 142–3.
30. See above, n.24.
31. P. Stafford, 'The reign of Æthelred II, a study in the limitations on royal policy and action', in *Ethelred the Unready*, ed. D. Hill (BAR 59, 1978), 29.
32. H.P.R. Finberg, 'The ancient shire of Winchcombe', *Early Charters of the West Midlands* (1972), 228–35.
33. *ASC* 'A', 917.
34. III Æthelred *passim*.
35. On Rutland see F.M. Stenton, *Victoria County History, Rutland*, I (1908), 121–36, and C. Phythian-Adams, 'Rutland reconsidered', in Dornier, *Mercian Studies*, 63–84.
36. Phythian-Adams, *op. cit.*, 68 and 73, and his 'The emergence of Rutland and the making of the realm', *Rutland Record*, I (1980), 5–12.
37. IV Edgar 6, *EHD*, I, 435.
38. A.K.G. Kristensen, 'Danelaw institutions and Danish society in the Viking age: *sochemanni, liberi homines* and *Königs freie*', *Medieval Scandinavia*, VIII (1975), 83.
39. H.M. Cam, '*Manerium cum Hundredo*: the hundred and the Hundredal manor', *Liberties and Communities in Medieval England* (1963), 83 and 90.
40. *Ibid.*, 90.
41. B. Cox, 'Leicestershire moot sites – the place-name evidence', *Trans.* Leics. *Archaeological and Historical Soc.*, XLVII (1971–2), 14–21.
42. P. Bigmore, *The Bedfordshire and Huntingdonshire Landscape* (1979), 73, and cf. *The Place-names of Bedfordshire and Huntingdonshire*, ed. A. Mawer and F.M. Stenton (1926), 99, for *Shirhacche* in Willington.
43. Bigmore, *op. cit.*, 71.
44. Cox, *op. cit.*, 16.
45. O. Arngart, 'Three English hundred names', *Namn och Bygd*, LXVI (1978), 13–17, but cf. Cox, *op. cit.*, 17.
46. G. Fellows-Jensen, *Scandinavian Settlement Names in the East Midlands* (Copenhagen, 1978), 341–6.

10　Social Structure

1. R. Bradley, 'Anglo-Saxon cemeteries, some suggestions for research', in *Anglo-Saxon Cemeteries*, 172.
2. See the salutary warnings of I. Hodder, 'Social structure and cemeteries: a critical appraisal', *ibid.*, 161–76.
3. B. Chapman, 'Death, culture and society: a prehistorian's perspective', *ibid.*, 61–4.
4. *Beowulf*, ed. C.L. Wrenn (1953), ch. 43, ll. 3137ff.
5. E.-J. Pader, 'Material symbolism and social relations in mortuary studies', in *Anglo-Saxon Cemeteries*, 143–59.
6. Meaney, *Gazetteer*, 39.
7. *Ibid.*, 73.
8. C. Hills, 'The archaeology of Anglo-Saxon England in the pagan period, a review', *ASE*, VIII (1979), 321.
9. N. Brooks, 'Arms, status and warfare in Late Saxon England', in *Ethelred the Unready*, ed. D. Hill (BAR 59, 1978), 82–3.
10. *The Blickling Homilies*, ed. R. Morris (Early English Text Society, 73, 1880), 213.
11. Pader, *op. cit.*, 155–6.
12. C. Arnold, 'Wealth and social structure: a matter of life and death', in *Anglo-Saxon Cemeteries*, 120.
13. Meaney, *Gazetteer*, 41–2.
14. W. Smith and H. Wace (eds.), *Dictionary of Christian Biography*, I, 736 and 738; *Fl. Wig.*, I, 265.

15. Felix, *Life of Guthlac*, ed. and trans. B. Colgrave (1956), ch. 20.
16. Bede, *Eccles. Hist.*, 146–8.
17. Stenton, 'The historical bearing of place-name studies: the place of women in Anglo-Saxon society', *Preparatory*, 320.
18. *Chron. Ram.*, 126.
19. C. Hart, 'Eadnoth first abbot of Ramsey and the foundation of Chatteris and St. Ives', *Procs. Cambs. Antiquarian Soc.*, LVI–LVII (1964), 61–7.
20. S.792.
21. *Chron. Ram.*, 57–8.
22. Stenton, 'The historical bearing of place-name studies', *Preparatory*, 318–20.
23. *Chron. Ram.*, 52.
24. *Ibid.*, 135–6.
25. E. Searle, 'Women and the legitimisation of succession at the Norman Conquest', *Procs. of the Battle Conference on Anglo-Norman Studies, 1980*, ed. R. Allen Brown (1981), 159–70.
26. Stenton, 'The historical bearing of place-name studies', *Preparatory*, 329.
27. *DB*, I, 220v.
28. *Ibid.*, 231v, 283v, 284r, 280r.
29. *Chron. Ram.*, 59–60.
30. *Liber Eliensis*, 103.
31. S.1493.
32. S.1233.
33. *ASC* 'D', 943.
34. M. Campbell, 'Queen Emma and Ælfgifu of Northampton: Canute the Great's Women', *Medieval Scandinavia*, VI (1971), 66–79.
35. *DB*, I, 280v.
36. A. Klinck, 'Anglo-Saxon women and the law', *J. Medieval History*, VIII (1982), 112.
37. H.C. Darby, *Domesday England* (1977), 86–7.
38. A. Boddington and G. Cadman, 'Raunds, an interim report on excavations 1977–80', in *Anglo-Saxon Studies in Archaeology and History*, 2, ed. D. Brown, J. Campbell and S. Chadwick Hawkes (BAR 92, 1981), 111ff.
39. L. Wilkinson, 'Problems of analysis and interpretation of skeletal remains', in *Anglo-Saxon Cemeteries*, 229.
40. Meaney, *Gazetteer*, 37–8.
41. *Anglo-Saxon Cemeteries, 1979*, 338, cist grave 57/32.
42. *Ibid.*, grave H.B.I.
43. C. Arnold, 'Wealth and social structure: a matter of life and death', in *Anglo-Saxon Cemeteries*, 132–4.
44. K.R. Fennell, 'Pagan Saxon Lincolnshire', *Arch. J.*, CXXXI (1974), 285–6.
45. Meaney, *Gazetteer*, 79.
46. *Ibid.*, 72.
47. T.H.Mck. Clough, A. Dornier, R.A. Rutland, *Anglo-Saxon and Viking Leicestershire* (1975), 13 and 72 no. 97.
48. P. Addyman, K.R. Fennell and L. Biek, 'A dark-age settlement at Maxey, Northamptonshire', *Med. Arch.*, VIII (1964), 20–73.
49. T.M. Charles-Edwards, 'Kinship, status and the origins of the hide', *Past and Present*, LVI (1972), 3–33.
50. S.1805 and Bede, *Eccles. Hist.*, 336.
51. Mirce, 2, *EHD*, I, 470.
52. Norðleoda laga, 10, *EHD*, I, 469.
53. Geþyncðo, 2, *EHD*, I, 468.
54. *Ibid.*, 3, *ibid.*, 468.
55. See, e.g., W. Ullmann, *History of Political Thought: The Middle Ages* (1965), 31.
56. *DB*, I, 280v.
57. Map and discussion in *Anglo-Saxon Charters, II: Charters of Burton Abbey*, ed. P.H. Sawyer (1979), xvi, xxiii–xxxiv.
58. Hugh Candidus, *Chronicle*, 29–30.
59. *DB*, I, 234r.
60. *Ibid.*, 212r.
61. *Ibid.*, 285r.
62. *Ibid.*, 284v.
63. *Ibid.*, 233v.
64. Robertson, Appendix 2, 9.
65. R. Lennard, *Rural England, 1086–1135* (1959), 358 and 362.
66. R.H. Hilton, *A Medieval Society, The West Midlands at the end of the Thirteenth Century* (1966), 121–3.
67. S. Harvey, 'Evidence for settlement study, Domesday Book', in *Medieval Settlement, Continuity and Change*, ed. P.H. Sawyer (1976), 195–9.
68. *EHD*, II, 892–3.
69. *DB*, I, 281r.
70. M.I. Finley, *Ancient Slavery and Modern Ideology* (1983), 68–71.
71. F.M. Stenton, *The Free Peasantry of the Northern Danelaw* (1969), 6–8.
72. *Ibid.*, *passim*.

73. *Liber Eliensis*, 98–9.
74. *DB*, I, 280v.
75. Eddius, *Life of Wilfrid*, ed. and trans. B. Colgrave (1929), ch. 21.
76. *Law of the Northumbrian Priests*, 1 and 2, *EHD*, I, 472.
77. *EHD*, I, 604–5.
78. Felix, *Life of Guthlac*, ed. Colgrave, chs. 20 and 26.
79. *Ibid.*, chs. 16 and 17.
80. *Blickling Homilies*, ed. Morris, 213.
81. S.1487.
82. III Æthelred, 3 and 4, *EHD*, I, 440.
83. *Ibid.*, 4.
84. *Chron. Ram.*, 79–80.
85. S.1536 and 1487.
86. 'The Wanderer', *Anglo-Saxon Poetry*, trans. R.K. Gordon (1954), 73–4.
87. E.g. II Edward 6; VI Athelstan 1 §4 etc.
88. Wergeld, printed in F. Liebermann, *Die Gesetze der Angelsachsen* (Halle, 1903), I, 392–4.
89. H. Loyn, 'Kinship in Anglo-Saxon England', *ASE*, III (1974), 197–209.
90. B. Davison, 'Excavations at Sulgrave, Northamptonshire, 1968', *Arch. J.*, cxxv (1968), 305–7.
91. G. Beresford, 'Goltho manor, Lincs: the buildings and their surrounding defences', *Procs. of the Battle Conference on Anglo-Norman Studies*, 4, 1981, ed. R. Allen Brown (1982), 13–36.
92. Davison, *op. cit.*, 307; D.M. Wilson, 'Defence in the Viking Age', in *Problems in Economic and Social Archaeology*, ed. G. de G. Sieveking, I.H. Longsworth and K.E. Wilson (1976), 443–4.
93. *DB*, I, 205r.
94. *Chron. Ram.*, 52–3.
95. *Ibid.*, 135–6.
96. *Ibid.*, 63–4.
97. Boddington and Cadman, 'Raunds', *op. cit.* in n.38, 109.
98. P. Everson, 'An excavated Anglo-Saxon sunken-featured building and settlement site at Salmonby, Lincs., 1972', *Lincs. History and Archaeology*, VII (1973), 61–9.
99. P. Rahtz, 'Buildings and rural settlement', in *The Archaeology of Anglo-Saxon England*, ed. D.M. Wilson (1976), 75–6.
100. E.g. P.V. Addyman, 'Late Saxon settlements in the St Neot's Area III, The village and township of St

Neot's', *Procs. Cambs. Antiquarian Soc.*, LXIV (1972–3), 70–5.
101. *Ibid.* and cf. C.F. Tebbutt, 'An eleventh-century boat-shaped building at Buckden, Hunts.', *Procs. Cambs. Antiquarian Soc.*, LV (1961), 13–15.
102. D. Perring, *Early Medieval Occupation at Flaxengate* (Archaeology of Lincoln, Report no. IX.1, 1981), 36–40.
103. K. Kilmurry, *The Pottery Industry of Stamford, Lincolnshire, c.A.D. 850–1250* (BAR 84, 1980), 26–7.
104. F.H. Thompson, 'Anglo-Saxon sites in Lincolnshire, unpublished material and recent discoveries', *Antiquaries J.*, xxxvi (1956), 193–9.
105. Law of the Northumbrian Priests, 15, *EHD*, I, 473.
106. B. Eagles, *The Anglo-Saxon settlement of Humberside* (BAR 68.2, 1979), nos. 130, 225, 289 etc.
107. J.E. Mann, Early Medieval Finds from Flaxengate (Archaeology of Lincoln, Report no. XIV.1, 1982), 43.
108. Meaney, *Gazetteer*, 155.
109. *Ibid.*, 41–2.
110. D. Kennett, 'Seventh-century cemeteries in the Ouse Valley', *Beds. Arch. J.*, VIII (1974), 100, no.34.
111. D. Brown, 'So-called needle cases', *Med. Arch.*, XVIII (1974), 151–4.
112. Clough, Dornier and Rutland, *op. cit.* in n.47, 14–15 and 73 no.103.
113. Meaney, *Gazetteer*, 74.

11   Religion and Belief

1. 'The Wanderer', *Anglo-Saxon Poetry*, ed. R.K. Gordon (1954), 74–5.
2. I. Hodder, 'Social structure and cemeteries: a critical appraisal', in *Anglo-Saxon Cemeteries*, 161–76.
3. C. Hart, *The Early Charters of Eastern England* (1966), 150–5.
4. A.E. Brown and A. Hannan, 'Watling St and the Gartree Road, some work on two Roman roads in Northamptonshire', *Northants. Arch.*, XIII (1978), 91.
5. D. Bonney, 'Early boundaries and estates in Southern England', in *Medieval Settlement: Continuity and Change*, ed. P.H. Sawyer (1976),

72–82.

6. Meaney, *Gazetteer*, 40 and 42, cf.192.
7. *Ibid.*, 73.
8. M. Gelling, 'Further thoughts on pagan place-names', in *Place-name Evidence for the Anglo-Saxon Invasion and Scandinavian Settlements*, ed. K. Cameron (1977), 99–114.
9. *Law of the Northumbrian Priests*, 54, *EHD*, I, 475.
10. *ASC* 'C', 626.
11. A. Boddington and G. Cadman, 'Raunds, an interim report on excavations 1977–80', in *Anglo-Saxon Studies in Archaeology and History*, 2, ed. D. Brown, J. Campbell and S. Chadwick (BAR 92, 1981), 111ff.
12. II Edgar 2, *EHD*, I, 431.
13. *Ibid.*, 5.2.
14. *Chron. Ram.*, 53.
15. *Ibid.*, 66.
16. R. Bailey, *Viking Age Sculpture* (1980), 85–100.
17. M. Jones and B. Gilmour, 'Lincoln, St Mark's Church', *Lincs. History and Archaeology*, XII (1977), 76.
18. T. Kendrick, *Late Saxon and Viking Art* (1949), 81–2.
19. E.M. Jope, 'The Saxon Building-stone industry in southern and midland England', *Med. Arch.*, VIII (1964), 101f.
20. D. Rollason, 'Lists of saints' resting places in Anglo-Saxon England', *ASE*, VII (1978), 82–3, 86.
21. *Chron. Ram.*, 127–8.
22. *Ibid.*, 118–19.
23. *Ibid.*, 55.
24. *Chronicon Abbatiae de Evesham*, ed. W.D. Macray, Rolls Series, 29 (1863), 83.
25. *Chron. Ram.*, 158.
26. Hugh Candidus, *Chronicle*, 50–1.
27. *Ibid.*, 52–6.
28. *Chronicon Abbatiae de Evesham*, ed. Macray, 325–37, and D. Rollason, *The Search for Saint Wigstan*, Vaughan Paper no. 27 (Univ. of Leicester, 1981).
29. H.M. Taylor, 'Repton reconsidered: a study in structural criticism', in *England before the Conquest*, ed. P. Clemoes and K. Hughes (1971), 351–89 and *St Wystan's Church, Repton: A Guide and History* (1979).
30. H.M. Taylor, *Anglo-Saxon Architecture*, III (1978), 1022.
31. P. Brown, *The Cult of the Saints: its rise and function in Latin Christianity* (Chicago, 1981).
32. Felix, *Life of Guthlac*, ed. and trans. B. Colgrave (1956), ch. 35.
33. P. Brown, 'The rise and function of the Holy Man in late Antiquity', *Society and the Holy in late Antiquity* (1982), 103–52.
34. Acts of the Council of Clofesho, 12, in *Councils and Ecclesiastical Documents relating to Great Britain and Ireland*, ed. A.W. Haddan and W. Stubbs, III (1871), 366.
35. *Tatuini Opera Omnia*, Corpus Christianorum, Ser. Latina, 133 (1968), 186.
36. *Ibid.*, 196.
37. *ASC* 'C', 1016; *Chron. Ram.*, 117–18.
38. Life of Oswald, quoted *EHD*, I, 914.
39. P.H. Sawyer, *Charters of Burton Abbey* (1979), xxii-iii.
40. Stenton, 'Medeshamstede and its colonies', *Preparatory*, 182.
41. P. Clemoes, 'Cynewulf's image of the Ascension', in *England before the Conquest*, ed. P. Clemoes and K. Hughes (1971), 301–2.
42. *Chron. Ram.*, 115, 120, 148.
43. *Ibid.*, 153.
44. Abbo of Fleury, *Vita Sancti Eadmundi*, Patrologiae Cursus Completus, ed. J.P. Migne, 139 (Paris, 1880), col. 507, and the *Vita Sancti Abbonis auctore Aimoini Monachi*, *ibid.*, col. 391.
45. C. Hart, 'The Ramsey computus', *EHR*, LXXXV (1970), 29–44.
46. H. Mayr-Harting, *The Venerable Bede, the Rule of St Benedict and Social Class*, Jarrow Lecture, 1976.
47. Law of the Northumbrian Priests, 1, *EHD*, I, 472.
48. *Ibid.*, 61–4.
49. R. Bailey, *The Early Christian Church in Leicester and its Region* (Vaughan Paper no. 25, Univ. of Leicester, 1980), 4–11.
50. Stow and Lincoln have both been suggested as sites for the original see of Lindsey; see D.P. Kirby, 'The Saxon bishops of Leicester, Lindsey (Syddensis) and Dorchester', *Trans. Leics. Arch. and Hist. Soc.*, XLI (1965–6), 1–8. In view of the preference for Roman sites in the seventh century, Lincoln seems by far the more probable.
51. Stenton, 'Medeshamstede', *Preparatory*, 182.
52. VIII Æthelred 5, *EHD*, I, 449.
53. *DB*, I, 280r.

54. *Ibid.*, 143v, discussed by R.V. Lennard, *Rural England* (1959), 401–2.
55. *DB*, I, 377r.
56. Acts of the Council of Clofesho, 8, *Councils and Ecclesiastical Documents*, ed. Haddan and Stubbs, III, 365.
57. Stenton, 'The founding of Southwell minster', *Preparatory*, 364, and S.659.
58. P.H. Sawyer, *From Roman Britain to Norman England* (1978), 248.
59. II Edgar 2, *EHD*, I, 431.
60. Boddington and Cadman, 'Raunds', *op. cit.* in n.11, 106–7.
61. Geþyncðo, 2, *EHD*, I, 468 n.7.
62. *Vita Wulfstani*, ed. R. Darlington, Camden Ser. 50 (1928), 45, and *DB*, I, 292v.
63. *Ibid.*, 336r.
64. C. Hart, 'The church of St Mary of Huntingdon', *Procs. Cambs. Antiquarian Soc.*, LIX (1966), 105–11.
65. F. Barlow, *The English Church, 1000–1066* (1963), 193.
66. C. Brooke, 'The Church in the towns, 1000–1250', in *The Mission of the Church and the propagation of the Faith*, Studies in Church History, VI, ed. G.J. Cuming (1970), 66; *DB*, I, 280r.
67. Lennard, *op. cit.*, 309.
68. Barlow, *op. cit.*, 160–2.
69. Boddington and Cadman, *op. cit.*, 107.
70. Brooke, *op. cit.*, 79.
71. R.I. Moore, 'Family, community and cult on the eve of the Gregorian Reform', *TRHS*, 5th ser., XXX (1980), 46–69.
72. *Chron. Ram.*, 153.
73. *Law of the Northumbrian Priests*, 41, *EHD*, I, 474.
74. *Ibid.*, 37, 29 and 30.
75. *Ibid.*, 38 and 39.
76. *Ibid.*, 13–18.
77. *Ibid.*, 33, 42.
78. *Wulfstan's Canons of Edgar*, ed. R. Fowler (Early English Text Society, 266, 1972).

Bibliography

Æthelweard, *The Chronicle of Æthelweard*, ed. A. Campbell (1962).

Abbo of Fleury, *Vita Sancti Eadmundi*, Patrologiae Cursus Completus, ed. J.P. Migne, 139 (Paris, 1880).

Adams, L., 'Early Islamic pottery from Flaxengate, Lincoln', *Med. Arch.*, XXIII (1979), 218–19.

Addleshaw, G.W.O., *The Development of the Parochial System from Charlemagne to Urban II*, Borthwick Papers no. 6 (1970).

Addyman, P.V., Fennell, K.R. and Biek, L., 'A dark-age settlement at Maxey, Northamptonshire', *Med. Arch.*, VIII (1964), 20–73.

—'Late Saxon settlements in the St Neot's area, I, The Saxon settlement and Norman castle at Eaton Socon, Beds.', *Procs. Cambs. Antiquarian Soc.*, LVIII (1965), 38–73; 'II, Little Paxton', *ibid.*, LXII (1969), 59–93; 'III, The village or township of St Neot's', *ibid.*, LXIV (1972–3), 45–99.

—'The Anglo-Saxon house: a new review', *ASE*, I (1972), 273–307.

—and Whitwell, J.B., 'Some middle-Saxon pottery types in Lincolnshire', *Antiquaries J.*, L (1970), 96–102.

Anglo-Saxon Chronicle, trans., *EHD*, I, ed. D. Whitelock (2nd edn, 1979); II, ed. D.C. Douglas and G. Greenaway (2nd edn, 1981).

Anglo-Saxon Chronicle, in *Two of the Saxon Chronicles Parallel*, ed. J. Earle and C. Plummer (1892–9).

Arngart, O., 'Three English hundred names', *Namn och Bygd*, LVI (1978), 13–17.

Arnold, C., 'Wealth and social structure: a matter of life and death', in *Anglo-Saxon Cemeteries*, 81–142.

Asser, *Life of King Alfred*, ed. W.H. Stevenson (1959).

Attenborough, F.L., *Laws of the Earliest English Kings* (1922).

Aymo, *Vita Sancti Abbonis auctore Aimoini monachi*, Patrologiae Cursus Completus, ed. J.P. Migne, 139 (Paris, 1880).

Bailey, R., *Viking Age Sculpture in Northern England* (1980).

—*The Early Christian church in Leicester and its Region* (Vaughan Papers no. 25, Univ. of Leicester, 1980).

Barley, M.W., 'Lincolnshire rivers in the middle ages', *The Architectural and Archaeological Society of the County of Lincoln. Reports and Papers* (1938), 1–21.

—'Medieval borough of Torksey, Excavations', *Antiquaries J.*, XLIV (1964), 165–87.

—(ed.), *European Towns, their Archaeology and Early History* (1977).

—and Straw, I.F., 'Nottingham', in *Historic Towns*, I, ed. M.D. Lobel (1969).

Barlow, F., *The English Church, 1000–1066* (1963).

Barrow, G.W.S., 'Northern English society in the early middle ages', *Northern History*, IV (1969), 1–28.

—*The Kingdom of the Scots* (1973).

Barrow, V., 'Early Anglo-Saxon Settlement in Leicestershire and Rutland', *Trans. Leics. Arch. and Hist. Soc.*, LIII (1978), 55–63.

'Barton-upon-Humber, Castledyke south', *Med. Arch.*, XXVII (1983), 184.

Bateman, T., *Vestiges of the Antiquities of Derbyshire* (1848).

—*Ten Years digging in Celtic and Saxon Grave Hills* (1861).

Bede, *Ecclesiastical History of the English People*, ed. and trans. B. Colgrave and R.A.B. Mynors (1969).

Beresford, G., 'Goltho manor, Lincolnshire: the buildings and their surrounding defences', *Procs. of the Battle Conference on Anglo-Norman Studies*, ed. R. Allen Brown, 4, 1981 (1982), 13–36.

Beresford, M.W. and Finberg, H.P.R., *English Medieval Boroughs, a Hand-list* (1973).

Biddle, M., 'The evolution of towns: planned towns before 1066', in *The Plans and Topography of Medieval Towns in England and Wales*, ed. M.W. Barley (CBA Research Report no. 14, 1976), 19–32.

Bigmore, P., *The Bedfordshire and Huntingdonshire Landscape* (1979).

Bishop, M.W., 'Multiple estates in late Anglo-Saxon Nottinghamshire', *Trans. Thoroton Soc.*, LXXXV (1982 for 1981), 37–47.

Bishop, T.A.M., 'The Norman settlement of Yorkshire', *Essays in Economic History*, ed. E.M. Carus-Wilson, II (1962), 1–11.

Blackburn, M., Colyer, C. and Dolley, M., *Early Medieval Coins from Lincoln* (Archaeology of Lincoln, Report no. IX.1, CBA, 1981).

—and Metcalf, D.M., 'Five finger exercises on the List hoard', *Viking Age Coinage in the Northern Lands*, ed. M.A.S. Blackburn and D.M. Metcalf (BAR International Ser. 122, 1981), 495–524.

Blake, E.O., ed., *Liber Eliensis*, Camden, 3rd ser., 92 (1962).

Bloch, M., 'The rise of dependent cultivation and seignorial institutions', *Cambridge Economic History of Europe*, I, ed. M.M. Postan (1971).

Blunt, C.E., 'The coinage of Offa', in *Anglo-Saxon Coins*, ed. R.H.M. Dolley (1961), 39–62.

—'The coinage of Athelstan, King of England 924–939', *BNumJ*, XLII (1974), 35–159.

—Lyon, C.S.S. and Stewart, I., 'The coinage of southern England, 796–840', *BNumJ*, XXXII (1963), 1–74.

Boddington, A., 'A christian Anglo-Saxon graveyard at Raunds, Northamptonshire', in *Anglo-Saxon Cemeteries*, 373–8.

—and Cadman, G., 'Raunds – an interim report on excavations, 1977–80', in *Anglo-Saxon Studies in Archaeology and History*, ed. D. Brown, J. Campbell and S.C. Hawkes, 2 (BAR 92, 1981), 103–22.

Bonney, D., 'Early boundaries and estates in southern England', in *Medieval Settlement, Continuity and Change*, ed. P.H. Sawyer (1976), 72–82.

Bradley, R., 'Anglo-Saxon cemeteries, some suggestions for research', in *Anglo-Saxon Cemeteries*, 171–6.

Britnell, R.H., 'English markets and royal administration before 1200', *Economic History Rev.*, 2nd ser., XXXI (1978), 183–96.

Brooke, C.N.L., 'The missionary at home: the Church in the towns, 1000–1250', in *The Mission of the Church and the Propagation of the Faith* (Studies in Church History, ed. G.J. Cuming, 6, 1970), 59–73.

—'The medieval town as an ecclesiastical centre; general survey', in *European Towns, Their Archaeology and History*, ed. M.W. Barley (1977), 459–74.

Brooks, N., 'The development of military obligations in eighth- and ninth-century England', in *England before the Conquest*, ed. P. Clemoes and K. Hughes (1971), 69–84.

—'Arms, status and warfare in late-Saxon England', in *Ethelred the Unready*, ed. D. Hill (BAR 59, Oxford, 1978), 81–103.

Brown, A.E., 'Roman Leicester', in *The Growth of Leicester*, ed. A.E. Brown (1972), 11–18.

—and Hannan, A., 'Watling Street and the Gartree Road, some work on two Roman roads in Northamptonshire', *Northants. Arch.*, XIII (1978), 87–95.

—Key, T.R. and Orr, C., 'Some Anglo-Saxon estates and their boundaries in south-west Northamptonshire', *Northants. Arch.*, XII (1977), 155–76.

Brown, D., 'So-called needle cases', *Med. Arch.*, XVIII (1974), 151–4.

Butler, L., 'The churchyard in Eastern England, A.D. 900–1100. Some lines of development', in *Anglo-Saxon Cemeteries*, 383–9.

Cam, H.M., 'Manerium cum hundredo, the hundred and the hundredal manor', *Liberties and Communities in Medieval England* (1963), 64–90.

Cameron, K., *The Place-names of Derbyshire* (1959).

—'Anglo-Saxon and Danish period', in *Nottingham and its Region*, ed. K.C. Edwards (British Association for the Advancement of Science, 1966), 195–204.

—'*Eccles* in English place-names', in *Place-name Evidence for the Anglo-Saxon Invasions and Scandinavian Settlements*, ed. K. Cameron (English Place-Name Society, 1977), 1–7.

—'Scandinavian settlement in the territory of the Five Boroughs: the place-name evidence', *ibid.*, 115–38.

—'Scandinavian settlement in the territory of the Five Boroughs: the place-name evidence, part II, Place-names in thorp', *ibid.*, 139–56.

—'Scandinavian settlement in the territory of the Five Boroughs: the place-name evidence, part III, the Grimston-hybrids', *ibid.*, 157–71.

—'The minor names and field names of the Holland division of Lincolnshire', in *The Vikings*, Proceedings of the Symposium of the Faculty of Arts of Uppsala, ed. T. Andersson and K.I. Sandred (Uppsala, 1978), 81–8.

—'The Scandinavian settlement of eastern England: the place-name evidence', *Ortnamnssallskapets i Uppsala Årsskrift* (1978), 7–17.

Campbell, J., 'Bede', in *Latin Historians*, ed. T.A. Dorey (1966).

—'The first century of christianity in England', *Ampleforth J.*, LXXVI.1 (1971), 12–29.

—'Bede's words for places', in *Names, Words and Graves, Early Medieval Settlement*, ed. P.H. Sawyer (1979), 34–54.

—*Bede's reges and* principes, Jarrow Lecture, 1979.

Chadwick, H.M., *Studies on Anglo-Saxon Institutions* (1905).

Chapman, B., 'Death, culture and society: a prehistoric perspective', in *Anglo-Saxon Cemeteries*, 55–99.

Charles-Edwards, T.M., 'Kinship, status and the origins of the Hide', *Past and Present*, LVI (1972), 3–33.

—'The distinction between land and moveable wealth in Anglo-Saxon England', in *Medieval Settlement, Continuity and Change*, ed. P.H. Sawyer (1976), 180–7.

Cherry, B., 'Ecclesiastical Architecture', in *The Archaeology of Anglo-Saxon England*, ed. D. Wilson (1976), 151–200.

Clemoes, P., 'Cynewulf's image of the Ascension', in *England before the Conquest*, ed. P. Clemoes and K. Hughes (1971), 293–304.

Clutton-Brock, J., 'The animal resources', in *The Archaeology of Anglo-Saxon England*, ed. D. Wilson (1976), 373–92.

Colyer, C., [Lincoln], *Lincs. History and Archaeology*, X (1975), 57–8.

—[Lincoln], *Lincs. History and Archaeology*, XI (1976), 59.

— and Gilmour, B., 'St. Paul-in-the-Bail, Lincoln', *Current Arch.*, no. 63, VI.4 (1978), 102–5.

—and Jones, R.H., 'Flaxengate', *Lincs. History and Archaeology*, XII (1977), 75–6.

Cooper, J., *The Last Four Anglo-Saxon Archbishops of York* (Borthwick Papers, no. 38, 1970).

Coppack, G., 'The excavation of a Roman and medieval site at Flaxengate, Lincoln', *Lincs. History and Archaeology*, VIII (1974), 73–114.

Courtney, P., 'The early Saxon Fenland: a reconsideration', in *Anglo-Saxon Studies in Archaeology and History*, ed. D. Brown, J. Campbell and S.C. Hawkes, 2 (BAR 92, Oxford, 1981), 91–102.

Cox, B.H., 'Leicestershire moot sites – the place-name evidence', *Trans. Leics. Arch. and Hist. Soc.*, XLVII (1971–2), 14–21.

—'The significance of the distribution of English place-names in -*hām* in the Midlands and East Anglia', in *Place-name Evidence for the Anglo-Saxon Invasions and Scandinavian Settlements*, ed. K. Cameron (1977), 55–98.

—'The place-names of the earliest English records', *J. of the English Place-Name Soc.*, VIII (1976), 12–66.

Cramp, R., 'Anglo-Saxon sculpture of the Reform period', in *Tenth-century Studies*, ed. D. Parsons (1975), 184–199.

—'Schools of Mercian Sculpture', in Dornier, *Mercian Studies*, 191–233.

—'The Anglian tradition in the ninth-century', in *Anglo-Saxon and Viking Age Sculpture and its Context*, ed. J. Lang (1978), 1–32.

Darby, H.C., 'The Fenland frontier in Anglo-Saxon England', *Antiquity*, VIII (1934), 185–201.

—*The Medieval Fenland* (1974).

—*Domesday England* (1977).

Darlington, R., 'Ecclesiastical reform in the late Old English period', *EHR*, LI (1936), 385–428.

Davis, R.H.C., 'East Anglia and the Danelaw', *TRHS*, 5th ser., V (1955), 23–39.

—'Brixworth and *Clofesho*', *J. British Archaeological Ass.*, 3rd ser., XXV (1962), 71.

—'Alfred and Guthrum's frontier', *EHR*, XCVII (1982), 803–10.

Davies, W., 'Middle Anglia and the Middle Angles', *Midland History*, II (1973), 18–20.

—'Annals and the origins of Mercia', in Dornier, *Mercian Studies*, 17–29.

—and Vierck, H., 'The contexts of Tribal Hidage, social aggregates and settlement patterns', *Frühmittelalterliche Studien*, VIII (1974), 223–93.

Davison, B.K., 'Excavations at Sulgrave, Northamptonshire, 1968', *Arch. J.*, CXXV (1968), 305–7.

Dickinson, T., 'The present state of Anglo-Saxon cemetery studies', in *Anglo-Saxon Cemeteries*, 11–34.

Dolley, R.H.M., 'Two Anglo-Saxon notes: an enigmatic penny of Edward the Martyr', *BNumJ*, XXVIII (1955–7), 499–504.

—'Three late Anglo-Saxon notes: a new Anglo-Saxon mint', *ibid.*, 88–92.

—and Strudwick, J.S., 'A note on the mint of Torksey and on some early finds of English coins from Nottinghamshire', *Numismatic Chron.*, XVI (1956), 293–302.

—'A possible sixth Anglo-Saxon mint in Lincolnshire', *BNumJ*, XXIX (1958–9), 51–4.

—*Viking Coins of the Danelaw and of Dublin* (British Museum, 1965).

—'The Anglo-Danish and Anglo-Norse coinages of York', in *Viking Age York and the North*, ed. R.A. Hall (CBA Research Report 27, 1978), 26–31.

—and Metcalf, D.M., 'Reform of the English coinage under Eadgar', in *Anglo-Saxon Coins*, ed. R.H.M. Dolley (1961), 136–68.

Dornier, A., 'The Anglo-Saxon monastery at Breedon-on-the-Hill, Leicestershire', in Dornier, *Mercian Studies*, 155–68.

Dumville, D.N., 'Kingship, genealogies and regnal lists', in *Early Medieval Kingship*, ed. P.H. Sawyer and I.N. Wood (1977), 72–104.

—'Sub-Roman Britain: history and legend', *History*, LXII (1977), 173–92.

Dyer, J., 'Earthworks of the Danelaw frontier', in *Archaeology and the Landscape*, ed. P.J. Fowler (1972), 222–36.

Eagles, B., *The Anglo-Saxon Settlement of Humberside* (BAR 68.1 and 68.2, 1979).

—'Anglo-Saxons in Lindsey and the East Riding of Yorkshire in the fifth century', in *Anglo-Saxon Cemeteries*, 285–7.

Eddius, *The Life of Bishop Wilfrid*, ed. and trans. B. Colgrave (1927).

Elmore Jones, F., 'A note on the mint of Horncastle', *BNumJ*, XXXVII (1968), 191–2.

Everitt, A., 'The primary towns of England', *Local Historian*, XI.5 (1975), 263–77.

Everson, P., 'An excavated Anglo-Saxon sunken-featured building and settlement site at Salmonby, Lincolnshire, 1972', *Lincs. History and Archaeology*, VII (1973), 61–9.

—'Some Anglo-Saxon potters of North Lincolnshire', *ibid.*, 16–19.

Ewig, E., 'Residence et capitale pendant le haut Moyen Age', *Revue Historique*, CCXXX (1963), 25–72.

Felix, *Life of Guthlac*, ed. and trans. B. Colgrave (1956).

Fellows-Jensen, G., *Scandinavian Personal Names in Lincolnshire and Yorkshire* (Copenhagen, 1968).

—'The Vikings in England, a review', *ASE*, IV (1975), 181–206.

—'Place-name evidence for Scandinavian settlement in the Danelaw. A reassessment', in *The Vikings*, Proceedings of the symposium of the Faculty of Arts of Uppsala, ed. T. Andersson and K.I. Sandred (Uppsala, 1978), 89–98.

—*Scandinavian Settlement Names in the East Midlands* (Copenhagen, 1978).

Fenger, O., 'The Danelaw and the Danish law', *Scandinavian Studies in Law*, XVI (1972), 85–96.

Fennell, K.R., 'Pagan Saxon Lincolnshire', *Arch. J.*, CXXXI (1974), 283–93.

Finberg, H.P.R., 'The ancient shire of Winchcombe', *Early Charters of the West Midlands* (2nd edn, 1972), 228–35.

—(ed.), *The Agrarian History of England and Wales*, I.ii (1972).

Finley, M.I., *Ancient Slavery and Modern Ideology* (1983).

Fletcher, E., 'Brixworth, was there a crypt?', *J. Brit. Arch. Ass.*, 3rd ser., XXXVII (1974), 88–96.

Foard, G., 'Saxon settlement in Northamptonshire', *World Arch.*, IX (1978), 358–74.

Fowler, P.J., 'Agriculture and rural settlement', in *Archaeology of Anglo-Saxon England*, ed. D. Wilson (1976), 23–48.

Gelling, M., 'The charter bounds of Æscesbyrig and Ashbury', *Berks. Arch. J.*, LXIII (1967), 5–13.

—'The evidence of place-names', in *Medieval Settlement, Continuity and Change*, ed. P.H. Sawyer (1976), 200–11.

—'Introduction', in *Place-name Evidence for the Anglo-Saxon Invasions and Scandinavian Settlements*, ed. K. Cameron (1977), ii–v.

—'English place-names derived from the compound *wīchām*', *ibid.*, 8–26.

—'Further thoughts on pagan place-names', *ibid.*, 99–115.

—*Signposts to the Past: place-names and the history of England* (1978).

Gilbert, E., 'Brixworth and the English basilica', *Art Bull.*, xlvii (1965), 1–20.

Gildas, *The Ruin of Britain and Other Documents*, ed. and trans. M. Winterbottom (1978).

Gilmour, B., 'The Anglo-Saxon church at St Paul-in-the-Bail, Lincoln', *Med. Arch.*, xxiii (1979), 214–18.

Gordon, R.K., ed. and trans., *Anglo-Saxon Poetry* (1926).

Gover, J.E.B., Mawer, A. and Stenton, F.M., *Place-Names of Northamptonshire* (1933).

—*Place-Names of Nottinghamshire* (1940).

Graham-Campbell, J., 'The Scandinavian viking-age burials of England, some problems of interpretation', in *Anglo-Saxon Cemeteries*, 379–82.

Haddan, A.W. and Stubbs, W. eds., *Councils and Ecclesiastical documents relating to Great Britain and Ireland*, III (1871).

Hall, D. and Martin, P., 'Brixworth, Northants. – an intensive field survey', *J. Brit. Arch. Ass.*, cxxxii (1979), 1–6.

Hall, R.A., 'The pre-conquest *burgh* of Derby', *Derbys. Arch. J.*, xciv (1976 for 1974), 16–23.

Hallam, H.E., *The New Lands of Elloe* (Dept of English Local History, Univ. of Leicester, Occ. Paper ser. 1, no. 6, 1954).

—*Settlement and Society, a study of the early agrarian history of south Lincolnshire* (1965).

—*Rural England, 1066–1348* (1981).

Hart, C., 'Eadnoth, first abbot of Ramsey and the foundation of Chatteris and St Ives', *Procs. Cambs. Antiquarian Soc.*, lvi–lvii (1964), 61–7.

—'The Church of St Mary of Huntingdon', *ibid.*, lix (1966), 105–11.

—*The Early Charters of Eastern England* (1966).

—'The Ramsey computus', *EHR*, lxxxv (1970), 29–44.

—*The Hidation of Northamptonshire* (Dept of English Local History, Univ. of Leicester, Occ. Papers, ser. 2, no. 3, 1970).

—'The Tribal Hidage', *TRHS*, 5th ser., xxi (1971), 133–57.

—'Athelstan half-king and his family', *ASE*, ii (1973), 115–44.

—*The Hidation of Cambridgeshire* (Dept of English Local History, Univ. of Leicester, Occ. Papers, ser. 2, no. 6, 1974).

—'Hereward the Wake', *Procs. Cambs. Antiquarian Soc.*, lxv (1974), 28–40.

—*The Early Charters of northern England and the north Midlands* (1975).

—'The Kingdom of Mercia', in Dornier, *Mercian Studies*, 43–61.

—'The Peterborough region in the tenth century: a topographical survey', *Northants. Past and Present* (1981–2), 243–5.

Harvey, S., 'Evidence for settlement study, Domesday Book', in *Medieval Settlement, Continuity and Change*, ed. P.H. Sawyer (1976), 195–9.

Hassall, J. and Baker, D., 'Bedford: aspects of town origins and development', *Beds. Arch. J.*, ix (1974), 75–94.

Hatcher, J., *Plague, Population and the English Economy, 1348–1530* (1977).

Hawkes, C.F.C., 'The exhibition [on pagan saxon Lincs.]', *Arch. J.*, ciii (1946), 89–94.

Hawkes, S.C. and Dunning, G.C., 'Soldiers and settlers in Britain, fourth to fifth century', *Med. Arch.*, v (1961), 1–70.

Hebditch, M., 'A saxo-Norman pottery kiln discovered in Southgate St, Leicester, 1964', *Trans. Leics. Arch. and Hist. Soc.*, xliii (1967–8), 4–9.

Hill, D., 'Late Saxon Bedford', *Beds. Arch. J.*, v (1970), 96–100.

—'Continuity from Roman to medieval: Britain', in *European Towns, their Archaeology and Early History*, ed. M.W. Barley (1977), 293–302.

—*An Atlas of Anglo-Saxon England* (1981).

Hill, J.W.F., *Medieval Lincoln* (1948).

Hills, C., 'The archaeology of Anglo-Saxon England in the pagan period, a review', *ASE*, viii (1979), 296–329.

Hilton, R.H., *A Medieval Society, the West Midlands at the end of the thirteenth century* (1966).

Hodder, I., 'Social structure and cemeteries, a critical appraisal', in *Anglo-Saxon Cemeteries*, 161–76.

Hodges, R., 'State formation and the role of trade in middle Saxon England', in *Social Organization and Settlement*, ed. D. Green, C. Haselgrove and M. Spriggs (BAR International Ser., suppl. 47.2, 1978), 439–53.

—'Trade and market origins in the ninth century: an archaeological perspective of Anglo-Carolingian relations', in *Charles the Bald, Court and Kingdom*, ed. M. Gibson, J. Nelson and D. Ganz (BAR International Ser. 101, 1981), 213–33.

Hoskins, W.G., *The Midland Peasant: economic and social history of a Leicestershire village, Wigston Magna* (1957).

Hunter Blair, P., 'The Northumbrians and their southern frontier', *Archaeologia Aeliana*, 4th ser., xxvi (1948), 98–126.

—'The battle at *Biedcanford* in 571', *Beds. Mag.*, xiii (1971), 27–30.

Hurst, J.G., 'The pottery', in *The Archaeology of Anglo-Saxon England*, ed. D.M. Wilson (1976), 283–348.

Jackson, E. Dudley and Fletcher, E.G.M., 'The apse and nave at Wing, Buckinghamshire', *J. Brit. Arch. Ass.*, 3rd ser., xxv (1962), 1–20.

Jackson, K., *Language and History in Early Britain* (1953).

John, E., *Orbis Britanniae and Other Studies* (1966).

Jones, G.R.J., 'Early territorial organization in northern England and its bearing on the Scandinavian settlement', *Fourth Viking Congress, 1961*, ed. A. Small (1965), 67–84.

—'Early territorial organization in Gwynedd and Elmet', *Northern History*, x (1975), 3–27.

—'Multiple estates and early settlement', in *Medieval Settlement, Continuity and Change*, ed. P.H. Sawyer (1976), 15–40.

Jones, M. and Gilmour, B., 'Lincoln, St Mark's Church', *Lincs. History and Archaeology*, xii (1977), 76.

Jones, M.E., 'Climate, nutrition and disease: an hypothesis of Romano-British population', in *The End of Roman Britain*, ed. P.J. Casey (BAR 71, 1979), 231–51.

Jope, E.M., 'The Saxon building-stone industry in southern and Midland England', *Med. Arch.*, viii (1964), 91–118.

Kendrick, T.D., *Late Saxon and Viking Art* (1949).

Kennett, D., 'Pottery and other finds from the Anglo-Saxon cemetery at Sandy, Bedfordshire', *Med. Arch.*, xiv (1970), 17–33.

—'Seventh-century cemeteries in the Ouse valley', *Beds. Arch. J.*, viii (1974), 99–108.

Kent, J.P.C., 'From Roman Britain to Saxon England', in *Anglo-Saxon Coins*, ed. R.H.M. Dolley (1961), 1–27.

Kilmurry, K., *The Pottery Industry of Stamford, Lincolnshire, c.A.D. 850–1250* (BAR 84, 1980).

King, E., *Peterborough Abbey 1086–1310, a study in the land market* (1973).

—'The town of Peterborough in the early Middle Ages', *Northants. Past and Present* (1980–1), 187–95.

Kirby, D.P., 'The Saxon bishops of Leicester, Lindsey (Syddensis) and Dorchester', *Trans. Leics. Arch. and Hist. Soc.*, xli (1965–6), 1–8.

Klinck, A., 'Anglo-Saxon women and the law', *J. Medieval History*, viii (1982), 107–21.

Knowles, D.M., *The Monastic Order in England* (1966).

Krause, J., 'The medieval household, large or small', *Economic History Rev.*, 2nd ser., ix (1957), 420–32.

Kristensen, A.K.G., 'Danelaw institutions and Danish society in the Viking age: sochemanni, liberi homines and Königsfreie', *Medieval Scandinavia*, viii (1975), 27–85.

Kuhlicke, F.W., 'The Bedford mint', *Beds. Mag.*, xiii (1972), 167–71.

Kuurmann, J., 'An examination of the -ingas, -inga- place-names in the East Midlands', *J. English Place-Name Soc.*, vii (1975), 11–44.

Lang, J.T. ed., *Anglo-Saxon and Viking Age Sculpture and its Context*: Papers from the Collingwood Symposium (BAR 49, 1978).

Lennard, R.V., *Rural England 1086–1135* (1959).

Lethbridge, T.C., 'The Anglo-Saxon settlement of Eastern England', in *Dark Age Britain, Studies presented to E.T. Leeds*, ed. D.B. Harden (1956), 112–22.

Levison, W., *England and the Continent in the Eighth Century* (1946).

Liebermann, F., *Die Gesetze der Angelsachsen*, 3 vols (Halle, 1903–16).

Liebermann, F., *The National Assembly in the Anglo-Saxon period* (Halle, 1913).

Lincolnshire Domesday and the Lindsey Survey, ed. C.W. Foster and T. Langley, Intro. by F.M. Stenton (Lincoln Record Soc., 19, 1924).

Loyn, H.R., 'Anglo-Saxon Stamford', in *The Making of Stamford*, ed. A. Rogers (1965), 15–33.

Loyn, H.R., 'The hundred in the tenth and early eleventh centuries', in *British Government and Administration*, Studies presented to S.B. Chrimes, ed. H. Hearder and H.R. Loyn (1974), 1–15.

'Loveden Hill, Lincolnshire', *Med. Arch.*, xvii (1973), 146.

Lund, N., 'Thorp-names', in *Medieval Settlement, Continuity and Change*, ed. P.H. Sawyer (1976), 223–5.

Lyon, C.S.S., 'Historical problems of the Anglo-Saxon coinage: 4, The Viking Age', *BNumJ*, xxxix (1970), 193–204.

—'Variations in currency in late Anglo-Saxon England', in *Mints, Dies and Currency, Essays in memory of Albert Baldwin*, ed. R.A.G. Carson (1971), 101–20.

—'Some problems in interpreting Anglo-Saxon coinage', *ASE*, 173–224.

McK. Clough, T.H., Dornier, A. and Rutland, R.A., *Anglo-Saxon and Viking Leicestershire* (Leicestershire Museums, Art Galleries and Records Service, 1975).

Mackey, W.F., *Bilinguisme et contact des langues* (Paris, 1976).

Macray, W.D., ed., *Chronicon Abbatiae Ramesiensis* (Rolls Series, 83, 1886).

Mahany, C., 'Stamford', *Current Arch.*, i (1968), 266–70.

—Burchard, A. and Simpson, G., *Excavations in Stamford, Lincolnshire, 1963–9* (*Med. Arch.*, Monograph Series, 9, 1982).

—and Roffe, D., 'Stamford, the development of an Anglo-Scandinavian borough', *Anglo-Norman Studies*, ed. R. Allen Brown, v (1983), 197–219.

Mann, J.E., *Early Medieval Finds from Flaxengate: objects of antler, bone, stone, horn, ivory, amber and jet* (Archaeology of Lincoln, Report no. XIV.1, CBA 1982).

Margary, I., *Roman Roads in Britain* (rev. edn, 1967).

Martin, G.H., 'Church life in medieval Leicester', in *The Growth of Leicester*, ed. A.E. Brown (1972), 27–37.

—'New beginnings in North West Europe', in *European Towns, their History and Archaeology*, ed. M.W. Barley (1977), 405–15.

Mayr-Harting, H., *The Coming of Christianity to Anglo-Saxon England* (1972).

Meaney, A., *A Gazetteer of Early Anglo-Saxon Burial Sites* (1964).

—'Notes on the coincidental burials', in *Place-name Evidence for the Anglo-Saxon Invasion and Scandinavian Settlements*, ed. K. Cameron (1977), 51–2.

Mellows, W.T. (ed.), *The Chronicle of Hugh Candidus, a monk of Peterborough* (1949).

Metcalf, D.M., 'How large was the Anglo-Saxon currency?', *Economic History Rev.*, 2nd ser., xviii (1965), 475–82.

—'Monetary affairs in Mercia in the time of Æthelbald', in Dornier, *Mercian Studies*, 87–106.

—'Geographical patterns of minting in medieval England', *Seaby's Coin and Medal Bull.* (1977), 314–17, 353–7 and 390–1.

—'The ranking of boroughs, numismatic evidence from the reign of Æthelred II', in *Ethelred the Unready*, ed. D. Hill (BAR 59, 1978), 159–212.

—'Continuity and change in English monetary history, c.973–1086', I, *BNumJ*, l (1980), 20–49; II, *ibid.*, li (1981), 52–90.

Millward, R., 'Saxon and Danish Leicestershire', in *Leicester and its Region*, ed. N. Pye (British Association for the Advancement of Science, 1972), 218–34.

—and Robinson, A., *The Peak District* (1975).

Morris, J., review of J.N.L. Myres, *The Anglo-Saxon Cemeteries of Caistor-by-Norwich and Markshall*, *Med. Arch.*, xviii (1974), 225–32.

Morris, R. (ed.), *The Blickling Homilies* (Early English Text Society, Old Series, 58, 63 and 73; repr. as one vol., 1967).

Mossop, H.R., *The Lincoln Mint* (1970).

Musset, L., 'Pour l'étude des relations entre les colonies scandinaves d'Angleterre et de Normandie', in *Melanges de linguistique et de philologie, In memoriam F. Mosse* (Paris, 1959), 330–9.

Myres, J.N.L., *Anglo-Saxon Pottery and the Settlement of England* (1969).

Nicolaisen, W.F.H., Gelling, M. and Richards, M., *The Names of Towns and Cities in Britain* (1970).

O'Connor, T.P., *Animal Bones from Flaxengate* (Archaeology of Lincoln, Report no. XVIII.1, CBA, 1982).

O'Donovan, M.A., 'An interim revision of episcopal dates for the province of Canterbury, 850–950', I, *ASE*, I (1972), 23–44; II, *ibid.*, II (1973), 91–113.

Owen, A.E.B., 'Hafdic, a Lindsey name and its implications', *J. English Place-Name Soc.*, VII (1974–5), 45–56.

Owen, D.M., *Church and Society in Medieval Lincolnshire* (1971).

Owen, D., 'Chapelries and rural settlement; an examination of some of the Kesteven evidence', in *Medieval Settlement, Continuity and Change*, ed. P.H. Sawyer (1976), 66–71.

Ozanne, A., 'The Peak dwellers', *Med. Arch.*, VI–VII (1962–3), 15–52.

Pader, E.-J., 'Material symbolism and social relations in mortuary studies', in *Anglo-Saxon Cemeteries*, 143–59.

Pagan, H.E., 'Coinage in the age of Burgred', *BNumJ*, XXXIV (1965), 11–27.

Page, R.I., 'Anglo-Saxon episcopal lists', I and II, *Nottingham Medieval Studies*, IX (1965), 78–95; III, *ibid.*, X (1966), 2–24.

—'How long did the Scandinavian language survive in England? The epigraphical evidence', in *England before the Conquest*, ed. P. Clemoes and K. Hughes (1971), 165–81.

Page, W., 'Some remarks on the churches of the Domesday Survey', *Archaeologia*, 2nd ser., XVI (1915), 61–102.

Parsons, D., 'Two nineteenth-century Anglo-Saxon finds from Lincolnshire', *Antiquaries J.*, LIII (1973), 78–81.

—'A note on the Breedon angel', *Trans. of the Leics. Arch. and Hist. Soc.*, LI (1975–6), 40–3.

—'Brixworth and its monastery church', in Dornier, *Mercian Studies*, 173–90.

—'Past history and present research at All Saints church, Brixworth', *Northants. Past and Present* (1979), 61–71.

—'Brixworth and the Boniface connexion', *ibid.* (1980–1), 179–83.

Payling, L.W.H., 'Geology and place-names in Kesteven', *Leeds Studies in English* (1935), 1–13.

Perring, D., *Early Medieval Occupation at Flaxengate* (Archaeology of Lincoln, Report no. IX.1, CBA, 1981).

Phillips, C.W., 'The present state of archaeology in Lincolnshire; the Anglo-Saxon period', *Arch. J.*, XCI (1934), 137–52.

Phythian-Adams, C., 'Rutland reconsidered', in Dornier, *Mercian Studies*, 63–84.

—'Jolly cities, goodly towns: the current search for England's urban roots', *Urban History Yearbook* (1977), 30–39.

—'The emergence of Rutland and the making of the realm', *Rutland Record*, I (1980), 5–12.

Potts, W.T., 'The pre-Danish estate of Peterborough Abbey', *Procs. Cambs. Antiquarian Soc.*, LXV (1974), 13–27.

Powell, R., 'The Lichfield St. Chad gospels', *The Library*, 5th ser., XX (1965), 26.

Raban, S., *The Estates of Thorney and Crowland, a study in medieval monastic land tenure* (Univ. of Cambridge Dept. of Land Economy, Occ. Papers, 7, 1977).

Raftis, J., *The Estates of Ramsey Abbey* (Toronto, 1957).

Rahtz, P.A., 'Caistor, Lincolnshire', *Antiquaries J.*, XL (1960), 175–87.

—'Buildings and rural settlement', in *The Archaeology of Anglo-Saxon England*, ed. D.M. Wilson (1976), 49–98.

—Dickinson, T. and Watts, L. (eds.), *Anglo-Saxon Cemeteries, 1979*, The fourth Anglo-Saxon symposium at Oxford (BAR 82, 1980).

Ralegh Radford, C.A., 'A lost inscription of pre-Danish age from Caistor', *Arch. J.*, CIII (1946), 95–9.

—'The later pre-conquest boroughs and their defences', *Med. Arch.*, XIV (1970), 83–107.

—'Pre-Conquest minster churches', *Arch. J.*, CXXX (1973), 120–40.

—'The pre-conquest boroughs of England, ninth to eleventh centuries', *Procs. British Academy*, LXIV (1978), 132–53.

Revill, S., 'King Edwin and the battle of Heathfield', *Trans. Thoroton Soc.*, LXXIX (1975), 40–9.

Reynolds, S., *Introduction to the History of English Medieval Towns* (1977).

—'Law and communities in Western Christendom, c. 900–1140', *American J. of Legal History*, XXV (1981), 205–24.

Rix., M., 'The Wolverhampton cross-shaft', *Arch. J.*, CXVII (1960), 71–81.

Rodwell, W. and K., 'Barton-on-Humber', *Current Arch.*, no. 78 (1982), 209–15.

Roesdahl, E., Graham-Campbell, J., Connor, P. and Pearson, K., *The Vikings in England*, catalogue of the exhibition 1981–2 (1981).

Rogers, A., *A History of Lincolnshire* (1970).

—'Parish boundaries and urban history: two case studies', *J. Brit. Arch. Ass.*, 3rd ser., XXXV (1972), 46–64.

—'The origins of Newark, the evidence of local boundaries', *Trans. Thoroton Soc.*, LXXVIII (1974), 13–26.

Roffe, D.R., 'Rural manors and Stamford', *South Lincs. Archaeology* (1977), 12–13.

Rollason, D.W., 'List of Saints' resting places in Anglo-Saxon England', in *ASE*, VII (1978), 61–93.

—*The Search for Saint Wigstan* (Vaughan Papers no. 27, Univ. of Leicester, 1981).

—'The cults of murdered royal saints in Anglo-Saxon England', in *ASE*, XI (1983), 1–22.

Routh, T.E., 'Corpus of pre-conquest carved stones of Derbyshire', *J. Derbys. Arch. and Natural History Soc.*, 71 (1937), 1–46.

Rumble, A., 'Hrepingas reconsidered', in Dornier, *Mercian Studies*, 169–72.

Russell, J.C., *British Medieval Population* (Albuquerque, 1948).

Salter, H.E., ed., *The Eynsham Cartulary*, I (Oxford Historical Soc., 49, 1907).

Salway, P., *Roman Britain* (1981).

Sawyer, P.H., 'The density of Danish settlement in England', *Univ. of Birmingham Hist. J.*, VI (1957–8), 1–17.

—*The Age of the Vikings* (1962).

—'The wealth of Britain in the eleventh century', *TRHS*, 5th ser., XV (1965), 145–64.

—'The charters of Burton abbey and the unification of England', *Northern History*, X (1975), 28–39.

—(ed.), *Medieval Settlement, Continuity and Change* (1976).

—'Early medieval English settlement', in *ibid.*, 1–7.

—*From Roman Britain to Norman England* (1978).

—(ed.), *Names, Words and Graves: Early Medieval Settlement* (1979).

—(ed.), *Anglo-Saxon Charters, II: Charters of Burton Abbey* (1979).

Simeon of Durham, *Opera Omnia*, ed. T. Arnold (2 vols., Rolls Series, 1882–5).

Sims-Williams, P., 'The settlement of England in Bede and the Chronicle', *ASE*, XII (1983), 1–42.

Smith, W. and Wace, H., *Dictionary of Christian Biography, Literature, Sects and Doctrines* (4 vols., 1877–87).

Smyth, A.P., *Scandinavian York and Dublin*, I (Dublin, 1975), II (Dublin, 1979).

Sørensen, J.K., 'Place-names and settlement history', in *Names, Words and Graves; Early Medieval Settlement*, ed. P.H. Sawyer (1979), 1–33.

Stafford, P.A., 'Historical implications of the regional production of dies under Æthelred II', *BNumJ*, XLVIII (1978), 35–51.

—'The laws of Cnut and the history of Anglo-Saxon royal promises', *ASE*, X (1982), 173–90.

Steane, J., *The Northamptonshire Landscape, Northamptonshire and the Soke of Peterborough* (1974).

Stenton, F.M., *Types of Manorial Structure in the Northern Danelaw*, Oxford Studies in Legal History (1911).

—'Introduction' to Domesday survey, *Victoria County History of Derbyshire*, I (1905), 293–355.

—'Introduction' to Lincolnshire Domesday, *Lincoln Record Soc.*, XIX (1924).

—*The Free Peasantry of the Northern Danelaw* (1969).

—'Lindsey and its kings', in *Preparatory*, 127–37.

—'The Danes in England', *ibid.*, 136–65.

—'Medeshamstede and its colonies', *ibid.*, 179–92.

—'The road system of medieval England', *ibid.*, 235–52.
—'The historical bearing of place-name studies: the Danish settlement of Eastern England', *ibid.*, 298–313.
—'The historical bearing of place-name studies: the place of women in Anglo-Saxon society', *ibid.*, 314–24.
—'The founding of Southwell Minster', *ibid.*, 364–70.
—*Anglo-Saxon England* (3rd edn, 1971).
Stewart, I.H., 'The Stamford mint and the connexion with the abbot of Peterborough under Æthelred II', *BNumJ*, xxviii (1955–7), 106–10.
—'The St Martin coins of Lincoln', *ibid.*, xxxvi (1967), 49–54.
Tallis, J.H. and Switsur, V.R., 'Studies on South Pennine peats, VI: a radio-carbon pollen diagram from Featherbed Moss, Derbyshire', *J. Ecology*, lxi (1973), 743–51.
Tatwine, *Tatuini Opera Omnia* ed. M. de Marco, Corpus Christianorum, Ser. Latina, 133 (Rome, 1968).
Taylor, C.S., 'The Origin of the Mercian shires', in *Gloucestershire Studies*, ed. H.P.R. Finberg (1957), 17–52.
Taylor, H.M. and J., *Anglo-Saxon Architecture*, I and II (1965).
Taylor, H.M., *Anglo-Saxon Architecture*, III (1978).
—'Belfry towers in Anglo-Saxon England', *North Staffs. J. of Field Studies*, viii (1968), 9–18.
—'Corridor crypts on the continent and in England', *ibid.*, ix (1969), 17–52.
—'Repton reconsidered: a study in structural criticism', in *England before the Conquest*, ed. P. Clemoes and K. Hughes (1971), 351–89.
—*The Anglo-Saxon Crypt*, Repton Studies, 1 (1977).
Tebbutt, C.F., 'An eleventh-century 'boat-shaped' building at Buckden, Hunts.', *Procs. Cambs. Antiquarian Soc.*, lv (1961), 13–15.
Tenhagen, H.P., *Das Northumbrische Priestergesetz* (Dusseldorf, 1979).
Thompson, F.H., 'Anglo-Saxon sites in Lincolnshire, unpublished material and recent discussion', *Antiquaries J.*, xxxvi (1956), 181–99.
Todd, M., *The Coritani* (1973).
Wainwright, F.T., 'Early Scandinavian settlement in Derbyshire', in *Scandinavian England*, collected papers by F.T. Wainwright, ed. H.P.R. Finberg (1975), 281–303.
Wakelin, M.F., *English Dialects* (2nd edn, 1977).
Walmsley, J.F.R., 'The *censarii* of Burton abbey and the Domesday population', *North Staffs. J. of Field Studies*, viii (1968), 73–80.
Watkin, J.R., 'A Frankish bronze bowl from Barton-on-Humber', *Lincs. History and Archaeology*, xv (1980), 88–9.
Watts, V.E., 'Comment on the evidence of place-names by Margaret Gelling', in *Medieval Settlement, Continuity and Change*, ed. P.H. Sawyer (1976), 212–22.
Weinreich, U., *Languages in Contact* (The Hague, 1966).
Wheeler, H., 'Aspects of Mercian art: the Book of Cerne', in Dornier, *Mercian Studies*, 235–44.
Whitelock, D., 'The pre-Viking age church in East Anglia', *ASE*, 1 (1972), 1–22.
—'The conversion of the Eastern Danelaw', *Saga Book of the Viking Society*, xii (1941), 159–76.
Whitwell, J., 'St Chad's, Barrow-on-Humber', *Lincs. History and Archaeology*, xiii (1978), 76.
—*The Coritani, some Aspects of the Iron Age Tribe and the Roman* civitas (BAR 99, 1982).
Wildgoose, R.H., 'Defences of the pre-conquest borough of Nottingham', *Trans. Thoroton Soc.*, lxv (1961), 19–26.
Wilkinson, L., 'Problems of analysis and interpretation of skeletal remains', in *Anglo-Saxon Cemeteries*, 221–31.
William of Malmesbury, *De Gestis Pontificum Anglorum*, ed. N.E.S.A. Hamilton (Rolls Series, 1870).
William of Malmesbury, *The Vita Wulfstani of William of Malmesbury*, ed. R.R. Darlington (Camden Ser., 50, 1928).
Williams, J., 'Northampton', *Current Arch.* no. 46 (1973–4), 340–8.
—'The early development of the town of Northampton', in Dornier, *Mercian Studies*, 131–52.

—'Northampton', *Current Archaeology.*, no. 79 (1982), 250–4.

Wilson, D.M., 'The Vikings' relationship with Christianity in northern England', *J. Brit. Arch. Ass.*, xxx (1967), 37–46.

—*The Anglo-Saxons* (1971).

—*The Viking Age in the Isle of Man* (Odense, 1974).

—'Craft and industry', in *The Archaeology of Anglo-Saxon England*, ed. D.M. Wilson (1976), 253–81.

—'The Scandinavians in England', *ibid.*, 393–403.

—'Defence in the Viking age', in *Problems in Economic and Social Anthropology*, ed. G. de G. Sieveking, I.H. Longsworth and K.E. Wilson (1976), 439–45.

Wood, M., 'Brunanburh revisited', *Saga Book of the Viking Society*, xx.3 (1980), 200–17.

Wormald, P., 'The uses of literacy in Anglo-Saxon England and its neighbours', *TRHS*, 5th ser., xxvii (1977), 95–114.

—'Bede, Beowulf and the conversion of the Anglo-Saxon aristocracy', in *Bede and Anglo-Saxon England*, ed. R.T. Farrell (BAR 46, 1978), 32–95.

Index

(The following abbreviations have been used: B = Bedfordshire, D = Derbyshire, H = Huntingdonshire, Le = Leicestershire, Li = Lincolnshire, N = Nottinghamshire, Nt = Northamptonshire, R = Rutland.)